Advance Praise for Jeff Blackman's

Peak Your Profits

"*Peak Your Profits* by Jeff Blackman is loaded with ideas and strategies to maximize your profits. Breaking even is over. The time for breaking records is now!"

—Jeffrey Gitomer, Author of *The Little Red Book of Selling*

"This great book will work miracles in your career...and your life!"

—Og Mandino, Author/Speaker

"This fast-moving, entertaining book is 'must' reading for every person who is serious about getting more business—better, faster and generating higher profits—in the shortest period of time."

—Brian Tracy, Author/Speaker

"My relationship with Jeff Blackman spans three companies, several years and lots of successes. He has literally traveled the country to share his message and strategies with my people. My feeling about *Peak Your Profits* can be summed up in 3 simple steps: 1. Read it. 2. Do it! 3. Pray your competition hasn't already bought a copy!"

—Jim Alland, CEO or President of 3 companies dramatically impacted by Jeff and the strategies of *Peak Your Profits*

"Chock full of useful ideas for growing your business and increasing profits. Jeff's years of experience helping clients improve now benefits you. Read this book!"

—Mark Sanborn, Author of *The Fred Factor* and *The Potential Principle*

"How to compete and win, while staying honest. Practical, witty and incisive. Jeff gives you a crystal-clear vision for success in all aspects of your life. He delivers a fast-paced, fun and rock-solid collection of strategies—for a lifetime of achievement. Greatness awaits you."

—**Denis Waitley, Author/Speaker**

"*Peak Your Profits* is a distinctive business book. Jeff Blackman has over three decades of high-level, intensive research into what makes businesses grow and leaders succeed. He delivers insights grounded in real-world experience. Plus, Jeff demonstrates clearly how to generate greater sales, higher returns, and peak profits. What a book! What if your competition reads it—and you don't?"

—**Scott McKain, Author of *Create Distinction***

"Jeff is a terrific writer with an astute understanding of today's intensely competitive, fast-changing marketplace. I suggest you read his book now, and keep a copy of it close by at all times."

—**Scott DeGarmo, Former Editor-in-Chief & Publisher,**
SUCCESS

"How can you improve your performance and get better results using the resources you already have? Jeff Blackman answers this question with the new edition of *Peak Your Profits*. It's written for anyone seeking greater business success. Jeff has spent decades advising business professionals, and this book is a collection of some of his best ideas for today's marketplace. Buy this book. It's a great investment in yourself and your business!"

—**Joe Calloway, Author of *Becoming a Category of One***

"*Peak Your Profits* is jam-packed with solid sales and relationship-building ideas to help you win. You'll read it—and keep it forever! With writing in the margins, underlined segments and highlighted gems of wisdom. Get it today and prosper!"

—Don Hutson, #1 Best-selling author, Hall of Fame Speaker, and CEO of U. S. Learning

"Certain business books are required reading, *Peak Your Profits* is now one of them. It's literally filled with hundreds of innovative ideas that will significantly contribute to the success of any individual or enterprise. Not only are the ideas practical, but they're easy to implement. That makes it even easier to generate rapid and profitable results."

—Roger Dawson, Author of
Roger Dawson's Secrets of Power Negotiating

"This book is loaded with powerful and profitable business strategies. Plus, it's one of those rare books that is on-target, thought-provoking and fun to read."

—Dr. Tony Alessandra, Author of
The Platinum Rule* and *Collaborative Selling

"For years, Jeff Blackman's strategies have been impacting some of the top companies in the world, including ours. Now, he can impact your business too. Without question, this is one of the most valuable books on what it takes to build relationships and grow a business."

—David Lasky, Former President,
Bresler's Ice Cream & Yogurt

"*Peak Your Profits* is not just another 'how-to' book. It's really a powerful guide filled with insight and practical experience that helps anyone on their journey to future success."

—Dan Burrus, Technology Forecaster,
Author of *Technotrends*

"This easy-to-read book presents the best explanation of key business success factors I've ever seen published. Jeff Blackman shows you how to apply these disarmingly simple strategies with powerful and predictable results. Jeff is a dedicated 'business scientist'—a man devoted to knowing what works, what doesn't and why. He knows things you don't. No one in business should try to transact a day's more business until they read every page. If conducting business with integrity and increasing your results are important, this book virtually guarantees you a 10 percent to 50 percent improvement within three months or less."

—Jay Abraham, Author and Marketing Guru

"Great strategies. Great insights. Great stories. An essential business companion."

—Susan RoAne, Author of *How to Work a Room*
and *The Secrets of Savvy Networking*

PEAK YOUR PROFIT$

THE EXPLOSIVE BUSINESS-GROWTH SYSTEM

Finally, a results-oriented book that gives you a phenomenal competitive edge! Jeff Blackman reveals, after 36 years of testing, research and development, his explosive business-growth system that shows you step-by-step how to *Peak Your Profits*.

You'll quickly outdistance your competition and reach new levels of unprecedented success. Jeff shares proven, positive and profit-producing strategies on the crucial areas of business development. He helps you build opportunities and enhance your top and bottom lines.

Peak Your Profits is unique because it's the first book to collectively focus on key or core business-growth skills: sales, marketing, relationship building, client development, negotiations, customer service and more. It's your blueprint for remarkable success. And it even includes client case studies.

Peak Your Profits helps you grow your business and skyrocket your profitability—quickly, ethically and dramatically—even in a tough economy. You'll add dollars to your bottom line. Fast!

The numerous clients already benefiting from Jeff's strategies include individuals, small business owners, entrepreneurial-driven companies, associations and even corporate giants like FedEx, Enterprise, New York Life Insurance, AT&T, Marriott, Hilton, IBM, Diner's Club and Nabisco.

Jeff is an award-winning speaker, bestselling author, success coach, broadcast personality and lawyer. He heads Blackman & Associates—a results-producing business-growth firm in the Chicagoland area. Since 1985, Jeff has shared his positive and profit-producing messages with audiences throughout the world.

In 2008, Jeff was inducted into the National Speakers Association's *Speaker Hall of Fame.* He was awarded the *CPAE: Council of Peers Award for Excellence* and is one of approximately thirteen percent of professional speakers to receive the CSP or *Certified Speaking Professional* designation from NSA. Also in 2008, Vistage, the world's leading CEO organization, named Jeff *Fast Track Speaker of the Year,* based upon the quality and impact of his content and delivery.

Jeff graduated with honors from both the University of Illinois and the Illinois Institute of Technology Chicago Kent College of Law. He's also a happy husband, devoted father, veteran softball player, avid bike rider and a loyal (or nutty) Chicago Cubs fan!

Now, it's time for Jeff to help you—*peak your profits*!

Peak Your Profits

Jeff Blackman

Networlding
Publishing

Peak Your Profits

Soft | 978-1-944027-16-2
Digital | 978-1-944027-14-8

First printing, 1996
Second edition, revised, 1999
Third edition, revised, 2002
Fourth edition, revised, 2007
Fifth edition, revised, 2018

Networlding Publishing

10 9 8 7 6 5

Also by Jeff Blackman

Stop Whining! Start Selling!
A profit powerhouse book

RESULT$: Proven Sales Strategies for Changing Times
A strategic sales book, plus CD

Carpe A.M. • Carpe P.M. / Seize Your Destiny™
A strategic life book

Opportunity $elling® / Your Path to Profit®
A sales/quotation book

Opportunity $elling® - Six Profit-Producing Steps to Multiply Your Earnings
An audio business-growth system

Profitable Customer Service
A video-based learning-system

How to Set and Really Achieve Your Goals
A video-based learning-system

Opportunity $elling® Style Analysis instruments
Assessment tools for sales behavior and performance

Management Style Analysis instruments
Assessment tools for leadership behavior and performance

Customer Service Style Analysis instruments
Assessment tools for customer service behavior and performance

Please see www.jeffblackman.com and
click on "Business-Growth Tools"

To my many clients—
who give me the privilege to serve,
learn and grow.

To Mom and Dad—
who are qvelling. And who taught me
at an early age, that if you do good work,
you'll succeed, but if you give "just a
little bit extra," you'll succeed beyond
your wildest expectations!

To my family—
my wife, Sheryl, and my kids—Chad,
Brittany and Amanda—who help me
realize the commitment to serve, help
and grow others—happens not just in your
business, but also in your home!

Acknowledgments

If I've learned one thing, from the time I started writing and finally completed *Peak Your Profits*, it's that writing a book isn't an immediate event. It's more akin to a gestation period! It's an evolution of ideas over long days and late nights. It's also by no means a singular effort. It requires hard work, dedication and contributions from lots of special people. The following folks, either directly or indirectly, helped turn my dream into a reality. And to all of them, I'll forever be grateful.

My wife Sheryl and my children—Chad, Brittany and Amanda—for always letting me create, yet still never letting me miss a sporting event, a diaper change, a bedtime story, a dance recital, ice skating competition or band trip—during PYP versions 1 thru 4. Now, with this new edition, you "kids" have become adults. And I still love you, more than you'll ever know. You too Sheryl, for after 36 years of marriage, you're still my date for life!

Irv Blackman—my Dad, the best friend and mentor a boy could ever have.

Sallie Blackman—my Mom, for putting up with my early-morning, mid-day and late-night brainstorming sessions with Dad, during the initial creation of *Peak Your Profits*.

Leo and Beverly Kantor—my in-laws, for accepting that their son-in-law doesn't practice law. (I miss you both.)

John Willig, my agent—for his persistence and faith. Betsy Sheldon, Ellen Scher, Regina McAloney, Larry Wood, Fred

Nachbaur and Ron Fry—my original editorial and promotional team, for their keen eyes and counsel.

Ron Willingham—for his knowledge and inspiration.

Bill Brooks—for his friendship and guidance. (Think about you everyday, "Coach.")

Angela Graham—my high school English teacher, for teaching me to love and value the written word.

The National Speakers Association—for giving me an international network of friends and advisors.

Frank Bucaro—my dear, longtime friend, a.k.a. Frankie or Babe. He was kind enough and smart enough to say "Hey, you oughta talk to Melissa at Networlding Publishing, she's really smart!" Boy, was he right!

Melissa Wilson and Jon Malysiak at Networlding—for your talent, expertise and enthusiasm. Plus, your ongoing commitment to results, while always making the entire process fun and easy!

The Chicago Cubs—for encouraging me as a lifelong loyal fan—to always hope and dream!

Contents

Introduction

Get Ready...to Peak Your Profits

If you're like most business people, you simply don't have the time or the luxury to learn all the crucial essentials of business development:

- Sales
- Marketing
- Negotiations
- Customer service
- Competing in a changing marketplace, etc.

Plus, you can no longer solve today's business problems with yesterday's solutions!

So finally, after 36-plus years of testing, research and development, I'm ready to reveal a *business-growth system* that helps you *Peak Your Profits.*

You'll learn proven, positive and profit-producing strategies in the key areas of business development—strategies to outdistance your competition and reach new levels of unprecedented success.

In this practical, entertaining and results-oriented book, you'll be bombarded with ideas that'll help you build opportunities and peak profits!

There has always been a demand for books I call "revenue generators." *Peak Your Profits* is one such book: A shot-in-the-arm to guide you to spectacular success and remarkable results!

No long-winded theories. No boring lectures. Just fast-paced, street-smart, straight-to-the-point, ethical, detailed specific actions and strategies that make you more money. Starting now!

Innovative, Yet Applicable

Ideas only have real value if they're used. I often tell clients and seminar-workshop participants that it's not just what you know, it's what you *do* with what you know, and *how* you do it that brings value. *Peak Your Profits* focuses on action, implementation and execution.

Peak Your Profits is unique because it's the first book to collectively focus on the key or core business-growth skills: sales, marketing, client development, relationship building, negotiations, customer service, etc. It's your blueprint for success.

Simple, Informative, Interesting

As a businessperson, you're immersed in "stuff." The last thing you need is some technical or academic book on business.

Yet you'll gobble-up an information-loaded book on business-growth that's also presented in a fun and entertaining format. This book is filled with personal experiences from "in the trenches." War stories, if you will. Tales from the front.

I'm convinced, you, like others, only invest in one thing—and that's a more favorable future. I wrote this book to help you *attain a more favorable future* and *to improve your condition.*

Timing

Timing is everything. And the time for *Peak Your Profits* is now. The present. And to be continued into your future.

In your competitive marketplace, you're continually looking for the "little things" that give you *big* results. Especially, with increased competition, downsizing, changing distribution channels, "turbo" technology and decision-makers who are more sophisticated, as well as disloyal. Now, you must search for, demand and require the right strategies to succeed.

And if you're like me, you don't like to wait for successful results. Thankfully, with *Peak Your Profits*, your wait is over. You can now improve, enhance or jump-start your business. Immediately!

A Proven Track Record

For four decades, I've been criss-crossing the world, helping clients enhance their performance, productivity and profitability. Those already benefiting from the strategies of *Peak Your Profits* include Fortune 500 corporations, young-growth organizations, entrepreneurial-driven companies, associations and their memberships, and individuals.

The annual sales volume or assets of my clients range from less than half-a-million dollars to in excess of $100 billion. However, they all share one thing in common: they're "peak profiteers!" They've heard and most importantly, *applied* my strategies with profound results!

The greatest compliments I receive aren't the glowing accolades and enthusiastic words of praise immediately following a speaking engagement, workshop or results-session. Instead, they're the letters, calls, and emails that come a day, or a week or a month later, where clients tell me how they've applied my strategies to their business—and generated dramatic results!

Somewhat sheepishly they admit, "Well, I wasn't sure it would work, so I tried your approach, just to see what would happen." The results are incredible. Thank you!"

Michael Blitstein, a C.P.A., investment advisor and client, informed me within two weeks of our first strategic session together that he applied my strategies and made $20,000. He was ecstatic! To me, Michael and all my clients (many of whom have doubled or tripled their income), that's the best kind of satisfaction—results!

How do I know my strategies peak profits? My clients tell me. After all, they are and should be the only barometer for determining success and results. Now you, too, can reap the same benefits!

In addition to the case studies that are sprinkled throughout the book, a sample of comments I've received from clients follows:

A real winner!
"Jeff, we were inspired, motivated and laughed, all in the same hour. Your presentation was a real winner. Your ability to integrate real IBM-specific names and occurrences was amazing. Thank you for being such a valuable asset."
—*Tim McChristian, General Manager / IBM*

Will double revenues!

"There is little doubt, with discipline and work, to implement the many excellent strategies for improving our business development and sales processes taught by Jeff, that it will have a substantial impact on our efficiency and effectiveness in BD pursuits, sales closures and bottom line. Embraced and executed by our team, I would expect this training to be the most significant factor in doubling our revenues over the next 5 years."

—*Steve Hill, President & CEO / The AEgis Technologies Group*

Valuable tools!

"Jeff, your dedication to learn about our business was apparent. Because you were so well prepared and committed to delivering a strong negotiations message about how we can build our business, your presentation was a success. Your performance was informative and humorous. Our team gained valuable tools. Thanks for your contributions and for being a great partner!"

—*Brenda Gaines, (Brenda served as President and CEO of Diners Club North America, a subsidiary of Citigroup)*

Increased profits, easily six-figures!

"Having built sales organizations for over 25 years as a CEO and business owner, I've tried several sales training programs and consultants, none come close to the immediate impact and results realized from Jeff Blackman. The increased profitability from using Jeff's strategies and techniques is easily in the six-figure range. Wish I found him sooner!"

—*Jay VanOrden, CEO / Worldwide Supply*

Significant improvements and results!

"My firm, a commercial insurance program management company, engaged Jeff as a sales training advisor. He initially worked with our leadership team to understand our needs and then designed a customized training and reinforcement program for our sales team. Jeff likes focusing on results. Our results are measured primarily by our revenue. And I can say that since working with Jeff for over a year now, our revenue is up over 35 percent year-over-year.

Jeff's interactions with my team are always very positive. This creates a more constructive learning environment. In addition to his people skills, Jeff is consistently prepared for meetings and has excellent follow-up, with our team and even 1:1 counsel. We're extremely pleased with his approach and, most important, our team's significant improvements and results. That's why we have an ongoing relationship with Jeff, and I enthusiastically recommend him for your professional sales training and coaching."
—Chris Randall, CEO / Ultra Risk Advisors

A catalyst for proven and relevant results.

"Jeff is a catalyst for proven, relevant results. We observed immediate benefits, within a day. Our people improved their preparation and listening skills in ways deeply satisfying to our leadership, our prospects and, most importantly, our clients. For our senior people, the lessons shared were an overdue refresher of tried and true disciplines that Jeff brings to life in new relevant ways. For others more junior, Jeff created a foundation that'll serve their careers faithfully for years to come. With so many business challenges today, I'd highly recommend Jeff now more than ever."
—Derrick Van Grol, Vice President of Global Sales / IDI Billing Solutions

Introduction

Roadmap to success!

"Jeff's results-oriented sales and personal development program provides individuals and organizations with can't-miss tools and strategies to drive true bottom-line results and great personal development. When you and your team put the time and effort in to make positive changes in ethical and logical ways, then Jeff is your roadmap to great success."

> *—Rob Stern, Vice President of Business Development /*
> *Werner Electric*

Substantial order at a very high margin!

"Jeff, I have high expectations. I immediately implemented several of the techniques I learned in a very tough sales cycle I was engaged in with a customer...well known for being notoriously cheap and grinding their vendors. They always start each project pricing discussion with, 'You're killing me with your prices...!'

Armed with the recent knowledge your course taught me, I held my ground and reinforced our value. Looks like this customer will be giving me a substantial order at a very high margin! Longer term, I see where I can optimize my selling techniques to grow my deals larger, make them more profitable, and bring them in sooner! Jeff, you kept me riveted the entire day!"

> *—John Lapadat, Senior Account Executive / ZENTRA*

Quick application, measurable results!

"Wow, Jeff! In the past, I've experienced a short-lived high from motivational speakers, so I had a tall order for you. I asked for a long-term strategy, with measurable ROI and specific tools our team could use to grow our business. Having your customized message, with direction, and how to apply your recommendations...resulted in quick application and measurable results. Jeff,

I'm impressed with your follow-up, the longevity of your message, and your ability to effectively communicate to a diverse group. The results you enabled my staff to achieve exceeded my expectations."

—*Dan Cologna, Director Sales & Marketing / Liturgical Publications, Inc.*

Greater Chicago...is greater!

"Thank you for making our annual meeting a great success. You received terrific praise from our newest and most experienced advisors alike. Your ability to tell stories, connect and give concrete examples kept them engaged and attentive. To a person, they were able to take away very practical, easy to implement ideas and techniques."

—*Alan Levitz, CEO - President / GCG Financial - Greater Chicago Group*

Valuable. Resonated!

"Thanks for your program at our National Distributor meeting in Montreal. It was very entertaining and provided a lot of energy at the end of a long day. More importantly, the distributors and employees thought it was valuable and even expressed interest in going beyond the 90 minutes. I've heard much talk from our distributors and team about creating their 'power probes.' That certainly resonated!"

—*Tom Watson, President / Petro-Canada America, a Suncor Energy business*

Jeff delivers...to FedEx!

"Outstanding! Our Senior Managers were genuinely surprised that an 'outsider' could know and understand so much about FedEx. Many expressed the feeling they were 'listening to someone who has worked at FedEx for years.' This is a real tribute to your professionalism as one who really does his homework and skillfully builds on this to establish rapport and connect with his audience. I appreciated what you said and how you said it. Your topic was an ideal fit, credible and relevant to our personal and business needs. Thanks for your significant contribution. You added great value!"

—*Diane Stokely, Vice President / FedEx*

Stupendous. The hit of our conference!
"'Stupendous, exciting, motivating, refreshing, current and personal!' Those words and more are what I heard from our AT&T professionals following your program. Jeff, you were definitely *the hit* of our two-day conference!"

—*James Croll, Vice President / AT&T*

The best in 9 years, a grand slam!
"Jeff, the feedback is the best I've received in 9 years of coordinating our *Forward* meetings. You scored a Grand Slam! Thank you for doing such a great job, in preparing and motivating our team."

—*David Wallach, President / Barclay Street Real Estate*

Highly impactful • A new direction!
"We have an experienced team, exposed for many years to individuals and speakers who can help us. Yet when Jeff Blackman spoke, I received comments like, 'Awesome!' 'Highly impactful!' 'Learned things I never knew, even after 25 years of selling.' 'I'll now take a different direction on how I present our value and work with customers.'—and much more."

"Jeff changed and improved what we all do daily. And he made

29

us think in more positive and creative ways. Our team now has better skills and is better prepared to deal with our daily challenges. Plus, take advantage of opportunities."

"Jeff's attention-to-detail and fact-gathering made him better prepared in learning about our culture and team than any previous speaker. And it showed! I highly recommend Jeff as an impact-player who can make any individual or company better!"
      —*Gerry LoDuca, President / DUKAL Corp.*

Fantastic kick-off!
"From the moment we met Jeff, he was interested in knowing our business at a fundamental level. He spent multiple sessions with our team, learning our merger challenges, interviewing customers and suppliers, and tailoring his 'change' message. He then set our conference tone with a fantastic kick-off. I highly recommend Jeff to anyone looking to launch a new initiative or jump-start their organization with new energy and direction. We value his hard work and preparation and were thrilled with his presentation."
      —*Paul Dean, Executive Vice President / LBM Advantage*

Entertaining, thought-provoking!
"We engaged Jeff as our keynote speaker at our annual national sales event. We're embarking upon a challenging time, and Jeff's assignment was designed to resonate and inspire. Jeff was, by far, the most engaging, entertaining and thought-provoking speaker we've ever had. So much so, elements of his presentation are still, (weeks later), reverberating around our organizational communication chain, at all levels. Thanks Jeff for a job well done!"
   —*Michael J. Kelley, President & COO / Glantz Holdings, Inc.*

And the following year, Glantz asked Jeff back…

Hit the mark!

"Jeff, I am writing this note as a letter of appreciation for an outstanding sales training and development workshop you led for our sales team and specialist group during our National Sales Meeting. Your development track on *Opportunity Selling* hit the mark! However, the greatest differentiator is **YOU!** You received the highest ratings from the post-meeting survey…and the buzz throughout the meetings was the energy driven from this training. While some programs stop there, you continue to work with us and our team on how to reinforce these skills and build upon them."

—*Mark Christie, Vice President Sales, Marketing and Strategic Sourcing / N. Glantz & Son*

Energized. Quickly leveraging. Jeff gets it!

"When we hired Jeff, I was lucky enough to have already known him for a few years. My confidence in him was already high. And when he started working with our team, I realized how he had developed masterful methodologies based on his experience and ethics. From the first day of the program and learning-system, our team was energized, eager to prepare for ongoing meetings and quickly leveraging the techniques. Knowledge builds confidence and practice builds skills. Jeff gets it."

—*Tim Padgett, CEO, Founder & Eye Candy / Pepper Group*

Positive impact. Ideas have stuck!

"Jeff has had a powerful, positive impact on our company. We reference his teachings on a daily basis. And his generous and ongoing email and phone availability, plus counsel and support have kept us engaged. Most important, Jeff's strategies and ideas have stuck!"

—*George Couris, President / Pepper Group*

Focused on results!

"Our experience with Jeff Blackman has been nothing less than excellent! Jeff is the consummate pro. His focus on results is coupled with intuitive people skills, providing an insight unique to his craft. Our team has greatly benefited through Jeff's natural style and adaptable strategies and tactics. We highly recommend working with Jeff to get your company focused on results you deserve!"
—*Dan Gabriel, Manager of Sales / Petro-Canada America - A Suncor Energy business*

I'll never forget the wise client who once told me, right before I was to conduct a program, "Jeff, we expect you to fill our hearts with hope, our tummies with desire and our minds with lots of good stuff!"

That, too, is my mission here. To fill your mind—and bank account—with "lots of good stuff!" I'm here to enrich your life and business. To positively push, pull, urge, cajole and propel you first and foremost. To propel you to have more fun. More achievement. More success. More knowledge. More productivity. More profitability. And more happiness.

I wouldn't dare waste your time, energy and money on strategies that only might, perhaps or possibly help you grow your business. This book has a singular purpose: *results*. The emphasis of this book is always on results—with lots of "how-to's" and a wee bit of inspiration.

Peak Your Profits helps you grow your business and skyrocket your profitability—quickly, ethically and dramatically. Even in a tough economy. You'll add dollars to your bottom line. Fast! Now get ready to *Peak Your Profits*.

CASE STUDY

Principal Financial Group and CitiMortgage Increase Sales, Market Share and Profits!

CHALLENGE:

How to create customized business-growth solutions to continually drive results in a very competitive marketplace.

GAME PLAN AND APPROACH:

For four consecutive years, I worked closely with Phil Kuhn, Vice President of the Correspondent Lending Division at the Principal Financial Group and CitiMortgage. Phil engaged me to create customized training for his Management Team, Account Executives and Operations Leaders. Their results-sessions were custom-designed to deliver advanced sales and account management skill-building, along with metrics for goals, performance, sales and profits. Plus, I also created a follow-up, or reinforcement program, to monitor progress and results.

C
A
S
E

S
T
U
D
Y

RESULTS:

Phil Kuhn exclaimed, "With Jeff's help we…"

1. increased sales by 25 percent
2. became the lender or partner of choice with many of our clients
3. improved Account Executive and Operational effectiveness by 30 percent

4. executed an overall strategy to become a dominant player in the market
5. increased market share and profits
6. exceeded short- and long-term strategic goals

Phil added, "Jeff's *results* format is well thought-out, strategic, ethical, and obviously, highly effective. I received overwhelmingly positive feedback from our team."

C
A
S
E

S
T
U
D
Y

CHAPTER 1

Willy Loman, Rest in Peace!

People invest in your ability to deliver to them
a more favorable future! And improve their condition!

1. Willy Doesn't Live Here Anymore!

Arthur Miller's play *Death of a Salesman* shares a rich and poignant slice of life. It's a story filled with emotion and pathos. Its richness lies in the fact that it freezes for all time the image of Willy Loman.

Willy is a classic peddler. He's a traveling man with only a shoeshine, a smile and friend in every town. He's forever optimistic in front of family, friends and associates that certain big sales will be landed, new territories conquered and greater commissions earned.

And once these are accomplished, he'll be a great man. A great man in the eyes of his proud family, admiring peers and thankful customers.

Unfortunately, Willy Loman is also a tragic character. His psychic and physical energies are focused on creating the wrong goals, performing the wrong activities and achieving the wrong results.

Willy Loman's life is filled with anxiety and frustration. He's jealous of others' success and confused as to why he isn't basking in the business glory. Willy Loman wrongly assumes success in business can only be realized by *who* you know—not *what* you know—and by who you *cheat*—not who you *serve*.

Stop This Business Treadmill...I Want to Get Off!

However, Willy is right about one thing. "Business" is extremely competitive. The demands are great, the pressures high. Businesspeople throughout the world often confide in me, saying, "My job has never been tougher." "The marketplace is changing," or "I feel like I'm on a treadmill and there's no *off* button."

Have you ever felt this way? I thought so!

You must be prepared on a daily basis. Prepared to confront the challenges of meeting deadlines, completing paperwork, prospecting, selling, serving, marketing, negotiating and even dealing with rejection.

Is the list of challenges endless? Perhaps. But guess what? So are the opportunities. Opportunities to penetrate new accounts, serve more customers and make more money.

2. The Future is Bright!

Business—especially today—isn't as simple as Willy Loman believed it should be. A businessperson can't simply show up, work the territory and depend upon friends to provide an order.

Today, running a business, prospecting, selling or serving customers or clients, marketing and negotiating have evolved into an art as well as a science. It's a new world of business. A world Willy Loman would never recognize.

Today, in order to be a successful business pro, you need to constantly be developing new skills. Customers are more demanding and less forgiving. Professionalism, quality and value are the norm and the expectation, not the exception.

Today's business professional must be a focused, strategic thinker with an unwavering commitment to serving others. Today's buyer or decision-maker doesn't simply want a product or a service, but instead expects a partner. A consultant. A strategic adviser. A *growth* specialist. Somebody or something that will help *grow* the business.

Slick manipulators won't survive in today's competitive marketplace. Today's business professional must know how to build relationships, gain rapport with prospects and draw out their wants and needs, handle their objections and get favorable decisions.

It's with that in mind that I created the *Peak Your Profits Business-Growth System*, a logical, organized and methodical approach to dramatic business growth and profitability.

It's simple, yet practical and results-oriented. It's designed for two purposes: 1) to help you market better, sell better and serve your customers or clients better; and 2) to help you make more money!

The Name of the Game is—Results

Whether you're just beginning your business career, you're on your way up, or you're already on top and want to stay there, *Peak Your Profits* was created to be both a philosophical and strategic powerhouse for your ongoing business strength, development and profitability.

What does *Peak Your Profits* do for you?

It helps you reach new and unprecedented levels of success:

- To market and penetrate new accounts or industries.
- To sell and serve more than you ever thought possible.
- To negotiate like a pro.
- To seize more opportunities.
- To realize the new freedom and flexibility that come with enhanced financial success.

You'll also have a profound, almost unfair advantage over your competition.

For all these great things to happen, however, *you* must play the crucial role. My role is really pretty simple. I'm the messenger. But *you* put the message into motion.

Our focus is more on action over knowledge, implementation over ideas, and execution over technique. I strongly suggest, unequivocally urge and repeatedly recommend you concentrate on not just what you'll learn, discover and soon know, but instead on what you'll *do* with your new knowledge. Whether you're reading this book at home, in your office or on an airplane, I suggest you read, reread and review these pages repeatedly. Underline. Highlight. Jot notes in the margin. Dog-ear the page corners.

Why? Because repetition leads to recognition. Recognition leads to reinforcement. Reinforcement leads to your understanding or internalization. Internalization leads to action, execution or implementation. And all these things added together lead you to...*peak your profits.*

3. Your System for Success!

To help you plan and prepare for your enhanced profitability, here's a brief overview of some of the many things you'll learn while reading or "internalizing" the *Peak Your Profits* business-growth system.

In Chapter 2, you'll learn how to:

- Prepare for and adapt to your changing business marketplace.
- Apply the eight core profit principles to capitalize—not cap-size—from change.
- Break through barriers, raise ceilings and more.

In Chapter 3, you'll learn how to:

- Lay a strong foundation, with the three-part philosophy of *Peak Your Profits* and the six profit-producing steps of business-development.
- Create value.
- Avoid the OUCH Impact and more.

In Chapter 4, you'll learn how to:

- Create your unique selling proposition (USP).
- Leverage your business with strategies such as value-investing, lifetime value and sponsorship.
- Optimize your relationship power...and more.

In Chapter 5, you'll learn how to:

- Maximize your long-term success and increased earnings with ethical business practices.
- Preserve and protect your integrity.
- Evaluate money, morality...and more.

In Chapters 6–11, you'll learn how to implement the individual steps of the *Peak Your Profits Business-Growth System*. You'll discover:

- The 30 profit points that are part of the system.
- 15 strategies to improve your listening skills.
- 12 questions to ask yourself to determine how quickly you're developing rapport or building relationships.
- More than 15 tips and techniques on questioning and probing prospects, customers or clients.
- More than 100 types of questions you can ask your prospects.
- 12 presentation strategies.
- 11 profit phrases to help you translate features into benefits.
- 51 power words.* (See the special bonus on the next page.)
- More than 25 negotiation strategies.
- The 14 decision-influencers and their impact on the four types of buying styles.
- More than 50 suggestions on how to adapt your business development and behavioral style to the style of your decision-maker.

- 8 guidelines to make sure you'll make the sale...and more.

---

* SPECIAL BONUS:

To help you during any stage of the *Peak Your Profits Business-Growth System*, I've compiled a list of 189 power words and phrases. Would you like to see the complete list? For free? Of course you would! Simply send an email to: sheryl@jeffblackman. com with the subject heading: PYP Power Words

---

In Chapter 12, you'll learn:

- How to focus on your customer commitment.
- The 10 dimensions of service and the 21 things you should never say to a customer.
- The 4-step S.E.R.V.™ problem-solving formula...and more.

In Chapter 13, you'll learn how to:

- Quickly collect bad debts.
- Increase your P/E ratio.
- Apply "psyche-kick" phenomena...and more.

And in Chapter 14, you'll learn a valuable lesson from a 6-year-old.

As you can tell, *Peak Your Profits* is filled with hundreds of strategies to develop and sharpen your skills, grow your business and peak your profits. You won't find academic lectures or ivory-tower business school rhetoric, but rather solid, proven and profit-producing strategies.

Peak Your Profits isn't designed to be a quick-hit, trendy or glib approach to business development. Instead, it's a hard-hitting, long-term, *business-growth system.* The benefits and successes are immediate. And they continue to build over time.

As you know, I'm here to help you get one thing, and one thing only...*results!* Results—especially the right results—are something Willy Loman searches for, but never finds. At the time of his death, he's a tired, bitter and exasperated man. He views business as a coldly competitive and ruthless game. He feels humanity is secondary to greed. And that trust, gratitude and respect serve no valuable purpose in a business relationship. Willy is wrong! Thankfully, we now know his perception of the marketplace is distorted.

To attain new levels of success today, the smart and highly successful business professional knows he or she must play a different role. A role with no resemblance to Willy Loman. Decision-makers and buyers don't want or need a "product pusher" or "service supplier." Instead, they demand and require a business partner or strategic ally. Vendors are expendable. Partners are invaluable!

With *Peak Your Profits,* you'll now be that ally, partner, strategic adviser or growth specialist—the type of individual who commits to the long-term relationship and reaps the significant rewards that accompany that commitment. And that commitment is always based on trust. For when trust is high, fear is low!

CASE STUDY

Burns Booms! Doubles Their Business!

BACKGROUND AND BRIEF HISTORY:

Meet the man who can put Michael Jordan, Susan Sarandon, Hugh Jackman, Shaun White, Mike Ditka, Mia Hamm or 20,000 other athletes, entertainers and celebrities on your team!

Since the fall of 1998, I've had the privilege to work with **Bob Williams, CEO & COO**, and his team at Burns Entertainment & Sports Marketing. Burns is the nation's leading entertainment and sports marketeer. They specialize in placing athletes, entertainers and celebrities with corporations, ad agencies, public relations firms and not-for-profits—in TV commercials, ad campaigns, speaking engagements and personal appearances. Burns emotionally connects consumers through entertainment, sports and music.

One of the things that makes Burns especially unique is they're not an "agent" that represents the athlete or entertainer. Instead, they represent the decision-maker who wants to hire a celebrity. And since Burns knows the "fair market value" of a current pro, retired All Star, coach, announcer, TV or film star, they can negotiate and reach agreements with athletes, celebrities and their agents at significant savings.

Burns has a forty-eight-year track record of results. And with Bob's leadership since 1993, Burns' revenues have increased over 500 percent. Plus the top media outlets in the world rely upon Bob and Burns for the inside scoop on sports marketing, mega endorsement deals and giant athlete contract signings. Bob is frequently quoted or interviewed for the *Wall Street Journal, New York Times, Fortune,* NBC, ABC, CBS, ESPN, Fox, etc. Bob is also the author of *The Brand Agent.*

RELATIONSHIP AND RESULTS:

Here's what Bob Williams, CEO and COO of Burns says about our working relationship:

> *I began working with Jeff in 1998 and he helped double our business at Burns with a blend of great ideas, structure and ongoing accountability—ensuring we followed through on the plan he helped create. I highly recommend Jeff to any company wanting to grow their business quickly. As good as Jeff is as a business-growth specialist, he's an even better person, who I call a friend.*

C
A
S
E

S
T
U
D
Y

IMPACT, IMMEDIATE AND LONG-TERM:

Here are excerpts from a conversation with Bob:

Q: What have been the results from your relationship with Jeff?

Bob Williams: As a business-growth specialist, Jeff looks at our company from a different perspective. We tend to think and act in terms of how things have always been done and are hesitant to change. Jeff identifies key areas for change that enhance what we do. He also suggests subtle, yet very powerful and profitable, upgrades, like the need to restructure our company. This change immediately translated into explosive sales with less effort. Jeff challenges us to achieve specific goals, yet he always provides the tools to help us meet and exceed these goals.

Q: What are some of the areas you have worked on together?

Bob Williams: There are many...

- Driving sales volume.
- Long-term planning.
- Goal-setting.
- Value billing.
- Restructuring.
- Discovering hidden profit centers.
- Elevating value perception.
- Referral generation.

Q: What do you value most about your relationship with Jeff?

Bob Williams: Jeff works as our partner. He brings an invaluable and unique business perspective. Plain and simple, he helps us produce ongoing results and profits.

CASE STUDY

CHAPTER 2

Change: Capsize or Capitalize!

There's nothing strange or mystical about creativity and change. Nothing superhuman. It's simply your willingness to take a step beyond.

4. Mirror, Mirror on the Wall…Here's the Future for One and All!

How would you like to predict the future with the confidence, assurance and knowledge that you'd be right? Believe it or not, you and I have the ability to do just that, and we need not even be a prognosticator, soothsayer or fortune teller.

How? Well, it's really quite easy. Because there's something that's going to happen daily. Guaranteed. And when it does, it'll be relentless. It'll be rapid. It'll be revolutionary. And it'll be reality.

It's truly the only thing you and I can be certain of. What is it? It's uncertainty or change!

David Thomas, Dean of Cornell Business School, once said, "The number one characteristic of students who later became company leaders is the ability to withstand uncertainty."

Have you ever experienced incredible professional or personal *change*, especially recently? Thought so. Get used to it. It won't stop. Yogi Berra, that wise business philosopher, once exclaimed, "The future ain't what it used to be!" Despite the absurdity of Yogi's thought process, he's right! Just think of some of the monumental, disruptive or unexpected historical or business changes we've witnessed—the fall of the Berlin wall, the rise of Apple, the evolution of the Internet, the emergence and ascension of Amazon, Facebook, Tesla, Airbnb, Uber, Netflix, YouTube, Google and social media, the demise of Toys R Us—and the Chicago Cubs finally winning a World Series championship after a 108-year drought!

5. Change: The Only Constant!

Now, and throughout the 21st century, change will be the only constant. For example, with genetic animal husbandry we can look forward to hogs that'll produce low-cholesterol pork and cows that'll deliver milk with pharmaceutical properties—such as insulin—already in place. And if you crave a fast-food burger and fries, *what* do you think will serve it to you? That's right, a robot!

Change is assured. Especially in three areas—computerization, communication and miniaturization. Over the past 60 years, computer performance has increased — are you ready for this? — more than a trillion fold! NASA's Apollo guidance computer, the one that helped astronauts head for the moon, had the processing power of two Nintendo Entertainment Systems. In 1946. ENIAC, the world's first large-scale multi-purpose computer filled 1,800 square feet—and stuffed inside it were 17,468 vacuum tubes. In 1974, my freshman year at the University of Illinois, my physics teacher, Steve Selbrede, predicted, "A computer that could fill this massive lecture hall...will one day, fit in the palm of your hand and be more powerful!" Some thought he was nuts. But he was right! (Imagine life without your Smartphone, tablet or iPad.) In 1985, the Cray-2 supercomputer was the fastest machine in the world. Its "power" was the equivalent of an iPhone 4! It's obvious, change—in technology, life and business—is a daily constant.

The only thing that appears to be speculative is whether you and I will have the ability to adapt to the changes within our market-place and world. Perry W. Buffington, Ph.D., professor of management at Georgia Southern University, once said, "The idea of change is one of the few constants in daily living. How we cope with it can spell the difference between successful and unsuccessful results!"

Now if you're like most people, change doesn't thrill you. It may even scare you. That's okay. That's typical. However, remember, *if you always do what you've always done, you'll always get what you've always got—or less!*

Therefore, if you want, need or demand more from your life, business, staff, customers, clients or prospects, you may have to *change*. The old way may no longer be appropriate or even work. Your past achievements may not be an accurate measurement of your future performance or future successes. Your past assures nothing. It's simply an influencer, not a guarantor. You must not allow your past to block your vision or mission for the future. Clinging to the *old way* for too long, just because "it has always been done that way," may thwart your implementation of new ideas, opportunities and solutions.

As an astute seminar participant once told me, "If you keep doing the same thing over and over, but expect different results each time, that's called insanity!" Therefore, you may have to ask yourself a series of questions:

- Do you choose to innovate?
- Do you choose to imitate?
- Or do you choose to vegetate?

And if you choose the latter, you might as well do what a client of mine suggests, and simply abdicate!

6. The Power and Plight of Change!

By effectively dealing with change, you turn reluctance into resilience, despair into desire and trepidation into triumph!

However, dealing with change may not come easy. Why? Because the pressures of change are both internal and external. Internal, as you wrestle with yourself and your new *you* and environment. External, as you combat the predictors of doom and gloom, the naysayers and the critics.

The stark reality of this struggle was driven home when I read the following framed quote on a wall behind a client's desk:

It should be borne in mind that there is nothing more difficult to arrange, more doubtful of success, and more dangerous to carry through than initiating changes.

The innovator makes enemies of all those who prospered under the old order, and only lukewarm support is forthcoming from those who would prosper under the new.

Their support is lukewarm partly from fear of adversaries, who have existing laws on their side, and partly because people are generally incredulous, never really trusting new things unless they have tested them by experience.

Without Change...

It's easy for me to encourage you to change, but first let's explore what might happen if you don't change and you stay as you are.

First, you must acknowledge that without confronting change, you're likely to limit growth. And without growth, you're likely to diminish opportunity. And without growth and opportunity:

- Your profits decline.
- You lose market share.
- You lose quality products and it gets tougher to obtain or create new ones.
- You lose enthusiasm, suppliers, your best people and customers or clients.

The following "fast facts" really drive home the glory of growth versus the devastation of decay:

- Intel is always working simultaneously on two sets of new products—the next product and the one that will replace it.
- During the boom days of the minicomputer, Digital

Equipment's CEO, Ken Olson, predicted the PC would be a bust in business. He attacked the workstation as a "snake oil" concept. In 1992, DEC posted a loss of $2.8 billion. Olson was canned!

- When *Fortune* magazine named Rubbermaid as America's most admired company, perhaps, it was because each year, Rubbermaid introduces 365 new products.

7. Bob Dylan is Right!

Of all the forces acting on us, change can be the most beneficial and the most cruel. As Bob Dylan once sang, "Oh the times, they are a changin'…"

If anybody knew about change, it was Sam Walton, the founder of Walmart. Some claimed Walton's middle name was "change." He spent little time on deliberation, but lots of time on action! This strategy enabled him to be a successful store owner. At the time of Walton's death in 1992, Walmart's annual sales were in excess of $55 billion dollars. Today, they surpass $486 billion dollars!

No Crystal Ball, But…

"The key to success will be a willingness to take long and major risks. The best companies will be better anticipators of change, willing to commit resources freely and determined to stay the course." Powerful words stated by a man who knew their value and truth—Robert W. Galvin, former Chairman of Motorola.

Galvin was at the helm of Motorola's vast corporate transformation in the late 1980s. Under his leadership, Motorola emerged as a world-class supplier in three rapidly expanding (at the time) electronics markets: two-way mobile radios, paging devices and cellular telephones, where they initially emerged as the global leader.

Galvin realized that to be competitive, to win, a company or an individual can't rest upon their laurels or previous accomplishments. He knew acceptance, comfort and complacency breed mediocrity. Quickly. Devastatingly. And usually unprofitably.

Many corporate marketers, entrepreneurs, and businesspeople fear brand loyalty is extinct. Today's demanding consumers expect quality and value, and if they don't get it, they're willing to change. Their vote is cast at the cash register, online payment link or purchase order.

However, leaders and visionaries know *change* also brings opportunity, even if it must be tempered by a wee bit of humility. Galvin admitted, "Challenging conventional wisdom is crucial to restoring a company's competitive edge. You have to acknowledge you don't know all the ways of doing things best." (Perhaps, Galvin's sentiment should have been embraced by future Motorola leaders? In 2001, Motorola's revenues plunged by almost $8 billion dollars. And their losses approached $4 billion dollars.)

8. Competing with Intellectual Capital!

So how do you *capitalize*, not capsize, from change? How do you compete profitably? Let's take a look at eight specific strategies that enable you to innovate with the power of your mind, or "intellectual capital."

1. Focus on Training, Development and Performance Enhancement.

Continually look at ways to improve the quality of yourself, your people, your services, your operations and your products. For example, many companies pursue a zero-defect manufacturing goal. And they also invest heavily in the ongoing training and education of its employees. If you're concerned about the expense of this training, consider this: If you think the cost of education is high, imagine the cost of ignorance!

Many organizations, also "educate" and "market" with a unique perspective. While quality is of course important to them, they seemingly no longer embrace only TQM, or Total Quality Management. Instead, they now exclaim the battle cry of *TBM—Total Business Management*. This revelation was actually shared with me by a client's director of quality assurance, who said, "Jeff, don't get me wrong. Quality is really important here, but it has to be quality with a purpose. It has to be quality that helps our customers and helps our business or bottom line."

2. Plan and Prepare. Better to be Proactive than Reactive.

How prepared are you for the future? How willing are you to change? No matter what, there will be some days when you must be reactive. Why? Because "stuff" happens! And on some days the "stuff" is piled higher and deeper. Fine—if you're prepared for the days when you must be "*re*active," that means you're already starting to be "*pro*active."

Too often, today's problems are caused by yesterday's solutions! But by being proactive, you're anticipating the future. You're preparing for the needs and goals of tomorrow by planning today. With a proactive approach, you're driven by creation, not reaction. And that's the way it should be. Mindless emulation of others' strategies will never catapult you into a more favorable future or an improved condition.

Believe it or not, I've had clients in the healthcare industry who were developing action plans for 25 years from now. Of course, they acknowledge, between now and then their plan might need drastic revisions. However, they were devoting the time now, to prepare for their future.

3. Establish "Teams."

Who goes to and wins the Super Bowl? That's right, a team. And hundreds of millions watch. And who plays in the National Football League's Pro Bowl? Individuals. And while some watch—who cares? Teams are essential for long-term success, because:

T together
E everybody
A accomplishes
M more

Teams can be created internally or externally—with customers, clients, suppliers and even fellow business professionals. It's unimportant whether you call it a team, study group, partnership or strategic alliance. The key is you have a team and actively participate. For the team to work though:

- The *T* (together) also requires *trust* at all levels. (Remember, when trust is high, fear is low!)

- The *E* (everybody) requires you be *empathetic* to others' needs, concerns and motivators.
- The *A* (accomplishes) requires you *appreciate* all individuals' personal contributions to the overall success.
- The *M* (more) requires you *manage* conflict. By the way, conflict is okay. It's healthy! If two or more people are always in agreement, at least one of them isn't necessary! The key is to manage the conflict, so you minimize any emotional war games. Reveal the problem. Discuss it. Then solve it!

Create an advisory group. One of the best ways to create a team environment is to establish an advisory group, almost like a board of directors. Here's what you do: Call five to ten key customers or clients, and ask them (and another key member of their team), to sit on your advisory board. Contact people who know you, like you and trust you—folks who will be brutally honest. The group should meet for two to three hours—perhaps two to four times annually. The purpose of the group is to provide feedback and insights—so you can better serve them and others.

An excellent example of teamwork is provided by a client of mine, EATON, a global manufacturer of highly engineered products, ranging from electrical power grids, switches and controls to even golf grips. EATON's sales in 1994 (when I worked with them) soared 37 percent and earnings climbed a whopping 55 percent. At the time, of its nearly $7 billion in corporate revenues, 80 percent were generated from products that were either number one or two in their respective markets. (Markets included automotive, truck, industrial, commercial construction, aerospace and marine.)

So what was the key to EATON's phenomenal performance in the 1990s? Teamwork! When the *Cleveland Plain Dealer* recognized EATON as "The Best in Area" and "The Best in State," in 1995, here's what then Chairman Stephen R. Hardis credited his company's success to: "Teamwork, at all levels of Eaton's sprawling form, put Eaton on top, and teamwork will keep it there." Even with new leadership, over the past twenty-plus years, the EATON team has had consistent and dramatic growth. EATON's sales today, is more than $20 billion dollars.

4. Define Goals that are Realistic, But that "Stretch" You.

To succeed, you must be a goal-seeking being. You should always be in pursuit of something. And you should give yourself every opportunity to succeed. However, if your goal is unrealistic, you'll be frustrated. If it's too easy, you'll have a diminished sense of success, a ho-hum feeling of accomplishment. However, if it "stretches" you beyond your perceived limitations, it brings euphoria!

5. Monitor Progress and Modify.

You should continually check how you're doing! Airplane pilots adjust their flight pattern. Coaches call time-outs. Business professionals review sales figures and expense reports. Why? To see if change is needed. If it is, do it! If it's not, see if you can enhance it, upgrade it or improve it. The old adage was, "If it ain't broke, don't fix it." The new adage should be, "If it ain't broke, test alternatives. Try to make it better."

6. "Pilot" Change Before Expanding.

Remember, change—and your successful adaptation to it—happens over time, not overnight! If you're unwilling to surrender yourself to *change*, why should those you market to, sell to or try to positively influence be any different? They won't be! They'll still cling to their artificial mental barriers and live within their personal prisons—unless you can help them discover the change that will help them attain a more favorable future and improve their condition.

People's lives are essentially driven by two very basic but powerful principles: 1) People do things for their reason, not yours; and 2) people search for ways to realize gain and/or avoid loss. So, it's important to complement change gradually. Don't become a Mutant Ninja Change Warrior! You'll frighten yourself and others! Instead, make things happen over time. Reprogram yourself and others toward positive action. Try to understand the sources of resistance and neutralize them.

7. Empower Yourself Before, During and After the Change.

"Empower" is more than a buzzword. Instead, it's really an overt expression of faith in your ability to take action and make good things happen. Webster Dictionary says it means "to authorize or to license." In other words, giving yourself the opportunity to take action, to learn and to succeed.

Empowerment is characterized by trust. Especially trust in yourself—you must possess an attitude and aptitude to "do it." You can make a decision on-the-spot, without looking to others.

Here's an empowerment story. At lunchtime, I like to drink iced tea—a tough drink to find in Chicago restaurants during the winter months. Apparently, iced tea is considered "out of season" at this time of year. (Now I never knew iced tea actually had a "season." I'm just beginning to understand when I can and can't wear white shoes!) Once, I was in a downtown Chicago restaurant on a frigid winter day. When I requested an iced tea, the waitress said, "I'm sorry sir, but during the winter, we don't serve iced tea." I asked, "Do you have hot tea?" "Yes," she replied. I asked, "Do you have ice?" Again, she responded affirmatively. "Do you think you could put the two of them together?" I suggested. To which she replied, "I'll have to ask the manager."

What?! Was she kidding?! No! *She* was *not* an empowered business professional! Management didn't empower her and she didn't empower herself to make a good on-the-spot decision.

8. Link Change to Rewards.

"You done good!" "Way to go!" "Hey, hey!" Whether it's words, money, material goodies or an afternoon off, when successful change happens, say "thank you" to yourself. Congratulate yourself! And when appropriate, don't forget to thank the rest of your team.

In my consulting work, my clients' employees sometimes complain about their environment, peers, management and compensation. Yet, you know what bugs them the most? When their work or contributions aren't recognized! I hear comments like, "We never know what they're thinking", "It would be nice to occasionally get a compliment" and "A pat on the back would sure be appreciated."

If an employee or someone you work with changes or has successfully altered their behavior in a positive way, praise them. Reward them. Thank them! If not, they'll be hesitant to change next time.

9. Breaking Barriers and Raising Ceilings

While the changes around you come fast and frequent, you might not adapt to them with the same sense of urgency or speed. While a key to your successful adaptation to change is physical—the actions you take because of change—first of all, it's mental: your mindset.

You and I may look at the world differently. We've each assigned to "our world" our own sense of order—or "how things should be done." We perceive our world based upon our set of assumptions or rules, which we usually take for granted. And when the world doesn't agree with these rules, we normally dismiss *those* ideas as being absurd or foolish.

How you interpret your world has a profound impact upon your future. You see your world with your own unique paradigm. The word paradigm comes from the Greek root "paradeigma," which means a pattern or a model.

Thomas Kuhn's book, *The Structure of Scientific Revolutions*, explored the phenomena of scientific paradigms. Kuhn studied how scientists never saw the world in its entirety, but instead in little pieces. Their paradigms acted as filters on reality. Scientists used their own paradigms or perceptions to either distort information until it fit their rules, or they simply dismissed the data.

Joel Barker, a futurist, also did extensive studies of paradigms in his book, *Discovering the Future: The Business of Paradigms*. He defines a paradigm as, "any set of rules or regulations that describes boundaries and tells us what to do to be successful within those boundaries."

Paradigms — whether they're business, social, global or local — influence our attitudes, actions, beliefs, and behaviors. Examples of paradigms might be:

- "Man will never walk on the moon."
- "Women shouldn't vote."
- "Television will never replace radio."
- "There's nothing left to be invented."

Paradigms can be very positive. Speed limits and parking spaces, for example, give us a sense of order or understanding to our daily lives. However, they can trick us into believing our way is the only way. And as a result, paradigms can thwart creativity, achievement and profitability. Marcel Proust once said, "The real act of discovery consists not in finding new land, but in seeing with new eyes." Therefore, you must begin to explore markets, products and people not only for what they are, but for what they can become.

Raise Your Ceiling!

Paradigm is a great word, but it's too fancy. Let me introduce you to another word with the same meaning—*ceiling*. Why ceiling? Several years ago, I left my home in the Chicagoland area for a three-week speaking and book tour throughout New Zealand

and Australia. The first leg of this journey took me from Chicago to San Francisco. The man sitting next to me was Al Wilkerson. I had never met him before. Yet I'll never forget him.

Al told me about a trip that he took several years ago with his daughter Alycia, when she was only 3. Al and Alycia had never traveled together before, let alone on an airplane. Alycia couldn't wait to get to the airport. As they walked through the terminal, Al clutched her hand. He sensed her excitement. As they walked down the jetway, her eyes grew bigger. Her heart pounded louder. After they boarded, Al took Alycia and plunked her small body into the great big leather seat that engulfed her. Then he turned her face to the window—so she could see the world from a whole new perspective.

As the 747 took off and started to climb toward 35,000 feet, Al stared at his daughter and watched as her expression changed—from fascination and glee to fear and panic. She kept looking up and then to him, up and at him, up and at him…until she finally exclaimed, "Daddy, Daddy, when do we hit the ceiling?"

I'm here you let you know—there are no ceilings, no paradigms, no parameters, no rules, no boundaries, unless *YOU* place them there!

One of my clients has actually placed an eight-inch by eight-inch ceiling tile on the desk of each employee in his company. Emblazoned on each tile are these words:

RAISE YOUR CEILING!

10. Your World of Infinite Possibility!

How high can you raise your ceiling? The answer is up to you. According to Don Winkler, former Chairman & CEO of Ford Motor Credit Company and former Chairman & CEO of Finance One—a subsidiary of Banc One, before it became part of Chase—and a client who I worked with at both Ford and Banc One, "We live in a world of infinite possibility. You just need to open your mind to all of the marvelous potentialities waiting to be discovered."

Don Winkler knew how to grow a business and his people. He once said to me, "Jeff, I'm really just a farmer. I pick the right seeds. Plant them. Nurture them. Grow them. And then harvest them." With that philosophy, Don's "farm" flourished.

When I was working with Don and his team at Finance One, they provided loans to borrowers for both personal and business needs. One of the Finance One Companies was Banc One Consumer Financial Services. They provided funding to borrowers for debt consolidation, mortgage refinancing, student-loan programs, tax-related services and other financial requirements. With Don's vision, this consumer finance company grew within five years—from receivables of $300 million to receivables of over $11 billion!

Because of this success, another "crop" was tilled on Don's turf: Banc One Credit Corporation provided commercial loans to dealerships, (automotive, marine, recreational vehicle, commercial, etc.) for their "floor plan" or inventory, as well as financed the retail purchases of their customers.

This division also grew with an "agricultural abundance." The loan portfolio of these companies, (Consumer Financial Services and Credit Company), soon totaled more than $38 billion!

So what was Don's secret?

He said, "It's a transformational approach to business. It's a discovery process that opens any organization and its people to a future of infinite possibilities and exponential growth."

Don firmly believed, "By changing unproductive attitudes and behavior, and harnessing experience and imagination, any individual, team or company can turn breakdowns into breakthroughs and garbage into gold!"

He also said, "There's not a business in this world that can't achieve compound annual earnings growth of at least 25 percent."

But how?

Don urges both individuals and companies to undergo a *metamorphosis.*

A Metamorphosis

Don Winkler was trained as an engineer. Therefore, he knows that entropy, or disorder, drains energy from essential work and results. And this *drain* is often the greatest enemy of any successful system, endeavor or business.

That's why he devised a process that replaces disorder with

direction. It replaces confusion with commitment. It turns the passive into the passionate.

Don Winkler's six steps to breakthrough results are:

1. Create a vision and a purpose. Get people out of their mental boxes and away from old assumptions. Create a new picture of what your business could be.

Don believes "true vision" is a mental image of the future the way you want it to be. It's not stagnant. It's evolutionary. It can be amended, expanded, refined and reconfigured. It allows for the realities of time, the marketplace and changing needs to shape its flexible form.

The "vision" must also be personal and defined in terms of your ideals and longings. And for staying power, it needs to be broad-based and must incorporate all aspects of your business.

Perhaps one of the best examples of a specific vision was when American president John Fitzgerald Kennedy set the goal that by the end of the 1960s, an American astronaut would be on the moon. Many laughed. Yet astronaut Jim Lovell wasn't one of them. As a Gemini and Apollo astronaut, Jim Lovell had a remarkable career. His harrowing and courageous experience during his Apollo 13 mission is told in the best-selling book *Lost Moon* and the movie *Apollo 13*.

When he was a guest on my television talk-show *Insight*, I asked Jim Lovell, "How did you react to President Kennedy's vision or goal?" He said, "Well when we first heard about the objective, we hadn't even flown a man into space and it was, 'Can we do it?'

He said before the decade is out…and that was just about 9 years away. It was quite a challenge for us, but as you know, everybody dug in, and as you well know, we finally accomplished it."

2. Analyze the status quo. Take a hard look at where your business is today and how things are being done.

3. Identify strategic issues. What is it about the status quo that could prevent the realization of your vision?

4. Plan and implement strategic initiatives. Design projects to knock down those barriers and pave the way to achieving your vision.

5. Set goals and objectives. Create specific targets to sustain investment. Support progress toward your vision.

6. Achieve true business breakthroughs. Although they're unpredictable at the start of the process, these breakthroughs are its end result: the realization of a vision with unique competitive advantages.

What makes Don's system different? He believes there are three reasons:

1. His definition of "vision" isn't based on numbers. Instead it's open-ended and infinite in scope—at the stimulating starting point and at the end-result of a bold discovery process.
2. The system resists setting specific numeric goals until the end, rather than at the beginning, of the discovery process.
3. His experience has proven that the process doesn't fizzle out over the long haul because it's both evolutionary and

self-propelling. It uses a project management system that keeps the ball rolling by assigning names and dates to every strategic initiative. This lays a strong foundation, or framework, for making and monitoring progress.

Thinking Out of the Box

The phrase "think out of the box" is a familiar rejoinder. Like "pushing the paradigm" or "raising the ceiling," it stresses the need for creativity and innovation. However, Don Winkler is the first person who ever defined for me "the box" and its sides. Don believes "the box" is a "strict interpretation of reality that constrains growth" with six sides: opinions/beliefs, habits, attitudes, rules/policies, assumptions and fears.

The Box

1. Opinions/Beliefs

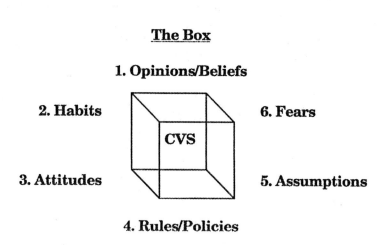

| 2. Habits | 6. Fears |
| 3. Attitudes | 5. Assumptions |

4. Rules/Policies

Don calls the view from inside the box the CVS, or the "Current View of the Situation." Yet, when you push out or break through any side of the box, it releases you to pursue the BVS, or the "Better View of the Situation." Why? Because it frees you to transcend the status quo and move beyond business as usual. Don further stresses, "This process is liberating as it gives you access to the infinite and harnesses your power of discovery. The spirit of inquiry is great...it invites participation and growth; questions are more stimulating than assertions."

To help his people actively pursue the BVS, Don had a simple but powerful response. When he heard someone claim, "It can't be done!" Don calmly and confidently stated, "Up 'til now!" His talented professionals then devoted themselves to a BVS, with a new vision, a new goal, a new dream, a new commitment—and a new result!

You, too, can think out of the box and envision a BVS. When somebody tells you, "It can't be done," take Don's advice. With a smile and a look of supreme optimism exclaim, "Up 'til now!"

(Note: The preceding is based upon personal conversations with Don Winkler and his article "Delivering True Business Breakthroughs." These comments and strategies are featured with Don's permission.)

11. On or Beyond the Edge!

To attain success in the future, you must continually push the paradigm—or raise the ceiling. It's on the edge or beyond the paradigm or ceiling where the real possibilities for your future happen.

If you're willing to wallow within your current paradigms or ceilings, you're likely to exist within a limited environment. We can describe it as having our growth stunted. While you're still enjoying success within your current ceiling, you should be proactively working toward your new ceiling. William James once said, "A new idea is first condemned as ridiculous and then dismissed as trivial, until finally, it becomes what everybody knows."

When it comes to change, remember six things:

1. You must accept change with the understanding that nothing comes to stay, but only to pass.
2. The most effective way to deal with change, is to change.
3. The best way to minimize the impact of change is to make the commitment to planning, ongoing knowledge and goal setting.
4. You play each game differently, not because you want to, but because you have to...because the marketplace and circumstances are always changing.
5. Your addiction to the past sets a trap for your future.
6. You must be willing to bust out of your zone of comfort, security and complacency.

To push your paradigm, to raise your ceiling, to attain new levels of business success, remember the words of Lester Thurow, who once said, "A competitive world has two possibilities for you. You can lose. Or, if you want to win, you can change."

12. Pictures in Your Eyes!

One morning, when our son Chad was 4, he wandered into our bedroom and said something my wife, Sheryl, and I will never forget. He exclaimed, "Mommy and Daddy, last night, I had pictures in my eyes!"

How prophetic—the wisdom of the sages in little ages! Chad's statement made me realize, as adults, we all too often take our lives too seriously. We can't "push the paradigm," "think out of the box" or "raise the ceiling" because we're hopelessly linked to the past and all too secure in the present. We cease creating. We let our lives be run by rigid rules. We refuse to change. We don't allow ourselves the luxury to dream. We don't "see the pictures in our eyes."

Whether your images of success are in black-and-white or color, 3D or holograms—make a commitment to change. Always have "pictures in your eyes"!

CHAPTER 3

Victory on the VINe: Building Relationships and Value

Always deliver more in perceived value
than you take in actual cash value.

13. A Vote for Value!

The *Peak Your Profits Business-Growth System* operates from a single basic principle, with three major elements. In order to be a successful business professional, you must be:

V Value-driven

I Integrity-based

N Non-manipulative

I refer to this three-step VIN strategy as the *VINe Principle*. To "swing" successfully and profitably from this *VINe*, you must possess each element. Let's briefly examine the *VINe* principle. First, *Value-driven*:

You must always be selling and delivering products and services of high perceived value. Now, I didn't say *actual* value—I said *perceived* value. There's a considerable difference. BMW, Lexus and Mercedes for example, have capitalized on the perceived value, pride, prestige and status of owning their automobiles in their advertising. A BMW magazine ad, (in the 1990s), proudly proclaimed:

BMW, for someone who knows the value of a buck and is willing to spend $40,000 of them!

Two ingenious print ads for Lexus conveyed "value" like this:

You're at a stoplight. It will last twenty seconds. This may be the only time some people ever see you. How do you want to be remembered?

You're torn. Do you park it outside so the neighbors can see it? Or inside, so the birds can't? You put it inside. But you leave the garage door up.

And when Mercedes first introduced its limited edition 600 series, a local dealership in the northern suburbs of Chicago simply posted this banner across the showroom's display window:

The 600 is here.

I actually know someone who bought the 600 for more than its list price. He paid $155,000. That's right, $155,000 for metal, glass, rubber and leather. In lots of places, that'll buy you a home!

Is a Mercedes, a Lexus or a BMW worth the amount of money

a buyer is willing to pay or invest? The answer is—it depends! It depends on whether the buyer/decision-maker perceives the value to be worth it.

Perceived Value and Cash Value

Whatever the required investment for your product or service, you should *always* deliver more in perceived value than you take in actual cash value. Let me repeat that. You should always deliver more in perceived value than you take in actual cash value.

Here's another interesting example of perceived automotive value, but unfortunately it's at the opposite end of the value spectrum. This message was posted on the marquis at a dealer's lot in Chicago just before the holidays:

> *Christmas is coming, yourself you should treat,*
> *Buy one of our cars, so we can eat!*

Now, would you have a lot of confidence buying a car from these folks? Me neither. People like to associate with winners. And if they perceive you're weak, desperate or in a survival mode, it greatly reduces or even removes any potential for you to make a sale, develop business or peak your profits.

Here's one more key point about value: In the absence of a value barometer, the relationship is reduced to a price eliminator. One more time: In the absence of a value barometer, the relationship is reduced to a price eliminator.

For example, if your decision-makers think your price or

investment is too high and isn't justified by the value you're providing, they'll use price to eliminate you. Let's say you're asking for $1,000 for your widget, but your customers think it's only worth $750. Why? Probably because you haven't shown them the perceived value to justify your request for $1,000. Therefore, what happens? They decline to purchase. Because, in the absence of a value barometer, the relationship is reduced to a price eliminator. Here the focus is price, *not* value.

Now, what if you're selling a widget for only $500, but your decision-makers think it's actually worth $1,000. Several things could happen. First, your decision-makers could let you know your product or service is grossly underpriced. But I wouldn't bet on this first scenario happening.

Second, your decision-makers quickly snatch up the widget for $500 because they know they've made the deal of a lifetime. Or perhaps even more likely, they'll refuse the offer, despite the seemingly incredible savings. Why? Because they're probably wondering, "What's wrong with this widget?" Is it defective? Stolen? Unlikely to perform as expected? Once again, what are the results? They graciously decline. Therefore, in the absence of a value barometer, the relationship is reduced to a price eliminator.

Perceived value is an interesting phenomenon. In 1989, a friend gave me a little card I've always hung onto: The card is called *Values* and it was written by John Ruskin. It says:

> *It's unwise to pay too much, but it's unwise to pay too little.*
> *When you pay too much, you lose a little money, that is all.*
> *When you pay too little, you sometimes lose everything,*
> *because the thing you bought was incapable of doing the*

thing you bought it to do. The common law of business pro-
hibits paying a little and getting a lot. It can't be done. If you
deal with the lowest bidder, it's well to add something for
the risk you run. And if you do that, you will have enough
to pay for something better.

When John Ruskin refers to something better, does that mean value can only be associated with a *premium price*? Definitely not. In the next Focus Section, you'll see how value can also be linked to *savings*.

14. The Price/Value Relationship

Here's a powerful example of the *price/value relationship*. Several deep-discount office supply stores are within minutes of my office. However, one of them does something I think is ingenious. It's a strategy I now see used by retailers, such as grocery stores and mass merchandisers. However, it's a philosophy that has easy application to your business. Here are the actual numbers from a receipt of mine. My office supply store receipt says:

Office catalog list prices would have cost you $131.20.
Our Low Everyday Price is $81.98.
You saved $49.22
That's a savings of 37%.

Wow! How's that for a powerful statement! What makes this receipt such a strong value-builder? It gives you tangible, substantive, and actual proof of significant savings.

Can you adapt this strategy to your product or service? I'd sure think so. All you need to do is quantify on a receipt, invoice, online order form or billing statement exactly how much you're saving your decision-makers.

15. Psychic Debt

Have you ever given a customer a product or service for nothing? Something you'd normally send them a bill or an invoice for, but because of the goodness in your heart, you decided to provide it for free? If you had charged the customer, how much would you have charged?

Believe it or not, I've had clients give their customers hundreds, sometimes even thousands of dollars' worth of goods and services for free! Now that's okay, but there's a better way. Next time, if you're going to give a customer something for free—something the individual would normally have paid for—send the individual a bill. That's right, send a bill—but cross out the amount owed and scribble across the statement something like, "This one's on us! No payment due. This is part of our commitment to better serve you!"

Why is this approach so effective? First, it lets your customer know you made an actual investment of time or money to provide the product or service. Second, it diminishes the potential that your decision-maker will expect something for nothing. But most important, what this strategy really does is create in a demonstrable way a business advantage with a unique name or label that I think you'll like.

This strategy is called *psychic debt*. And the satisfaction of that debt is likely to have a significantly greater value over the long-term future of your business than the few extra dollars you might have placed in your bank account now, from the payment of that one bill.

Here's one way I counseled a distributor client, Joe, about *psychic debt*. Joe told me he was providing free delivery to his customers and if he charged a delivery fee, some of his customers would be paying well in excess of $1,000 a month. Once Joe understood and applied the concept of *psychic debt*, he then sent his customers monthly, quarterly and yearly transportation or delivery invoices. The actual amounts they could have paid were crossed out. Customers now saw, on a regular basis, that Joe truly was providing them with incredible value and tangible dollar savings.

Does the concept of *psychic debt* only apply to a product? Of course not. It also applies to your time through consulting, training or the offering of a service. If you provide a client with, let's say, three hours of valuable guidance or training at no charge, assign a dollar value to that service and then send them a *psychic-debt* bill.

16. The Discount Dilemma or OUCH! Impact

Remember, value can be created in countless ways. Later, we'll talk about your values checklist and how it relates to the negotiation process. However, there's a big difference between value, psychic debt and discounting simply to make the sale. I'm not telling you not to negotiate, but it's essential you truly understand the impact of a price reduction on your long-term business relationship, career and bottom line.

Let's imagine your product or service regularly sells for $100 and the cost of sales is $75. Therefore, your gross margin is $25. Now, what happens if you cut your price? Let's say you trim your sale price by only 10 percent. Therefore, your new price is $90. Your cost of sales, though, is still the same $75. And $90 minus $75 equals a new gross margin of $15. You might be thinking, that's not a big deal to give up 10 percent to secure the deal. But with a 10 percent price reduction, how much new business must you bring in to regain the lost margin?

Believe it or not, to regain the lost margin, you'll have to get additional business of almost 67 percent! OUCH! And if you cut your price by 15 percent, you must get additional business of 150 percent! OUCH! OUCH! (To see me explain this frightening reality, please head to www.jeffblackman.com/results-tv/ then click on "Jeff Blackman interviewed on: Value vs. Price!")

When I ask workshop participants, "Why would you want to discount? What might the advantages or disadvantages be?" Here's how they respond:

Advantages of Discounting:

- Gains new accounts.
- Generates long-term business volume.
- Guarantees credit.
- Increases market share.
- Offers higher exposure to a new business/market.
- Secures long-term commitments.
- Gets "foot in the door."
- Generates positive exposure with high-profile account.
- Increases utilization during a slow time.
- Keeps business we may have lost.
- Takes business away from competition.

Disadvantages of Discounting:

- Reduces profits.
- Creates negative impact/perception on existing business.
- Lowers company's value to prospective customers.
- Makes it hard to raise prices later.
- Starts a bidding war.
- Erodes margins.
- May sacrifice availability.
- May sacrifice reliability.
- Lowers revenues.
- Lowers commissions.
- May create loss of trust.
- Generates "low-baller" perception.
- Creates an image of an inferior product/service.
- Creates equipment shortages.
- Causes hassles from management.
- Reduces company image to level of competition.
- Makes sales people lazy.
- Jeopardizes quality.
- Turns products and services into a commodity.
- Sets a scary precedent for future business.

Remember, a price reduction may cause you to work *harder*, not smarter. Plus, price wars can be demoralizing, exhausting and unprofitable.

17. Honesty Doesn't Require a Good Memory!

The second step in the VINe principle is *I*, for *Integrity-based*. Without integrity, truth and honesty in the business-development process, there's no need to even market, sell, negotiate or serve. Your *word* represents your credibility, reputation and character. A buyer and seller must forge a relationship. And there's no quicker way to destroy that relationship than by deceit.

Time magazine once devoted a cover story to business and societal ethics. The story was called, "Lying: Everybody's doin' it… honest!"

I overheard the following conversation, one person pointing his finger at another and accusing, "You're lying!" To which the other person replied, "You're right, but at least hear me out!" Sad, but true.

Do you know what the best thing is about honesty? It doesn't require a good memory!

The wise businessperson knows the value of integrity. And that by helping and serving others, we help ourselves. By hurting or abusing others, we hurt and abuse ourselves. Integrity must be built into everything we do. Its impact is powerful. It's characterized by goodwill and good sense. When you're an integrity-based individual, you possess a special power: an aura of influence.

Reputation rises above riches. Trust overshadows greed. Character commands commitment. Honesty reigns supreme.

In Chapter 5, we take an even closer look at integrity, the value of your word and how you can always keep your ethics in check and never jeopardize your professional or personal reputation.

18. Let 'Em Buy, not Battle!

The third step in the VINe principle is the *N*, which stands for *Non-manipulative*. A buyer or decision-maker who is manipulated is likely not to buy, to buy and later reject your product or service or, under either circumstance, tell countless others about the conniving businessperson he or she dealt with. Buyers are turned off by pushy, hard-sell, guerrilla tactics.

However, they seldom mind a polite and positive approach to persuasion and persistence. As Calvin Coolidge once said:

> *Nothing in this world can take the place of persistence.*
> *Talent will not, nothing is more common than unsuccessful*
> *men and women with talent. Genius will not; unrewarded*
> *genius is almost a proverb.*
> *Education will not; the world is full of educated derelicts.*
> *Persistence and determination alone are omnipotent.*
> *The slogan "press on" has solved and always will solve the*
> *problems of the human race.*

When I stress a "non-manipulative" approach to business in my keynotes, workshops and results-sessions, a few folks snicker or roll their eyes in disbelief. Some claim, "Jeff, there's a logical inconsistency! The art of persuasion requires manipulation."

Ridiculous! Manipulation only secures an initial or fleeting success, not the highly lucrative and profitable long-term relationship. And relationships are a must when you aim to peak your profits!

Remember, when value is high, when integrity is high, when

non-manipulation is high, and yes, sometimes even when the price, rate, fee or investment is high—what's low? Resistance!

19. Relationship Power!

Every business person I meet waxes rhapsodic about the importance of relationships. Bankers, lawyers, entrepreneurs, manufacturers, service professionals, advertising executives, accountants, retailers, wholesalers, distributors, independent reps—*everybody* tells me how their business is a "relationship business" and their success is "built on relationships."

Are they right? Well, of course they're right. Yet there's a difference between *right* and *results*. When others talk about relationships, they're usually referring to whom they know. Their network. Their circle of influence. Their clique. Their internal club.

But that's not enough! To truly maximize your relationships, two key elements of "relationship power" must exist:

- Your "little r."
- Your "BIG R."

Your "little r" refers to *traditional relationship-building*. It's your:

- Likeability.
- Trust.
- Humanity.
- Sincerity.
- Courtesy.
- Personality.
- Chemistry.

The "little r" focuses on your ability to get along. It's your inherent nature to be warm, caring and compassionate. You're empathetic to your customers, clients and prospects. In Yiddish, the word for "little r" is *mensch*. And a mensch is simply a good person!

People like to do business with people they like. However, "little r" alone isn't enough to peak your profits. You also need to optimize your "BIG R"!

"BIG R" focuses on your ability to deliver results! Never forget, people aren't only interested in *who* you are, ("little r"); they're also interested in *what* you can do for them, ("BIG R"). "BIG R" is your ability to be a growth-specialist. You, your products, services, company and team—have the expertise to help prospects, customers and clients attain a more favorable future and improve their condition by:

- Maximizing gain.
- Reducing loss.
- Increasing earnings.
- Slashing costs.
- Creating enjoyment.
- Assuring satisfaction.
- Providing security.
- Developing pride.
- Enhancing performance.
- Producing results.

Why is the attrition rate so high in professions that require business-development skills? Because once you sell to your friends and neighbors, who only bought because they wanted to be a "nice guy" and honor their "little r" commitment, you have no real marketable "BIG R" skills to the rest of the world.

Have you ever heard someone exclaim something like this? "Hey, don't get me wrong. Sue is a wonderful person, I really like her, but she just doesn't have the knowledge, product capabilities or company support I need!" This decision-maker acknowledges satisfaction with Sue's "little r" but expresses disappointment and doubt with her "BIG R."

On the flip-side, have you ever heard something like this? "Phil is really bright, he has a quality line, but there's something about him that hits me wrong. It's hard for me to explain or put my finger on, but I think it would be tough to work with him." Here, the decision-maker is firmly convinced about Phil's "BIG R," but is disturbed with his "little r."

Remember, your "little r's" and "BIG R's" can't be mutually exclusive. People invest in who you are *and* what you can do for them.

20. The Relationship Builder!

Information is valuable—but you must have the ability to capture it, remember it and then apply it. Although that's obviously easier said than done, it's crucial to your success. (It's often that casually uttered statement or seemingly unimportant piece of minutiae from a prospect's or customer's lips that gives you a distinct and profitable competitive advantage.) But you're bombarded with so much "stuff" during a day, it's usually hard to determine—let alone recall—which "stuff" is worth keeping and which can be tossed.

Relationship power (via the "little r" and "BIG R") requires your "awareness antenna" be operating at all times. Your eyes and ears should be prepared to capture the nuances of comments, non-verbal signals and other responses from those with whom you come into contact. It's these subtleties that help you maximize the strength, longevity and profitability of your relationships.

The dilemma, though, is how do you keep track of all that good stuff that someday might mean the difference between a suspect, a prospect and a customer?

I created the following *Relationship Builder* as an organized and efficient way to capture valuable information about an individual. Some of the questions are hard-hitting and business-oriented. Others deal with lifestyle, health and personal preferences. You may even consider some of the questions "off the wall," but I assure you, each one serves a purpose. And that purpose is—*results!* There's a direct correlation between trust, knowledge and business-growth. (Clients tell me the *Relationship Builder* and its content can easily be adapted or incorporated into their sales software or CRM system.)

One of the reasons my business has grown over the years is because I truly take an "active interest" in my clients' lives, on both the personal and professional level. They share with me their feelings and experiences about business and other aspects of their lives. Our discussions are vast and varied. The following is a mere sampling of actual discussion topics clients have initiated with me:

- Potty training.
- The death of a loved one.

- Ribald indiscretions of youth.
- Unique hobbies like hot-air ballooning.
- Divorce.
- Substance abuse and alcoholism.
- Embarrassing moments in the boardroom.
- Bizarre dreams or nightmares.
- Favorite recipes.

Obviously, our relationships are based on a high level of trust. And trust translates into opportunity and profitability. That's not a greedy or mercenary statement, but a fact. Once again, because it's worth repeating, when trust is high, fear is low!

However, let me emphasize, the motivation for my interest isn't solely dollars. First and foremost, it's important that I acknowledge that my client is a human being. And the best way to serve that individual, is to to know him or her better than any competitor.

The *Relationship Builder* with its 77 questions helps you do just that. Feel free to adapt the *Relationship Builder* so it works best for you. You may want to delete, skip or change certain questions. Or perhaps even add your own questions. Please do so.

May the *Relationship Builder* help you, like it has helped countless others to *peak their profits!*

Relationship Builder

Relationship Power = little r + BIG R

Customer • Prospect • Network Contact

Start Date _____

Update date _____ Updated by _____

Update date _____ Updated by _____

Update date _____ Updated by _____

❑ **Customer**   ❑ **Prospect**   ❑ **Network Contact**   ❑ **Other**

1. Name _____

Nickname _____

Title _____

2. Company / Association, etc.: _____

Address: _____

City: _____ ST: _____ Zip: _____

Telephone: Business: _____

Direct Line: _____ Fax: _____

e-mail: _____ Web: _____

Social media: LinkedIn, Facebook, Twitter, Skype

_____

3. Home

Address: _____

City: _____ ST: ___ Zip: _____ Country: _____

Telephone: H: _____ O: _____

Direct Line: _____

Fax: _____ e-mail: _____

4. Birth date _____

Birthplace _____ Hometown _____

5. Height _____ Weight _____

Physical conditions: (i.e., great shape, injuries, problems, etc.)

_____

_____

6. Secretary: Name: _____

                  Personal info: _____

                  Direct Line: _____

                  Fax: _____ e-mail: _____

   Secretary: Name: _____

                  Personal info: _____

                  Direct Line: _____

                  Fax: _____ e-mail: _____

Education

7. High School _____

Year graduated _____ Town & State _____

Sports/Special interests _____

_____

_____

College _____

Year graduated _____ Town & State _____

Sports/Special interests _____

_____

_____

College honors _____

Advanced degrees _____

Fraternity or sorority _____

8. If individual didn't attend college:
❑ touchy subject ❑ not a touchy subject
What did he/she do instead?

_____

_____

_____

_____

9. Military service
Years served _____ Branch _____
Rank _____
Feeling/opinion toward service/military _____

_____

_____

_____

_____

Family

10. Marital status: ❑ Single ❑ Married ❑ Divorced
❑ Widow(er) ❑ Engaged ❑ Significant Other / Dating

Spouse's / Boyfriend's / Girlfriend's / Partner's / Fiancé's
/ Fiancée's... Name _____
Occupation _____
Education _____
Interests/activities/affiliations _____

_____

Wedding anniversary date _____
Wedding location _____

11. Children:

Name _____ Age _____ Birthday _____
Activities/Problems/Education _____
_____
_____

Name _____ Age _____ Birthday _____
Activities/Problems/Education _____
_____
_____

Name _____ Age _____ Birthday _____
Activities/Problems/Education _____
_____
_____

Name _____ Age _____ Birthday _____
Activities/Problems/Education _____
_____
_____

Professional Experiences and Background

12. Previous employment:
Company _____
Location _____
Dates _____ Title _____

Company _____
Location _____
Dates _____ Title _____

Company _____
Location _____
Dates _____ Title _____

13. Previous position(s) at present company

_____

_____

Title(s)/ Dates _____

Length of service at present company _____

Special accomplishments _____

_____

14. Office: awards/recognition/memorabilia/quotes/books/
pictures/etc. _____

_____

_____

15. ❑ CHARMER ❑ DRIVER ❑ PACER ❑ ANALYZER
(Please see Chapter 10 • Focus Sections 71 - 76)

16. Buzzwords, likes to say: _____

_____

17. Professional associations - membership/holds office/
upcoming conventions or programs _____

_____

_____

18. Magazine/newsletter subscriptions, likes to read: _____

_____

_____

19. Mentors _____

_____

Networks with or knows _____

_____

20. Leaders admired/quoted _____
_____

21. Professional or personal relationship(s) with others at
our company _____
_____
_____

22. What do we already know about this individual or their
business? _____
_____
_____

23. How did we get introduced/meet/first establish contact?
_____

24. Attitude toward his/her department/company/staff/job
_____

25. Immediate or short-term goals _____
_____

26. Long-term goals _____
_____

27. Greatest professional challenge _____
_____

28. Pro-active or reactive? Looks to the future/reflects on
the past? _____
_____

Personal/Professional Interests

29. Clubs/Organizations/Associations _____

_____

_____

_____

_____

30. Political involvement? ❑ Y   ❑ N
Party _____
Supports/Donated to _____

_____

_____

_____

_____

31. Community involvement _____

_____

_____

_____

_____

32. Religion _____
Place of worship _____
Active ❑ Y   ❑ N

33. Is opinionated/passionate about: _____

_____

_____

_____

_____

Health and Well-Being

34. Topics not to be discussed (i.e., divorce, suicide, substance abuse, etc.) _____

_____

_____

_____

_____

35. Health _____

_____

_____

_____

_____

36. Drink? ❑ Never ❑ Occasionally ❑ Often
Favorite brand/drink/watering hole _____
Attitude toward drinking _____

37. Smoke? ❑ Y ❑ N
❑ Cigarettes ❑ E-Cigarettes ❑ Cigars ❑ Pipes
Brand _____
Attitude toward smoking _____

38. Works out? ❑ Y ❑ N   At _____
Type(s) of exercise/recreation _____

_____

_____

Special athletic/recreational accomplishments or goals

_____

39. Food - favorite places and dishes:

Breakfast _____

Lunch _____

Dinner _____

Other _____

Favorite foods _____

_____

40. Entertainment:

I/He/She treated on at _____ for $ _____

I/He/She treated on at _____ for $ _____

I/He/She treated on at _____ for $ _____

41. Hobbies, interests, activities _____

_____

_____

_____

Golf: Favorite course/best hole/funniest experience/
country club/etc. _____

_____

42. Reader? ☐ Y ☐ N

Favorite book(s) _____

_____

Favorite author(s) _____

_____

43. Favorite movie(s) _____

_____

Favorite director(s) _____

Favorite genre(s) _____

_____

Favorite actor(s) _____

_____

44. Vacation interests _____

_____

_____

_____

45. Spectator-sports interest: (i.e., sports and teams) _____

_____

_____

_____

46. Car(s) _____ License plate _____
    Car(s) _____ License plate _____
    Car(s) _____ License plate _____

47. Boat? ❏ Y ❏ N   Name _____
Docked at _____

48. Likes to talk about _____

_____

_____

_____

49. Pets _____

50. Musical interests, (artist, group, rock, ethnic, etc.) _____

_____

51. Conveys image of _____

_____

Business Image

52. Wants others to see/perceive him/her as: _____

_____

_____

_____

_____

_____

53. Adjectives to describe this person: _____

_____

_____

_____

_____

_____

_____

54. Greatest accomplishment: _____

_____

_____

_____

_____

_____

55. Short-term personal goal(s): _____

_____

_____

56. Long-term personal goal(s): _____

_____

_____

_____

_____

Our Relationship

57. Any ethical concerns? _____

_____

_____

58. Does he/she have allegiance, (perceived or actual) to me, our company, a competitor? What? How come? _____

_____

_____

_____

_____

59. How does our approach/action plan require him/her to alter the way he/she does things or disrupt his/her "culture"?

_____

_____

_____

60. Reaction to feedback/input from us or others: _____

_____

_____

_____

61. Ego: ❑ Small ❑ Healthy ❑ Out-of-control

62. Real challenges/problems/objections from his/her perspective: _____

_____

_____

63. Other problems that may exist, yet not articulated: _____

_____

_____

_____

64. What are the critical issues of his/her management/ board/committee? _____

_____

_____

_____

65. How's the relationship between this individual and his/her leadership? Any problems? _____

_____

_____

66. How can we solve these problems/issues? _____

_____

_____

_____

67. Is this individual a decision-maker? ❏ Y ❏ N

If a *decision-influencer*, who else must be influenced: _____

_____

Who is the real decision-maker(s)? _____

_____

Is this individual sensitive about not having final
authority? ❑ Y ❑ N

What's required to fund this project/investment? _____

_____

_____

68. Funny experiences/inside "stuff"/running joke _____

_____

_____

69. Previous products/services used from us _____

_____

_____

70. Previous products/services used from competitor(s)

_____

_____

71. Current relationship(s) with competitor(s) _____

_____

72. Golf:
Date: _____ Course: _____
He/She shot: _____ I shot: _____
Learned/Discussed: _____
My follow-up: _____

Date: _____ Course: _____
He/She shot: _____ I shot: _____

Learned/Discussed: _____

My follow-up: _____

Commonality/Influence:

73. Who does he/she know that I know:

Person: _____
Commonality, i.e., group, club: _____

Person: _____
Commonality, i.e., group, club: _____

Person: _____
Commonality, i.e., group, club: _____

74. Who does he/she know that I'd like to meet, know, do business with:

Person: _____
Business: _____

Person: _____
Business: _____

Person: _____
Business: _____

75. Who could this person "sponsor" (see Focus Section 28) or "introduce" us to?

- _____
- _____
- _____

76. Does anyone who I compete with on the planet earth, know more about this person / company / prospect / network contact / decision-maker / supplier / decision-influencer / partner and his or her life and business, than me? _____

_____

77. How will I use this information to best serve and help: My customer, contact or prospect? His or her business or life? My business or life? My company? Our relationship? _____

_____

_____

21. The Value of a Lifetime!

Now you obviously know the value or worth of your products and services. However, do you know the value or worth of your customers? If you don't, you need to. It's easy to calculate and it's crucial for your success.

The *lifetime value* of your customers focuses on their long-term significance to you and your business. While each transaction of every every customer is important, it's the multiple or lifetime-purchase decisions that yield your greatest profits.

To discover the *lifetime value* of a new customer, you only need a few numbers:

1. The size in dollars of your median, or typical, sale to this customer.
2. The size in dollars of your typical sales over a certain period of time (i.e., a month, a quarter, a year).
3. The number of years (prospective) you'll serve this customer.
4. Your average gross profit value (AGPV) or profit margin (the percent of profit you make on each sale).
5. Your acquisition cost (how much it cost you to acquire or "land" this new customer). You may consider the cost of advertising, direct outside sales, public relations, promotion, trade show exhibits, etc.

You might not know all of these figures immediately, but it's worth investing a little time to discover what they are. To show you why, let's go through the *lifetime value* equation with an example. Imagine that:

1. The size in dollars of your typical sale is $5,000.
2. The size in dollars of your typical sales over a year is $20,000. (Your typical sale with a typical customer is $5,000 per quarter.)
3. At a minimum, you determine you'll service this customer for at least another 10 years.
4. Your AGPV or profit margin on each $5,000 sale is 25 percent, or $1,250.
5. Your acquisition cost to acquire a customer is $1,500.

Now, let's plug these numbers into the *lifetime value* formula:

Median or typical sale: $5,000
Annual sales: $20,000
Years of prospective service: 10
Annuitization: (years of service multiplied by annual sales): 10 x $20,000 = $200,000

AGPV/Annual: 25% ($20,000 x 25%) = $5,000
Years of prospective service: 10 x $5,000
= $50,000
Less acquisition costs: - 1,500
Lifetime value: = $48,500

How often, would you invest $1,500 (in year one) to get back $48,500 over 10 years? All the time, right?

There are several advantages in knowing the *lifetime value* of your customer:

1. It helps you and your people focus on the long-term.
2. It emphasizes that your ability to "peak your profits" may not happen on your initial transaction, but it will with many transactions over the years.
3. It allows you to positively manipulate and better understand or justify your marketing and advertising expenditures.

Let's take a look at the last advantage. Let's go back to our example. Imagine, now, you own this business and you advertise your gizmos in a magazine and industry-related website. The cost for these ads is $10,000. They generate 100 leads, but only two $5,000 sales. On the surface, it looks like the ads are, at best, a "break-even" proposition. This might be your analysis—if you didn't know the lifetime value of your customer.

Yet now you know these customers should each buy another three times over the next three quarters. And they should buy another 36 times over the next nine years. Therefore, despite a $10,000 investment in the original ads, you'll still have a profit of $90,000 over 10 years from these two customers. Even if your acquisition cost is significantly higher, it's still a wise investment because of the *lifetime value* of these new customers.

Now, if you're a cynic, you might say, "Hey, nothing is guaranteed. These decision-makers could die tomorrow. Their relatives could open competitive businesses and steal away these accounts. Who knows if they'll still be loyal in 10 years?" You're right, all these things could happen. However, the following could also take place:

- You serve these accounts for more than 10 years, increasing your profits.
- The size of these orders increases in dollars, increasing your profits.
- Your customers buy more often than four times per year, again increasing your profits.
- Your customers refer you to several others who then become long-term customers too.
- Not only do you get the benefits of *lifetime value* from these new customers, but you do so at a significantly reduced acquisition cost, thereby increasing your profits.

By knowing your customer's lifetime value, you can also begin to peak your profits for a lifetime!

22. Value-investing!

Have you ever provided your products or services to grateful clients and then said to yourself, "I know I could have charged more, and they would have gladly paid"? Or maybe you've had extremely satisfied clients who've said something to you like:

- "We're really happy. No question about it. Even if we paid more, it's still worth it!"
- "You're worth every penny...even more!"
- "I don't know how you do it! Great quality. Great service. And a great price. I bet if you charged more, you'd get it!"

If your answer to either question is a reluctant but resounding yes, welcome to the club. I, too, have said and heard the same things. And that's why I created the concept of *value-investing*. In a nutshell, it lets my clients—not me—determine the "value" of my work and, therefore, their appropriate "investment."

You may be thinking, "This is absurd! Why would somebody pay more if they don't have to?" I agree. This was my initial thought and fear, too. However, I was willing to experiment with this *value-investment* strategy just to see what the results might be. And the results have been amazing! This strategy may also be applicable to, and work for, your business, products and services. Here's an example of how I position or present the *value-investment* strategy.

My client, Ryan, and I have already predetermined his budget for a particular project through an extensive process of questioning and discussion. For example, let's say the "investment range" for this project is between $50,000 and $60,000. The "range" isn't in question, only the final investment. Ryan might say, "Jeff, when we're all done, how will I know what my actual investment is?"

My response goes something like this: "Ryan, it may be hard now for us to determine the final investment for a project that'll be completed in five months. Obviously, it'll be influenced by the extent of my research, customization and analysis. But most importantly, by your results. So tell me if you think this approach is a fair one: What if, when we're all done, you assess the value of my contribution to your success? And if you think the final investment should be $60,000 or any number between $50,000 to $60,000, that's fine, too. But of course, if you feel the final investment should be less than $50,000, that, too, is okay. Would that be fair?" Ryan's response: "Yeah, that's fair. Let's do it that way." And then, with a smile I say, "Ryan, I should let you know, this is a 'bet' I've never lost!" He, too, smiles and says, "I didn't think so! Let's get started!"

The following is actual language I've used many times with a client (like Ryan) where the value-investment strategy is part of our agreement.

As discussed and agreed upon, between you and Jeff:

- As agreed, an initial investment of $25,000 is requested now. This initial investment enables us to: 1) hold the dates for Ryan Enterprises and 2) be applied toward the "work in progress" of customization—interviewing your people, reviewing your literature, visiting your sites, etc.

- Subsequent to your learning-system, you'll determine the value of Jeff's contribution to the short and long-term success of Ryan Enterprises. Based upon that assessment, Ryan Enterprises will then make the remaining balance of the investment. The remaining balance of the investment, ($25,000 to $35,000) is requested within seven days of the completion of the learning-system.

- If in the unlikely event you determine the value of Jeff's contribution to the short-term and long-term success of Ryan Enterprises is less than $25,000 to $35,000, then your remaining investment will be for whatever you deem that value to be. And if you honestly believe the value is less than the $25,000 you had already invested, then Blackman & Associates will write you a check for the difference. Immediately. No hard feelings, either. Jeff's focus is on results, not rhetoric. Therefore, he provides this no-risk assurance to you and Ryan Enterprises. This is a "bet" Jeff has never lost. And you might be interested in knowing our long list of ecstatic clients must be happy with the results…because for a final or remaining balance, they've never chosen a reduced or "lower end of the range" investment!

To see our "No-Risk Assurance," as well as Jeff explain it in a video, please take a peek at:

http://www.jeffblackman.com/services/no-risk-assurance/

As unlikely or as strange as it seems, you did just correctly read that, "…for a final or remaining balance, (a client) has never chosen a reduced or 'lower end of the range' investment!"

I've even used the *value-investment* strategy for shorter programs, (for example, a 60-minute keynote or a half-day workshop) and the strategy still works. I leave presentations knowing my clients are extremely grateful and tremendously satisfied, but I have no idea as to what their final investment will be. It really makes for a fun sense of anticipation when, seven to ten days later, an envelope with their check arrives. And it always contains their maximum investment!

The *value-investment* strategy is usually more adaptable to *services* than products, but through creative positioning, it could also work for your products. The real power of this strategy is it places control in the minds and checkbooks of your decision-makers. Perceptions of value, returns on investments and results are their decisions and theirs alone. They are the sole judges of your *value* and *investment*. Yet superior results motivate your decision-maker to reward you with the highest number in the *value-investment* range.

Results! That's the name of the game in business. And results are easier to obtain when you're:

- Value-driven.
- Integrity-based.
- Non-manipulative.

As you embrace and execute this *VINe principle* daily, you'll have a distinct and powerful competitive advantage.

CHAPTER 4

Your Unique Selling Proposition!

"The imagination is the very eye of faith!"

—Henry Ward Beecher, 19th-century American clergyman

23. Remove the Mystery!

Despite popular belief, business development isn't characterized by manipulation, mind-reading, mysticism, magic or mystery. It requires hard work, a sustained effort and the sincere desire to help others. It has become increasingly difficult to attain success in our competitive marketplace. All too often, businesspeople and companies try to distinguish themselves from their competition through bland and almost generic statements such as:

- Lowest prices.
- Great service.
- Superior quality.
- Top-of-the-line.
- New and improved.
- Gold standard.
- Latest and greatest.
- Leading edge.

- Cutting edge.

Such claims are practically meaningless. They don't tell a prospective customer how low your prices are, how great your service is, the extent of your quality, what "top-of-the-line" really means, what you did to become "new and improved" or help substantiate any other boastful, insignificant drivel you assert about you, your team or company.

Sweeping and generalized statements don't allow a customer, client or prospect to perceive you and your product or service as being unique or different. Without any sense of inherent drama or uniqueness, you and your product can be relegated to a commodity perception.

What Makes You Different?

You must continually concentrate on your uniqueness or differential competitive advantage. One of the best ways to do this is by developing your *USP*—for you, your company, products and services.

USP stands for *unique selling proposition*. It's a strategy that comes from the world of advertising, yet it has direct application to the world of business development. A USP helps you rise above the clutter of other competitive sales, marketing and service messages.

An example of a USP might be a pizza place that assures you delivery within 30 minutes and if they're late, you get $3 off. Now that's unique! Sound familiar? With that simple and original USP, Domino's built a huge business.

What is Domino's really selling? It's not pizza. It's speed! Domino's lets you know, if you want a deep-dish, gourmet style, soufflé pizza, they're probably not the folks to call. But if you're hungry and need to satisfy your craving quickly, they're the *only* pizza place to dial.

Here are two more examples of creative and effective unique selling propositions. I spotted this one in a print ad in a Chicago newspaper, for an eye-care medical treatment center. The ad's headline read:

> *If your vision is not measurably improved after cataract surgery, the charges for your surgery will be refunded!*

A southern California accounting firm provides this assurance:

> *We guarantee you 10-day turnaround (after receipt of information) on your tax return. If we don't make our deadline, we pay you $50 per day for each day we're late.*

24. How to Create Your USP!

Here are five specific steps to help you develop your USP:

1. You must make a proposition to each customer who buys your product or service that he or she receives a specific benefit or benefits.
2. The proposition must be one your competition cannot or does not offer. It must be unique—either in the brand, the product, the service or the claim.
3. The proposition must be strong enough to move the masses

or attract new customers to you, your people and your product or service.

4. Your USP can be how your business is operated; how your product is developed, manufactured or marketed; or elements that go into your product or service that are of significantly higher quality, value or durability than your competitors.

5. Your USP can even highlight or be something your competitors are already doing, but have failed to explain it or make it known to their or your customers. Therefore, the first company to define that unique benefit, process or procedure and educate their customers takes a unique, powerful and profitable preemptive advantage.

To *preempt* means to replace, to do-away with or to take possession of. Therefore, even if your product or service offers the same benefit as that of a competitor's, guess what? If you're the first one to tell the marketplace, you now have a unique and profitable preemptive advantage. *You* are the leader. And even if your competitors now claim they too can offer these benefits, the marketplace perceives them as followers.

25. Hoist a Cold One to Results!

Claude Hopkins was one of the greatest advertising copywriters of all time. In the early 1900s, his words and ideas transformed products and services with weak sales histories into cash cows. Why? Because Hopkins knew how to capitalize upon the powerful, yet often overlooked, obvious or commonplace aspects of a product or service.

Here's how Hopkins used the power of a unique selling proposition and preemptive advantage with one of his advertising clients, Schlitz. Schlitz was a major Midwestern brewery, in fifth place among beer manufacturers. Part of the problem was that Schlitz, like all the brewers at that time, was exclaiming its beer was "pure." While this was true, the word "pure" meant nothing to beer drinkers because every manufacturer made the same claim.

Hopkins knew he could only create a vast distinction for Schlitz if he could discover something unique, out-of-the-ordinary or even commonplace about Schlitz that the beer-drinking world didn't yet know.

Research Plus Creativity Equals Results

Hopkins began to ask questions. Lots of them. He snooped around. He was like a detective in search of the missing clue. Hopkins' research uncovered that, at least in the early 1900s, brewers all made beer the same way. That's why they could all proudly boast their product was "pure." However, what they didn't tell you was *how* their beer became "pure."

Hopkins jumped on that oversight and turned it into a powerful, profitable and preemptive advantage. Hopkins began telling the beer-drinking world about:

- How Schlitz was brewed through great filters filled with white-wood pulp.
- How the pumps and pipes were cleaned twice daily to avoid contamination.
- How elaborate machinery cleaned every bottle four times.
- How the Schlitz artesian wells were dug 4,000 feet deep into the earth's surface to discover pure water.

- How the beer was aged in vats for six months.
- How the unique flavor of Schlitz was developed from a mother yeast cell that was the result of 1,200 experiments.

While other brewers continued to yell their beer was *pure,* Hopkins told beer drinkers in exacting detail how Schlitz *became* pure.

Within two months, Schlitz ascended from fifth place to within dollars of first place. All because Hopkins knew how to describe the common in an uncommon way. And most important, he did it first!

Remember, what you currently perceive about your business as being ho-hum or ordinary might present a preemptive advantage the world will marvel at, respond to and invest in. The key is to take advantage of the advantage first, before your competition.

26. Find the Frustration

In addition to the five USP steps you learned in Focus Section 24, here's a series of questions to help you develop your own unique selling proposition. Ask your prospects, customers or clients the following:

- What are the greatest frustrations you have with *our* industry?
- When it comes to dealing with others who market or sell related products or services to ours, what are your biggest challenges?
- If there was one thing you would change about *our* industry that would really make your business better or your life

easier, what would it be?

The answers to these questions usually reveal a common thread of pain, anguish, concern or frustration. Therefore, your USP should be designed to remove or eliminate these "undesirable threads." Your USP should create only positive benefits, high perceived value and dramatic results.

Remember, to attain results, there are only three ways to grow your business:

1. Get more customers.
2. Serve the same number of customers at the same dollar volume, yet at better margins.
3. Serve the same number of customers, but increase the *size* or *dollar volume* of their *orders,* by selling them more related or complementary products or services.

Your USP helps you find, serve and keep your customers as you grow your business in one or all of the preceding ways. After all, the business of *business* is about customer acquisition, satisfaction and retention.

27. B&A's USP

Here's how I developed the unique selling proposition for my firm, Blackman & Associates (B&A).

Like you, my clients—whether individuals, Fortune 500 companies, young growth organizations, entrepreneurial startups or international associations—invest in a more favorable future, improved condition and results! Whether I'm speaking, training or consulting, clients want ideas and information to help them improve performance, productivity and profitability. You may remember the client who told me, "Jeff, we expect you to fill our hearts with hope, our tummies with desire and our minds with lots of good stuff!"

Unfortunately, there are too many people within my business or industry who are only providing the "fluff" without the "stuff." Clients and prospects have told me their frightening horror stories about investing big bucks with others in my industry, and they have nothing to show for it. There was absolutely no return on their investment.

I'll never forget my first phone call with the president of a very large and successful chain of home supply centers. He tersely stated, "I don't like working with guys like you. You promise a lot and don't deliver. If you put your money where your mouth is, Jeff, I'll meet with you. If not, goodbye!"

I told him, "If I don't deliver, it won't cost you a penny!" We set the appointment and he eventually became a very happy client. Yet I'm convinced, if I didn't have a USP that addressed and removed his fears and frustrations, he never would have become a prospect or a client. Instead, he would have forever remained, a suspect.

Tell the World

Before I reveal my unique selling proposition, I should let you know the USP for Blackman & Associates appears everywhere—in emails to prospective clients, in every client agreement, and as part of every business-growth tool we offer—and it's always explained to prospects and clients on the telephone, in face-to-face meetings, and of course, on our website.

An important element of your USP is that you, your literature and all your employees tell it to the world. If you know it, but others don't, it may as well not exist. Customers, clients and prospects must become aware of your USP. Therefore, at every opportunity you must inform and educate them.

Everything I do, (keynotes, business-growth tools, services, training, consulting, coaching, learning-systems, etc.) comes with an unequivocal and unconditional no-risk assurance. The following is excerpted language from our website and agreement.

Here's the actual language, from our USP:

Jeff Blackman's
No-Risk Assurance
Jeff offers you special "bail-out" protection.

Jeff is a pretty light-hearted guy, but when it comes to helping you and your people grow your business, he's dead serious. Therefore, he provides this incredible no-risk assurance:

You and your people must be absolutely delighted with Jeff's message. Or, if you feel its value or profit-producing potential does not exceed your investment, then Jeff has authorized me to refund your money!* Immediately. Part of it or even all of it.

No hard feelings either. Only Jeff is at risk! But ask our many ecstatic clients. They'll tell you, with Jeff, there's no risk.

Only results!

* (You should know, Jeff has *never* lost this "bet!")

To see me explain our "No-Risk Assurance," please take a peek at: http://www.jeffblackman.com/services/no-risk-assurance/

My USP declaration also incorporates the strategy of *risk-reversal*. That's where Blackman & Associates, as the "seller," takes all the risk. My "buyer," or decision-maker, has NO risk. When I'm on the phone or in a meeting with a prospective client, I always tell him or her about our no-risk approach to doing business. And the responses are interesting. Prospects who became clients have said things like:

- "Wow, you wouldn't do that Jeff, unless you were really confident."
- "That's not only fair, it's an incredible way to run a business."
- "No one in your industry has ever made an offer, a guarantee or a promise like this one."
- "You can only afford to do that if you've got your act together."
- "I'm sure that's a bet you've never lost."

Of course, these are the exact types of responses I want to hear. One of the real keys to our USP is that it not only diminishes the risk, it actually removes it. This *risk-reversal* gives us a very distinctive differential competitive advantage.

And this USP risk-reversal strategy generates incredible amounts of new business—even if your price is high. It quickly enhances perceptions of quality, credibility, commitment, value, trust and expertise.

Now I know what you're thinking: "Jeff, why would you set your-self up so easily to get burned?!" Somebody could love your stuff, have great results, but still demand their money back!" You're right, that could happen. But it never has!

To date, my risk-reversal/USP strategy is a "bet" I've *never* lost. I really think that most, if not all, business professionals are honest and reasonable people. And if they choose to be deceitful, that's their problem, not mine.

The right unique selling proposition will quickly become a key business-growth weapon, to help you peak your profits!

28. And Now, A Word from Our Sponsor!

A unique way to influence and serve your marketplace is often not through the traditional front-door, but instead through the creative back-door. And an excellent way to do this is with *sponsorship*. Sponsorship allows you to capitalize on and leverage OPR—other people's relationships.

First, let's define *sponsor*. A *sponsor* is an individual, company, organization or association that pursues and benefits from the same or similar target markets or target customers as you. While your products and services are not competitive, they're likely to be complementary.

Here are some examples:

• If you sell computer, IT or management information systems to businesses, complementary vendors might include interior designers, space planners, computer accessory companies, software specialists, furniture distributors and lighting specialists.

- Let's imagine you're an accounting or financial services firm serving small businesses. Complementary service providers might be print shops, computer hardware or software companies, travel agents, photocopier dealers, banks and telecommunication resellers.

- If you're a remodeling company, complementary businesses could include carpet cleaners, kitchen and bath retailers or designers, landscape architects, floor and wallcovering dealers.

As you can quickly see, the potential *sponsorship* possibilities are seemingly endless. The only limit is your creativity.

Some of the advantages of *sponsorship* are:

- You benefit from an existing relationship between the sponsor and your prospect.
- You and the sponsor can jointly pursue a prospect.
- You can serve a new customer, because the sponsor has made the investment or a portion of the investment. For example, when I speak at national or international association meetings, my investment is sometimes paid by a sponsor that's a major supplier to the industry. The sponsor receives recognition in a variety of ways: on signage, in the program brochure, in my handouts or even in my presentation with a personal expression of thanks.
- You, your company, products and services are being positively positioned by the sponsor.

- Your credibility is enhanced by somebody else who is touting your talents.

Some of the advantages of sponsorship to your *sponsors* include:

- They have exposure to an audience or a customer base they value.
- There can be tangible evidence of their involvement, as their name and logo are seen on collateral and support materials. However, there's also a very high perceived value, because of their contribution to this particular customer's or market's success.
- They have distinguished their business from their competitors by finding another business that benefits their prospects and customers.
- They create tremendous goodwill, loyalty and the potential for future business opportunities with these prospects or customers.
- They might be able to now open and penetrate a market that has previously been inaccessible.

29. Marketing Magic, or Let's Go Fishin'!

I have a love/hate relationship with fishing!

What I hate about it, is that it's slow. It ruins a good boat ride. And it becomes a very expensive nap!

What I love about it, is that it teaches you important lessons. Personally and professionally.

What I especially love about it, is that it provides quality time with those who are important to me. My son. My Dad. My brother-in-law. My nephews. My friends. And their kids.

We have landed little nibbles and big ones—in lakes, rivers, gulf waters and oceans.

Some of the valuable lessons learned while fishing are:

1. Persistence pays.

2. Always seek new pools of possibilities.

3. Dangle the hook and bait in the water in front of the fish. (Sounds like marketing.)

4. When the fish bites, set the hook and reel him in. (Sounds like selling.)

5. Bait your hook, with what the fish likes to eat. (Sounds like negotiating.)

6. Once the fish is caught, keep him comfortable. (Sounds like customer service.)

7. Attitude matters, yet you're compensated for your behavior and results.

8. Listen to the experts, i.e., Captain Jimbo Hail who taught me how to jig in the Gulf of Mexico.

9. Don't brood over rejection. It's more fun to talk about the one you reeled in vs. the one that got away.

10. You've gotta be in the right place at the right time and then know what to do while you're there!

11. Reap the rewards, i.e., having red snapper that we hooked in the gulf, prepared by a gourmet chef at a local restaurant, within two hours from the time we caught it.

So how can you always find a great fishing hole with plenty of fish? Here's a simple, yet profit-peaking, exercise. Please answer the questions on the following pages as they apply to you, your products or services, your business, your prospects, your customers or clients and your marketplace. (And look for the answer in the question!)

Your answers to these questions will begin to reveal hidden assets, untapped markets, new opportunities and peak-profit potential. Remember, your USP helps you rise above the clutter of other competitive messages.

Your Peak-Profit Potential

1. What other companies, suppliers and vendors do your prospective customers know, like and trust?

2. Where is there a relationship you can benefit from, with a preexisting group of prospects, who have a predetermined need for your product or service?

3. Who's your target market?

4. What are your customers' CSCs—Critical Success Considerations? (What are the factors that matter most to them and influence whether they're willing to give you and your company approval?)

5. How many "active" customers do you serve?

6. How often do you serve them? (Daily? Weekly? Monthly?)

7. What have been your most successful strategies to build your business?

8. What "buying" trends are you seeing?

9. What types of previous marketing efforts and advertising have worked for your business? What hasn't worked for you?

10. How much money can you afford to invest in marketing and advertising?

11. What follow-up procedures are in place once you secure a new customer?

12. What sort of follow-up review or "postmortem" do you conduct if you lose the sale or a new customer?

13. What "postmortem" do you conduct if you lose a current customer?

14. What other organizations or businesses serve your prospects or target markets?

15. What professional organizations do your prospects belong to?

16. What industry publications or general interest magazines do your prospects and customers read?

17. What industry websites do your prospects / customers frequently visit?

18. What social media do your prospects / customers use?

19. What unique benefits or "hidden assets" do you or your company have, yet you're not telling the world about them?

20. What specific problems are you solving in a prospect's / customer's life?

21. What results/benefits/advantages/outcomes do you deliver to customers?

22. What are the top reasons anyone should buy from you vs. a competitor?

23. Who are your best customers?

24. How did you get them?

25. What are you doing for them that you could do for others?

26. If you could choose your next customer, who would it be? Why?

27. What are the characteristics of your "typical" customer?

28. How many/who of your customers are influential in their field or industry?

29. How could they "sponsor" you?

30. What noncompetitive businesses serve your target markets?

31. What nonprofit groups can you help?

32. Who can you position as a referral source or sponsor?

33. Who are the suppliers for your vendors?

34. How can you serve your vendors' customers?

35. Who could benefit from your customer base?

36. What value does your customer database have to other

vendors who might serve the same customer?

37. How can you let prospects "sample" your product or service?

38. What kind of ongoing, consistent service can you offer?

39. What additional products or services do your customers want and need that you offer?

40. What additional products or services do your customers want and need that you don't offer?

41. What related special events get prospects to "sample" your talents?

CHAPTER 5

Your Life and E.T.H.I.C.S.: A Banquet of Consequences

"Each time you are honest and conduct yourself with honesty, a success force will drive you toward greater success. Each time you lie, even with a little white lie, there are strong forces pushing you toward failure."

—Joseph Sugarman, entrepreneur

30. A Life. A Lie. A Legacy.

How would you respond to this question: "Are you willing to lie?" Yes? No? It depends on the circumstances?

How might you answer if the one asking the question is a current or prospective client or customer? And they claim, ironically, if you do lie, it's in *their* best interests.

In the fall of 1986, I was confronted with this question. I call it a question rather than a dilemma, because for me, lying isn't an alternative.

When my client, a vice president of a nationally known corporation, posed this question, I looked at him with surprise, as did the two other vice presidents with us. I paused and asked, "Al, when you say 'lie,' what do you mean?"

He explained that if I interviewed his salespeople to find out what was really on their minds, what was troubling them and what their honest feelings were about the executive team, I'd be in a better position to help management.

I agreed. However, Al continued, "Jeff, they'll really open up to you, if you tell them the information is just for your ears, and you won't share their feelings with us!"

I told him that the trust already developed between his people and me would be more than tarnished, it would be destroyed! Forever! The other two vice presidents sat silently, but nodded their heads in agreement. I further explained, that if we're all to work together, it must be with an underlying foundation of integrity intact. This commitment to integrity is so crucial to your success as a business professional, I've chosen to address it very early in *Peak Your Profits*.

What is Integrity?

Integrity is based upon truth. Oscar Wilde said, "Truth is never pure, and rarely simple." *Truth* indeed may not be simple, but the complexities of deceit and situational ethics are monumental. Remember, the greatest advantage of truth is it doesn't require a good memory!

I was thankful that once my position was known, the apologetic vice president withdrew his suggestion. He realized that lying, even when euphemistically defined as "creative research," wasn't a good idea. The other vice presidents agreed.

After leaving my client's office, I began to reflect upon this experience. Ethics and honesty have always been and always will be the basic tenet by which I live and work. But I don't offer this "true confession" in order to portray myself as a "paragon of principle" or "touter of truth," but rather to emphasize the importance of truth, especially in a business relationship.

Several years ago, I received a call from a prospective client, Stephen. He said, "Jeff, you come highly recommended and I'd like you to work with my sales team." I said, "Great! But first, please tell me more about your salespeople and what you want to accomplish." He did. And then I asked, "When is your meeting?" When he told me the date, I said, "That's unfortunate. I already have a previous commitment. But let me be a resource and recommend a friend, who is another talented professional speaker—Frank Bucaro." Stephen asked, "What does Frank speak on?" I said, "Business ethics." To which Stephen responded, "Jeff, I have no use for him. I told you, these are salespeople!"

At that moment, I made the decision, I'd never pursue a future relationship with Stephen and his company. Philosophically, he and I were operating from a different integrity or values base. If my prospects or clients opt to perform by another standard, that's their decision. However, I'm not willing to be a "co-conspirator"!

Upon further analysis, I realized there was something else in jeopardy when my client, (the vice president), suggested I lie— and that was my future relationship with this client. All our previous communications had been open and honest. There was a wonderful give and take. I wasn't perceived as some "smooth talkin' sales guy" or conniving consultant, but instead as a professional who helped them solve their problems, improve their future and get results.

Earlier, I had conducted an extremely successful business-growth program for another division of this client's company. At that workshop and results-session, one of the group vice presidents rose and declared, "Jeff not only shares these techniques and principles with you today, but he also practices and lives by them himself. That's been apparent in our previous dealings with him." I nodded a simple thank-you, but knew he had given me the greatest compliment I had ever been paid in business.

Knowing that's how he and his company felt about me and my work, how could I "blow it" with a casual agreement to lie?

31. Liars are Losers

Let's assume, in the interest of serving my client, that I agreed to lie. And my "research" revealed valuable information. It gave leadership great new insights. It provided me with tremendous awareness of existing problems. The staff left with a greater appreciation for management because of their keen perceptions. And the staff never knew I "snitched."

You might wonder, "Jeff, what's the big deal if nobody finds out and no one gets hurt?" It's because if my clients know I'm willing to lie or "bend the truth" in their interests, how do they know I'm not also willing to do the same thing, when it favors *me*?

You'll be Judged by What You Say and Do

Usually, you'll be judged by your actions, not just your words. However, if your words aren't believed, it's unlikely you'll be given the opportunity to take action. You never want a current or prospective client to wonder if your word is good. Seductive business skills and clever closes seldom, if ever, supersede truth. If someone doesn't trust you, they're not going to buy from you. Are there exceptions? Sure. But I bet the perpetrators only have short-term victories. They may smile after the encounter, but they seldom survive the long-term relationship!

Sometimes the pressure to win causes violations of the basic ethical rules of the game. And this turns winners into losers. It should be your creativity, tenacity, determination and integrity that enable you to continually succeed, not your ability to bend the truth. Buyers might expect you to sit at the bargaining table with a sharpened pencil, laptop computer and savvy negotiation strategy. But there should be no need for a lie detector, belief barometer or ethics evaluator. Your customers' or prospects' confidence, belief and trust in you will catapult you to unprecedented levels of success.

32. Integrity for Sale!

A joint study was conducted by the Korn/Ferry International consulting firm of New York along with the UCLA Graduate School of Management. The purpose of the study was to determine 16 key traits that maximize effectiveness. The respondents were 1,300 senior executives.

Now what success traits do you think were deemed to be

especially significant to these high-level and highly paid executives? Might it be time management? How about education? Interpersonal skills? Self-motivation? Nope. All important—but not the *most* important!

Believe it or not, 71 percent of the executives polled said the single most important success trait is *integrity*. That's right, integrity. Now isn't that refreshing news!

If integrity were a product that could be bought and sold in our competitive marketplace, one might think the demand for it would be high, but its availability is frighteningly low. And unfortunately, that suspicion or cynicism is frequently confirmed by the nightly news and daily headlines.

Throughout the 1980s, 1990s, 2000s, 2010s and today, millions of TV viewers and newspaper readers have had the opportunity to follow the daily foibles and ethical dilemmas of athletes, businesspeople, politicians and organizations. Some of those caught beneath our scrutinizing societal microscope include; Wall Street's Ivan Boesky, televangelist Jim Bakker, automotive entrepreneur John DeLorean, baseball's Pete Rose, speakers of the house Jim Wright and Newt Gingrich, figure skater Tonya Harding, hotel queen Leona Helmsley, President Bill Clinton, Martha Stewart, Enron's Ken Lay and Jeffrey Skilling, Tyco's Dennis Kozlowski, WorldCom's Bernie Ebbers, high-powered lobbyist Jack Abramoff, Ponzi-schemer Bernie Madoff, Illinois governor Rod Blagojevich, President Donald Trump, the Volkswagen Emissions scandal and soccer's FIFA corruption scandal.

So rampant were stories of ethical misconduct that *Newsweek* magazine labeled the 1980s as the "decade of greed!" That sentiment was brilliantly, but chillingly reinforced by actor Michael Douglas, in the movie *Wall Street,* when, as the ruthless Gordon Gekko, he defiantly declared, "Greed is good!" Well, if greed, deceit and situational ethics are good, then the future could become decades of disaster! Why? Because business relationships will then be characterized by an energy-sapping, mind-manipulating and profit-reducing game of "who do you trust?"

The era of distrust may have already begun. According to a *Time* magazine/CNN Poll, 63 percent of Americans have little or no confidence that government leaders "talk straight," while 75 percent believe there's less honesty in government today than a decade ago. During political elections, the topic of *trust* is always more than an issue. It becomes a battle cry for all the candidates and parties. The only name uttered more than the contenders is Pinocchio!

A Frightening New Card Category

While browsing through greeting cards at a local pharmacy, my eyes stared and fingers stopped in disbelief, when I discovered a new card category. Are you ready for this? You can now actually buy for those "special select few who play it straight, who are above board, who really do promise a lot and deliver more"—a card that proclaims on its front in bold black letters, "I am proud of your honesty!"

Have we become so mistrusting, so disbelieving, so fearful of being taken advantage of, that we now need to congratulate others when they're honest with us? I hope not!

As an ethical business professional, you may be perceived as unique. Just like a diamond is worth more when it's rare and unique, so are you. Your integrity base gives you a profound advantage over your competition. Your unwavering and unqualified commitment to integrity by you and all who work for your company will have a dramatic impact on your bottom line. Your prospects and customers will believe in you. They will trust you. And they will buy from you. Again and again.

33. E.T.H.I.C.S.: A Formula for Your Future!

As a business professional who is likely to be confronted with ethical considerations in the future, you might wonder, "How do I know what to do, and when do I need to do it?"

Perhaps we can answer that question by using the acronym E.T.H.I.C.S.—created and developed by my longtime, dear friend, Frank Bucaro, a fellow professional speaker, seminar leader and author.

Frank believes, and I agree with him, that the issue of ethics in a nutshell boils down to asking yourself a two-part question about the outcome of your decisions:

1. What price must I pay for this decision?
2. Can I live with that price?

Frank helps all of us find the answers to those questions through his E.T.H.I.C.S. formula. Let's start with the letter *E*, which stands for:

Experience. The experience or values you carry with you into adulthood and into your business career are likely to be those same values or experiences passed on to you by a parent, teacher, relative or some other role model. How you behave and the decisions you make speak much more loudly and convincingly than what you simply say. Because, as you may know, with lots of people, "When all is said and done, all too often, much more is said than done!"

The second letter, *T*, stands for:

Training: You must proactively train yourself to keep the question of ethics fresh in your mind. Certain ethical information may not seem to fit within or match up to your experiences, values and perceived reality. Therefore, you have a tendency to do away with that information. To toss it aside. That may or may not be the right course of action. The information may be accurate, truthful and beneficial, but the only problem is, you don't quite recognize its value.

The *H* represents:

Hindsight. Ask yourself what you have learned from others and from yourself regarding your personal and professional history. Your past reveals clues about a more successful future. What went right? What went wrong? What could be changed, improved or enhanced? An analysis of where you have been often helps you get to where you are going—a lot faster, a lot happier and a lot more profitably.

The *I* signifies:

Intuition. It's that gut feeling or sense you're doing the right thing or avoiding the wrong thing. Yet it's more than merely a hunch. It's closer to a guarded optimism toward your decision. And it activates you at both a logical and emotional level.

During the summer of 1978, I was traveling through Europe with my best friend, Mark Liss. Our budget? $22 a day. One evening, just after midnight, we found ourselves stranded in Cannes, France. We unfortunately missed the last train from Cannes to Nice and couldn't catch the next train until the morning. So, with little money, but lots of courage, we slept on a sidewalk in Cannes. Several hours later, we awoke to an early morning sunrise, the rumbling sounds of an automated street cleaner and the scent of delectable baked goods.

Fresh croissants were just delivered and left outside the door of a local restaurant that had not yet opened. Mark and I were tired, cold and hungry! We looked and saw no one. We knew this was our chance to have a quick and undetected breakfast. So we quickly grabbed and gobbled-up our four croissants! We also left two times the appropriate amount of francs for these flaky delicacies in the croissant box! Our intuition told us, *that* was the right thing to do.

The C symbolizes:

Company. It's the *company* or *corporate* factor in the ethical equation. It requires you to not only consider the decision to be made, but the long-term impact and implications that decision will have on the "big picture."

You may need to ask yourself questions such as: How does this decision affect my company? My reputation? My fellow professionals? My industry? My relationship with this client or customer? My relationship with other clients or customers? My relationship with future clients or customers?

Is the bottom line important? You bet! But for the short term, are you willing to sacrifice the goodwill, reputation and value of you and your company simply to improve it?

And finally, the *S* is for:

Self-esteem. How do you derive yours? Is it solely by the acquisition of more dollars or material goodies? If so, then perhaps ethical considerations don't play a major role in your decision-making process. But I doubt it, and so does Frank! He feels the greatest ethical decision is the one that builds your self-esteem while it simultaneously helps others. Your short-term decision might not seem like a winner, but the long-term implication is likely to represent a series of positive, productive and profitable victories.

When you're an ethical business professional, you're building and continuing to build long-term relationships. Relationships based upon mutual trust and confidence.

Any loss of personal integrity toward you, by your customer, even if it's only perceived, quickly and harshly jeopardizes that relationship. Goodwill is created by many actions, but it can be lost by only one. A strong ethical or integrity base breeds a positive self-esteem. And that makes it easy for you to look at yourself in the mirror and sleep well at night.

34. Money and Morality

Ethical abuses in business—such as gifts, bribes and payoffs—have been identified in a variety of studies. In the book *Ethics in Business*, Robert Bartels talks about "lubrication money" that's used to grease the palms of decision-makers in Asia, Africa, the Middle East and Latin America.

In Italy, businesspeople have been known to pass the *bustarella* or envelope stuffed with money to "motivate" a company to get the job done. By contrast, the *mordida* or "the bite" is commonplace in Mexico to assure that a government inspector *doesn't* do his job. And in North America, we euphemistically refer to "bag men," "gift-givers," "fat envelopes" and "money under the table."

Ethical decisions aren't easy to make. No one person can impose his or her ethical decision-making and value system upon another. Robert Bartels, Frank Bucaro or Jeff Blackman can't convince, cajole or command you to do that which you refuse to do. Our background, beliefs and perceptions are likely to be different. But, every decision you make reveals not only your past-self and current-self, but, as Robert Bartels says, "It also molds, for better or worse, your future self!"

One of my clients has taught his salespeople and other employees to ask themselves this question, "Would you be willing to explain your decision or action on network television?" How's that for a gut-check test?!

Let's Pause and "Reflect"

John Dewey, an American philosopher and educator, developed

a strategy for ethical decision-making that he called *reflective morality*. Dewey felt that upon reflection, thought and deliberation, a decision-maker could creatively imagine, rehearse and evaluate several courses of action before reaching a conclusion.

Adapting Dewey's framework, here are six steps to help business-people, entrepreneurs, managers and salespeople clarify responsibilities, eliminate misunderstandings and conduct their business with the highest possible professional standards.

To help your ethical decision-making process, you should evaluate six steps:

Step 1: Identify the topic or issue that's causing your ethical dilemma.

Step 2: List all of your possible choices.

Step 3: List the possible consequences of each choice.

Step 4: List the people affected by your choices.

Step 5: Trade places. Put yourself in an empathetic position to understand how those just listed in Step 4 are affected by your choices. Bury your ego. Minimize your needs. Instead, maximize, for example, your customers' or clients' needs. How do your choices affect their lives, their interests and their futures?

Step 6: Make a decision. Then, take action! For without action, the dilemma not only lingers, it magnifies.

These steps, along with Frank Bucaro's E.T.H.I.C.S. acronym, should offer you a framework for future success.

Oh, by the way, that vice president who asked me to lie? He's no longer with the company. But to this day, I still enjoy a very positive and ongoing relationship with the laudatory vice president, who stood to sing my praises. And he became the next president!

Ethical considerations should always play a major role in your performance, productivity and profitability as a business professional and peak profiteer. Products may be new and improved or obsolete. Services may be outdated or trendy. But your reputation lives forever. If you don't believe it's sacred, no one else will!

So what's the best course of action for you? That's your decision. It's your future. But perhaps the best place to start is by following the guidelines of *Peak Your Profits* and by asking yourself a simple question: "Am I willing to lie, cheat or steal, bend the truth, manipulate the facts or pass the envelope?" And if so, am I willing to explain my decision or action on the network news?"

CASE STUDY

38 Percent Above Forecast!
ATAS Puts Pedal to the Metal!

CHALLENGE:

ATAS was already a premier manufacturer of metal building and architectural solutions. Yet they wanted to learn new skills, attitudes and behaviors to exceed their goals.

GAME PLAN AND APPROACH:

I worked closely with ATAS's senior leadership team, i.e., President, Vice President of Marketing and National Sales Manager, to create an impactful ongoing business-growth learning-system.

IMPACT AND RESULTS:

Here are verbatim e-comments, received within one week of results-sessions kicked-off for the ATAS eastern team:

- "The solutions are based on an approach of absolute integrity and honesty, and we have plenty of support tools to help with implementation and ongoing reinforcement. Jeff presented powerful business-growth strategies in a positive, entertaining environment that stressed implementation, teamwork, action and follow-through."

- "After one week of using these new questions, got an answer from one customer who said they'd increase business with us by 40 percent."

C
A
S
E

S
T
U
D
Y

- "Double-digit, annual profitable growth can now be easily obtained."

- "The most immediate economic impact will be improved efficiency throughout the team. Proper information-gathering should allow for sales to improve profitability on a per sale basis. Ongoing, we can double our sales within a two-year time frame."

- "What a great meeting. Employees are genuinely excited. Initial increases should be on the order of 50 percent!"

MORE RESULTS:

C
A
S
E

S
T
U
D
Y

Based upon the eastern team's success, a few months later, (in the winter), I headed to Mesa, Arizona to continue the progress with the eastern team, and to kick-off the western team's results. Then in the fall, I met with the entire ATAS team again, to continue their road to results.

By the fall, only one year after the initial results-session, the ATAS team was 38 percent above their sales goal!

CHAPTER 6

Your Business-Growth System: Seize the Opportunity!

Selling has its real fascination in its ability to communicate, persuade and move others to action...and that is an art!

35. Results! The Name of the Game

Now that the philosophy of *Peak Your Profits*—from both an ethical and value perspective—has been established, let's take a closer look at how the specific steps in the *system* are used in the business-development process.

Remember, *Peak Your Profits* is a logical, chronological, methodical and profit-producing approach to business growth. It has helped other business professionals dramatically and quickly increase their revenues, earnings and commissions by 30 percent, 40 percent, 50 percent or more in less than eight weeks. Why? Because it's an organized step-by-step, *system for success.*

To help you achieve new levels of success, let's take a look at the six steps of *Opportunity $elling*® (O P R T N TY) that are part of the *Peak Your Profits system:*

1. **Open.** Your initial contact with your customer, client or prospect.
2. **Probe.** You ask open-ended, need-development questions to determine what problem must be solved, need fulfilled or dream realized.
3. **Reveal.** You present the ideas, products and services that best meet those pre-determined needs discovered in the probe.
4. **Translate.** You translate features into benefits—not what your product or service *is*, but what it *does* for your decision-maker.
5. **Negotiate.** You overcome objections and solve problems, but always in a win-win, value-driven, integrity-based and non-manipulative environment.
6. **The Yes.** You get your prospects, clients or customers to say "Yes."

The Yes is traditionally referred to as *the close.* But to me, this never made any sense. Why? Because it's not true! Something that's closed is over, done, finished, completed, terminated! And in business-development, *the close* is really just the beginning. Now, you have to do all the things you promised to do—like provide quality, on-time delivery, efficiency and dependability.

Close is a word of conclusion, not commencement. Therefore, I'll only share with you proven and profit-producing strategies that help you secure *the yes*—so you can always keep the door open for your next *opportunity.*

To maximize your understanding, application and reinforcement of the *Peak Your Profits* business-development stages, please take a look at the *Opportunity $elling®* chart below. It graphically displays the six stages:

- **O**   Open
- **P**   Probe
- **R**   Reveal
- **T**   Translate
- **N**   Negotiate
- **TY** The Yes

OPPORTUNITY $ELLING*

The horizontal continuum is a reflection of time—meaning the amount of time you devote to that step of *the system*. Where *should* you spend the greatest amount of your time? If you said in the *probe* stage, you're right!

Probing enables you to assess your customers' or clients' needs, wants and desires. Without discovering what's important to them, what they hope to accomplish, what their motivators and hot buttons are, it's extremely difficult for you to *reveal* an effective solution, product or service.

The vertical continuum is also a reflection of time, but with an important distinction. Here, each step is divided into the amount of time you should spend listening rather than talking. Most businesspeople are very adept at their "spiel, pitch or presentation," but they don't know or have never been trained in the *art* of listening. You have a greater likelihood of *listening* a customer into an *investment,* as opposed to *talking* them into a *buy!*

For how long do you listen? You should devote most of your listening time to the first two stages: the *Open* and the *Probe.* As a recommended guideline, 80 percent of your time in both of these stages should be spent listening and only 20 percent talking.

These and the other percentages on the OPRTNTY chart are, of course, only guidelines, but they establish the significance of listening, especially in the first two stages of *Open* and *Probe* by a 4 to 1 ratio. You really don't begin to "talk" or "present" until the *Reveal* stage.

36. Listen and Learn!

Listening is essential to your success and profitability. To help you become a better listener, here are 16 specific listening strategies:

1. Hold your comments and judgments until your prospect or client is done speaking.
2. Look for the benefits of good listening: what *you* can learn. Even if the information doesn't help you sell this particular

customer, it could be very valuable to securing or informing your next customer.

3. Try to keep your discussion on point.

4. Minimize the competition, meaning distractions like ringing telephones, buzzing smartphones or background noises.

5. Identify the objective of your conversation. Know the purpose of your call or meeting.

6. Use the words *you, your* and *yours* often. Use the words *I, me* and *my* seldom.

7. When appropriate, take notes. (We'll expand upon this concept later.)

8. Use periodic summaries to allow for confirmation or modification.

9. Ask questions that are on-point and open-ended to elicit customer responses.

10. Focus on all aspects of the communication: body language, word choice and intonation.

11. Never interrupt or argue.

12. Pretend it's your responsibility to repeat the speaker's message tomorrow at a national press conference.

13. Help your speaker. Make it easy for him or her to communicate.

14. Don't be afraid of appropriate silence—for example, when you allow your prospects or customers to reflect upon or contemplate their answers.

15. Maintain eye contact.

16. Work at listening. Practice. Practice. Practice.

Listening Helps You Reach Your Destination

Kids can often teach you great lessons in listening. My wife, Sheryl, and I have been incredibly blessed with three remarkable kids. Chad was born in 1989, Brittany 55 weeks later in 1990 and Amanda in 1994 on New Year's Eve! (That's called tax planning!)

Ever since the kids have been old enough to talk, Sheryl and I have asked them two simple questions. First, "What are you doing?" Their response? "Nothing!" Second, "Where are you going?" Their response: "Nowhere!" Now I've got the feeling that if you ask most businesspeople these same two questions, you'll probably get the same two answers.

One of the reason I developed the *Peak Your Profits system* is to help you get to where you're going, quickly, efficiently and profitably! When you travel, what's the first question a skycap asks you, "Where you going?" Could you imagine if you said to the skycap, "I don't know, why don't you pick the city!" (Out of curiosity, has that ever happened with your luggage?)

Recently, I was at the Las Vegas airport, heading back home to Chicago. When I hopped out of the cab, the skycap asked, "Sir, what's your final destination?" I looked up and said, "Heaven!" He panicked, because he couldn't find the right baggage check!

The *Peak Your Profits system* also helps you avoid panic, reach your destination quickly and keep you organized. Organized in the sense that you now have an action plan or step-by-step approach for business development. The steps aren't mutually exclusive. They all complement one another. However, to assure your success, they're presented chronologically. Without a successful opening, you need not worry about getting to *The Yes* decision.

Of these six steps in the system, where do you think most businesspeople begin? That's right—at the *reveal* stage. Why? Because the typical businessperson has a story to tell and is anxious to share it—whether or not the prospect or client is even interested in hearing it!

This approach is a basic mistake. You should never begin to sell, tell or reveal how you can help someone until you know what they need or want. And how do you know this, unless you properly *open* or greet them and then ask information-gathering need-development questions?

Years of experience have proven that of all these stages, the final stage—*The Yes*—is really the easiest. *The Yes* simply asks for a positive decision at the right time. However, asking for a yes decision or trying to perform the so-called *close* often causes anxiety and pressure. For whom? Actually, for both the *buyer* and the *seller*. But when you do the previous five steps right, then asking for and getting *The Yes* is really quite easy. And peak profiteers always find ways to do things easier, faster, better and more profitably.

37. The Open Stage: Get Comfortable!

The *Open* stage is your first opportunity to make a favorable impression on your prospects, customers or clients. As the old adage forewarns, you never get a second chance to make a first impression.

According to a popular psychological theory, we create our own self-image—favorable or unfavorable—from our judgments about the impressions we're making on others. A University of Virginia study suggests that most of us are incredibly poor judges about how we *impress* people.

If this is true, then what can be done to improve the impression we make on others? Elwood Chapman, author of *Your Attitude is Showing* says:

> *You are what you are, and you cannot become someone else. But you can change your habits, attitudes and behavior in working with people. By recognizing the importance of better human relations, you can go a long way toward fashioning a desirable image.*

The *Open* stage of a business relationship is influenced by a variety of personal factors, including, but not limited to, your vocabulary, attire, demeanor, body language, enthusiasm and confidence. The first impression can also be influenced by your company's offices, letterhead, packaging, product merchandising and online presence. A negative impression in any of these areas drastically reduces your potential to get *The Yes*. Your attention to detail enhances every aspect of your and your decision-maker's experience.

38. Image Impact!

Your image and your company's image are especially important if you're selling a service or an intangible. Fairly or unfairly, buyers allow first impressions to influence their decisions. When buyers can't physically hold or see your product, they try to find reassurance. Hopefully, that reassurance or peace of mind is provided by your presence and professionalism.

On a daily basis, decision-makers are bombarded by countless external stimuli: from travel, work, advertising, the media and your competitors. Many times these external factors are interpreted and analyzed quickly. Buyers make snap judgments and then are off and running, ready to solve the next problem. Therefore, you want to make sure judgments made about you are positive and favorable.

According to a personal friend of mine, Lynn Pearl, president of the Chicago-based company, Executive Image, "You only have five seconds when you enter a room to make a positive impression. A confident manner characterized by a strong stride, a friendly smile, good posture and a genuine sense of energy will command respect."

Her findings also show that people whose personality tests reflect confidence and self-assurance even walk with longer strides, while short-strided shufflers are unassertive and unhappy.

There's a little-known field of study called *semiotics*, which studies nonverbal language and the power of silent persuasion. According to William S. Pfeiffer, Ph.D. and chairman of the Humanities and Social Sciences Department at the Southern College of Technology, first impressions really do count. His findings show that simple things such as a firm handshake, good eye contact, or remembering names are especially critical in a business meeting, sales setting or persuasive situation.

"I Really Wish It Didn't Squish"

A decision-maker told me the *real* reason why she didn't select another company to help train and grow her people. She said Jean, the company representative, didn't "walk her talk." She didn't look, sound or act like a winner. She explained her people wouldn't listen to Jean because Jean conveyed no credibility or professionalism. She then said something I'll never forget: "I was especially turned off within the first minute of meeting Jean because her handshake was squishy!"

That's right: squishy! This was a high-level decision-maker who was offended by the squish factor! Jean never had the opportunity to develop a long-term relationship because her initial relationship-building skills were so weak—and squishy!

Be honest: How well do you begin or cement a relationship within the first few minutes of meeting someone? The following questions were designed to help you find the answer. Please check off the responses that best represent your business situation or style.

1. When you approach a prospect/client/customer, do you convey confidence?

☐ Always   ☐ Occasionally   ☐ Rarely

2. Do you offer to shake hands first—and is your handshake firm and strong?

☐ Always   ☐ Occasionally   ☐ Rarely

3. Do you repeat someone's name and make sure you're pronouncing it properly?

☐ Always   ☐ Occasionally   ☐ Rarely

4. Do you greet people with a smile in-person and on the phone?

☐ Always   ☐ Occasionally   ☐ Rarely

5. Do you focus on your prospect?

☐ Always   ☐ Occasionally   ☐ Rarely

6. Do you listen effectively?

☐ Always   ☐ Occasionally   ☐ Rarely

7. Do you show you were listening? Do you *recap* the individual's key points and ask appropriate follow-up questions?

☐ Always   ☐ Occasionally   ☐ Rarely

8. Do you interrupt others?

☐ Always   ☐ Occasionally   ☐ Rarely

9. Do your words, expressions and body language convey a positive attitude?

☐ Always   ☐ Occasionally   ☐ Rarely

10. When you make a *promise* to do something, do you do it?

☐ Always   ☐ Occasionally   ☐ Rarely

Your answers to these questions should reveal your strong areas, as well as those that need improvement.

39. The Eyes and Ears Have It!

1. Visual. It's everything your customer sees. How you're dressed. Are your products working properly and free of dust? Does your promotional literature convey a positive image? Does your car have that *showroom look* or is it ready for the junkyard? Does your company "look good"? When you meet somebody, do you confidently and professionally greet them or appear uninterested by their presence?

2. Vocal. It's not what you say, but how you say it. It's your vocal quality, intonation and inflection. Let's try this simple exercise. First, exclaim in a positive, upbeat tone, "Welcome, it's great to see you today. How can we help you?" Now, repeat the *exact same* words, but in a negative, demeaning and confrontational tone, "Welcome, it's great to see you today. How can we help you?" Hear the difference? And the only thing that changed, was the tone or *attitude* of your voice.

3. Verbal. It's the words you use to convey your message. Does your industry or company have a unique language? Of course. But are all customers going to understand this *language*? Probably not. They might need to be educated. Therefore, you should communicate, market, sell, negotiate and serve at the customer's level of understanding.

While conducting a business-growth workshop for a large Chicago law firm, one of the attorneys asked me, "All this information about easy-to-understand language is fine and good, but what if I want impress my clients with my technical expertise?" I replied, "Ask yourself this question: Which is more important, impressing your clients or having them understand you?"

The Visual Vote

If you purchased a computer from a high-tech manufacturer, you'd expect it to be innovative and and leading-edge, wouldn't you? Of course! And for that reason, I had a client, (a manufacturer of software to the health industry) remove the typewriters from their office. A typewriter conveyed the wrong visual and perceptual image for this client. Their office should say *dynamic*, not dinosaur!

The power of visual persuasion is significant. However, it's only one element of the business development process. While a strong *visual* may be used to lure a customer in the *Open* stage, it must be always accompanied by a sincere desire to help this customer.

I was once lured into a men's clothing store by a large sign, "Bargain, We Won't Be Undersold! Sale Today!" While sifting through a rack of suits, I heard a sales associate exclaim to his customer who just bought one suit, "As long as I've got you in a buying mood, I might as well take advantage of it!" The stupidity of his statement caused me to grab for pen and paper, record his "classic sales motivator," and send it to the Museum of Business History!

Let's analyze this salesman's not-so-clever "come-on":

1. *"As long as I've got you."* Although a fine haberdasher attempts to fit a man's entire body, this statement seemingly indicates the salesman may have truly had or "gotten" his customer by another part of his anatomy!
2. *"In a buying mood."* Are we ever in a "buying mood?" Sure! But what does that *mean*, especially while shopping for new clothes?

The *mood* of the new clothes shopper is often pride, recognition, status, enhanced self-image, accomplishment or personal value. The shopper isn't just buying clothes, he or she is investing in self-image. Products and services are bought with emotion, but rationalized with logic!

3. *"I might as well take advantage of it!"* This salesman was already counting his commission! His focus was on his *paycheck*, not his customer's satisfaction. He was truly selling pants and jackets rather than value, pride, self-esteem and quality.

This salesman may have *cleaned-up* with this customer, but long-term he's programmed for failure! One foolish utterance often destroys the rapport and trust of your business relationship! If he had a *value-driven, integrity-based* and *non-manipulative* approach to business, he may have asked, "With such a great sale and the biggest savings of the year, how would you like to take advantage of...?"

Successful business development gives your customers and clients the opportunity to first satisfy *their* wants and needs, not yours! But by giving them what they want, you eventually get what you want!

To optimize your earning power, here are five peak-profit points to help you *Open* effectively with your next prospect, client or customer:

1. Be positive and devote all attention to your customers.
2. Let them talk about their favorite subject—themselves.
3. Maintain eye contact and show empathy for their concerns.
4. Carefully listen to statements, questions and feelings.
5. Value their presence and make them feel important.

Just as a Broadway opening hopes to set the stage for a long and profitable theater run, your *opening* should also start a long and profitable relationship.

CHAPTER 7

Probe and Prosper!

"Curiosity is one of the most certain and permanent characteristics of a vigorous intellect!"

—Samuel Johnson, 18th-century English critic

40. He Said, She Said

Webster's Dictionary defines "probe" as *"to examine, to inquire thoroughly, to investigate."* Your ability to do just that may be one of your most important and profit-producing, business-growth tools.

All too often, businesspeople assume their success is dependent upon their ability to master their *pitch, spiel* or *presentation.* It's not! Of course, that's a major part of the business-development process, but in the long run, your investigative or *probing* skills help you rise to new levels of success and profitability.

The *Probe* stage enables you to discover what problems your customer, client or prospect has, what needs they'd like to fill and what dreams they'd like to realize. This strategy gives you tremendous insight into customer preferences, sense of commitment, budget, expectations and objectives. Failure to properly assess these things causes most businesspeople to flounder. And they wonder why. Their assumptions are: "Gee, I must be a poor closer! I guess I need more product knowledge," Or, "I knew that customer wasn't serious anyway!"

CASE STUDY

Thrivent Financial Breaks Records with *Question & Qualify!*

CHALLENGE:

The leaders at the Fortune 500 insurance company, Aid Association for Lutherans, now Thrivent Financial, were frustrated. Their sales team of FRs, or financial representatives, needed help asking better questions to drive sales and client satisfaction.

GAME PLAN AND APPROACH:

So they asked us to help them create the customized *Question and Qualify* sales and business-growth learning-system with; workbooks, audio and video reinforcement, a train-the-trainer manual and in-person results-sessions.

OUTCOMES / NEW RECORDS BROKEN:

FRs quickly discovered when applying their customized *Question and Qualify* strategies that it took:

1. 30 percent fewer client contacts to generate an interview.

2. 30 percent fewer interviews to generate a sale.

And that:

3. The sales being generated were 30 percent bigger.

We helped Thrivent, reduce the length of their sales cycle and increase the size of their sales!

41. Goodbye to Gab!

"What a smooth talker!" "She's got the gift of gab!" Or "He's a born salesman!" How many times have you heard remarks such as these? Lots? Of course. But to the best of my knowledge, businesspeople are never born! I have several friends who are obstetricians, and they assure me they've never hoisted a newborn high into the air and proudly announced to the parents, "Congratulations, you've just given birth…to a salesperson! An entrepreneur! No, no…it's a business executive!"

CASE STUDY

Successful businesspeople aren't born. They're nurtured, developed and trained. At least the top achievers are! They may have the ability to "gab or talk," but their real skill is their ability to probe or question. Questions help establish rapport, uncover concerns, reveal problems and peak profits. Questions are a natural way to get others to talk, so you can *listen* and *learn!*

As a radio and TV talk-show host, the real success of my interviews depended not upon my speaking ability, but instead my questioning ability. Questions gave me the opportunity to explore a guest's feelings, attitudes and opinions. Exactly like your *business interview.*

Are Your Decision-Makers Motivated?

Questions allow you to discover whether a customer has a motivated or unmotivated need. A customer with a motivated need has a problem to solve. An unmotivated need, no matter how eloquent your presentation or beautiful your product, is unlikely to lead to *The Yes*. Why? Because the customer has no "pain" to diminish, problem to solve or dream to realize.

Several years ago, I conducted a three-day business-growth workshop in Toledo, Ohio. Immediately following the conclusion of the first day's program, I changed into my jogging clothes and hit the pavement. At the half-mile point, it began to pour! Despite this unwelcome and unexpected drenching, I continued to run, eventually seeking protection in a nearby shopping mall.

Upon entering the mall, I was greeted by a cheery representative of a major department store. She immediately inquired, "Sir, how'd you like to fill out an application for our charge card?" I assured her, I didn't need more "plastic money!"

She then acknowledged my tired, cold and damp condition and asked, "Just for applying, you receive at no obligation—(she then reached beneath the counter, removed and held up an umbrella)—you'd find this umbrella helpful, wouldn't you?" I said, "Where do I sign?!" I had a *motivated* need!

Motivated needs are easily discovered through observation, a natural curiosity and especially, the question-and-answer process.

As a business professional, you should never sell, tell, reveal or demonstrate your product or service until you discover and understand your prospect's or decision-maker's motivated needs.

42. What's Up, Doc?

Think back to your last doctor's visit. Did you enter the office, linger in the lobby, wait in a cold examining room and then eventually have your doctor arrive to proclaim, "Looks like you're here for stress. No? Ummm, how about the flu? No, no, let me guess...a pulled muscle? How about..."

Like a physician, you can't precisely make a diagnosis of your customer's needs until you know more about the individual. A good doctor doesn't guess at the illness, but rather examines the patient, asking questions and observing closely.

For decades, my primary care doctor has been Gerry Lewis. (Yes, I know, it only makes sense, that *my* doctor, would have the same name as a comedian!) Gerry is a terrific doctor. Smart. Compassionate. Empathetic. And always accessible. Yet our conversations, in-person or over-the-phone, always begin the same way. Gerry asks me a simple, yet powerful question, "What's up?" I answer. He listens intently—then makes specific "next-step" suggestions. As a business professional, you, too, must examine, question and observe, first! Remember, prescription without diagnosis is malpractice!

Questions Equal Profits!

The benefits of asking questions are numerous. Here are seven:

1. Your customers share their feelings from *their* perspective.

2. You gain valuable insights into your customers as individuals.
3. You begin to appreciate their needs.
4. If you say something, it's likely to be true. If your customers say something, it's "gospel!"
5. When your customers speak, they may reveal a need or problem you had not previously considered.
6. The focus is on your *customers'* "presentation" of information instead of *your* pitch or "dog-and-pony-show."
7. Questions put you in control. Your customers may perceive they're dominating the information-gathering process, interview or probe with their ideas. That's fine. They think they're in control. Yet with questions, you are!

43. A Journalism Lesson

Just like a good journalist, your *need-development* questions should include the basic W's—*who, what, when, where, why, which*—and the H, *how*. Plus, *tell me more about*. These open-ended questions can be mixed with closed-ended questions, requiring a *yes* or *no*, i.e., qualifying or decision questions—to maximize your questioning results.

The following questions are designed to get your customers to *open up*. Are they all inclusive? Of course not. Can you use and apply all of them? Probably, although not necessarily in the same call, visit or meeting. But do they help you fine-tune your questioning and earning power? Definitely, yes! The results are remarkable. Adapt and work with the questions that best complement you, your personality, your customers, your product and your service or situation.

1. "How do you think our product or service can help you?"

2. "What aspects or features of our product or service will help you most?"

3. "How soon would you like to benefit from our product or service?"

4. "As a result of this investment, what benefits or outcomes are you expecting?"

5. "Have you spoken with my competitors?"

6. "What aspects or features of their products or services did you like?"

7. "Anything you didn't like? How come?"

8. "Aside from you, who else will approve this investment?"

9. "What's your budget for this investment?"

10. "What trends do you anticipate in your industry? And what trends do you anticipate in your business?"

11. "How has your business changed over the past few years?"

12. "What are your goals over the next (establish a specific time frame)?"

13. "How do you see our product or service helping you achieve these goals?"

14. "If you could design the perfect solution for this problem,

what would you do?"

15. "How and/or why did you first get involved in this business?"

16. "What are your key responsibilities?" (Or, "Tell me more about what you do…")

17. "What are your priorities?"

18. "What qualities/assets do you look for and value most in a sales professional?"

19. "What qualities/assets do you look for and value most from a company like ours?"

20. "How will you measure, quantify or determine the success of our product or service?"

21. "What's your biggest challenge right now?"

22. "What one thing do you wish your current product/service did? How come? Why would that be important or helpful to you?"

23. "What are your competitors doing, you wish, you were doing?"

24. "How do your customers/clients perceive you?"

25. "Aside from the information you've already shared, what else would you like to share with me, that'll help me help you?"

Remember, the response to each *core* question can help you develop your next question. Then, you can probe even deeper for results.

44. Categorize and Conquer!

Obviously, the list of questions you could ask a client are endless. As a *peak profiteer* and *Opportunity $eller,* you should create a list of potential power probes or need-development questions. And you can even organize them by key categories. For example, business history, marketing and sales, competition, operations, technology, physical facilities, management, training, lifestyle, personal dreams and goals or any logical category that makes sense for your product or service.

Let me open my *questions vault* and share with you some *category* questions. I assure you, these questions, like the preceding 25 *core* questions belong in a vault or safe, because they're incredibly valuable! For example:

Company Role/Personal Assessment

- What does being effective in your job mean?
- What is it about you, the job or its context that has contributed to this level of effectiveness?
- What are your major responsibilities?
- What occupies most of your time?
- What are the biggest problems or challenges you face?
- How effective are you in your job?
- What would make you even more effective?
- What are your greatest strengths?
- What are your greatest weaknesses?

- What have been your major accomplishments in the business?
- What personal goals would you like to realize in the business?
- What company goals would you like to realize in the business?
- How would you describe your management style?
- How has it changed over the past five years?
- If there's one thing you could change about your role in the organization, what would it be and why?

Business Overview

- What are the key characteristics of your industry?
- What are the key characteristics of your business?
- What are your principal products and services?
- What distinguishes your company from your competition?
- What is your company's total revenue or sales?
- What percentage of revenue is derived from each product or service? What percentage of profit?
- How many employees do you have? Leadership? Sales? Administrative? Production? Hourly? Union? Executive? Operational? Manufacturing?

Marketing and Sales

- How is your marketplace segmented?
- How would you describe your business: Seasonal? Cyclical?
- How would you describe your customers?
- What is the potential size of the markets you serve?
- Are these markets growing, stable or declining?
- How do your customers perceive your company?
- What changes would you like to make in these perceptions

over the next year, three years and five years?

- Do you have any new products and services? What? When will they be introduced?
- If not, what are your plans for developing new products and services?
- How much time and money does your company devote to research and development? New products? New services?
- How do you see your company expanding? Growing? Improving?

Competitive Analysis

- What distinguishes you from your competitors?
- Who do you consider competition?
- What's your USP—unique selling proposition?
- Is competition in your business/industry mostly price? Service? Quality? Image?
- What advantages do you have over your competition?
- What disadvantages do you have as compared to your competition?
- What new competition is entering your market?
- What is a competitor doing that you wish you could do?

Operations

- How efficient is your operation?
- How could it be improved?
- What procedures are in place to assure quality and customer satisfaction?
- What is the biggest problem area within your operation?
- What plans are being made for a company action plan or policy manual? When will it be completed?

Information Systems

- How does your computer system or CRM system satisfy or not satisfy your needs?
- What kinds of reports do you receive on a regular basis?
- How do these help you?
- What kind of ongoing information would you like to receive that you're not currently receiving?
- What "new technology" would help your business?

Physical Facilities

- How could your present facilities be changed to maximize customers' satisfaction and your profitability?
- How impactfully is the store merchandised within the store, your windows, your parking lots, dressing rooms, carpeting, waiting areas, lighting, reception desk?
- How impactfully is your office merchandised? What image does it convey?

Management

- Describe your organizational structure.
- How effective is it?
- What, if any, are weak links?
- Do you have a formal organizational chart? Do you need one?
- How often do you have management meetings?
- What's the focus of these discussions? Problem-solving? New opportunities? Or gripe sessions?
- Do you have any type of middle-management group? If not,

do you think one should be developed?

- What type of incentive plan is available for your managers?
- Is it effective? Does it need to be changed? How? What are the key things your managers and salespeople need to understand about your business and your organization, if they're to *truly understand* the environment in which they work?

Service

- If you asked your clients or customers to list your firm's strengths, what would they write? Have you ever asked them?
- Of the strengths listed, which three would they list as the strongest?
- What are your firm's weaknesses in the minds of the people you serve?
- Of your weaknesses, which three are most frequently mentioned?
- What strengths do you have that those you serve don't know about?
- What strengths do you have that your competition doesn't?
- What assets do you have that people want?
- What assets do you have that people need?
- What's your mission?
- Given your strengths, weaknesses, marketable assets and mission, what three goals seem appropriate for you and your team, department and company?
- How do you *listen* to customers and gain their feedback and opinions?

Personnel

- How do you classify your employees?

- How many people do you have in each department?
- Do you have a turnover problem?
- Do you have a morale problem?
- If so, what is the cause of these problems?
- How have you tried to solve the problems?
- What are the results?
- What type of systems, processes or training programs are currently in place to enhance the success of your company and your employees?
- What do you do to motivate employees?
- How is your current system for motivation working?
- Do you know what motivates your employees? On a group or an individual basis?
- Have you ever received employee input in this area? What did they feel motivated them?
- Have you ever used any type of an analysis or assessment instrument, with your employees to measure performance and behavior? If so, with what results? If not, how might this information be helpful to you?

To best familiarize yourself with these and other probing questions, I strongly suggest, unequivocally urge and repeatedly recommend you write them down! Pale ink is better than a faded memory! And you can even record your power probes onto your smartphone, so when you drive to appointments, run errands or workout, you're continually programming yourself for success.

Do you sequentially and painstakingly ask each *core* or *category* question? Of course not. Instead, your next question or series of questions is really dependent upon your prospect's or client's previous responses.

45. Why Q&A Pays

Questioning or probing techniques and skills have a dramatic impact on your bottom line. Business professionals who moan, "I'm lousy at getting a commitment!" are really poor probers or interviewers. They can't get *The Yes*, because they usually didn't discover the prospect's needs. Remember, it's tough to suggest or solve before you've asked or assessed.

When I meet a prospective client for the first time, he or she may ask me, "How can you help our company?" My response goes something like this: "I don't know yet. At this point, I'm really not quite sure, because it's likely your needs are different and unique from others we've already helped. Therefore, would it be okay if I ask you some quick questions—to better understand your particular needs, specific challenges and desired outcomes?" No one has ever said no!

To maximize your results during your *probe*, here are six tips:

1. **Let the individual know** you need to ask questions, so you can better help.
2. **Always ask for permission** before you start the probing process.
3. **When your decision-makers** are talking, don't interrupt.
4. **Take lots of notes.** There's great credibility in the printed word, especially when the words belong to your customers. Words not written are words forgotten. A law school professor of mine used to say, "An oral contract is as good as the paper it's written on!" Also, be sure to ask for permission to take notes. If you suddenly pull out a legal pad and start scribbling away, customers could become reluctant and unwilling participants.

5. **Converse, don't interrogate.** There's no need to play Sergeant Joe Friday from *Dragnet*—"The facts ma'am, just the facts." Instead, follow the example of TV's Detective Columbo. His questions are asked almost apologetically. They seem harmless. Yet, they uncover information that always leads to a solved case!

6. **Jot down your key** need-development questions or power probes, so they become automatic. Put them on a 3x5 card or record them onto your smartphone. Keep them close; in your briefcase, taped to your car's visor, on your desk, on your laptop—wherever they'll serve as a constant reminder for results.

46. He Said, "Sell Me!"

Years ago, I had a meeting with the head partner (we'll call him Mr. Big) of a large and well-recognized financial organization. The purpose of our meeting was to discuss a series of seminars in an ongoing learning-system for his professional staff. We had never met before and he was the final decision-maker.

My proposal or action plan had already been approved by the firm's marketing director, assistant director of human resources and director of human resources. They all told me they were confident it soon would get Mr. Big's okay.

When I entered Mr. Big's office (about the size of Texas), the marketing director and assistant director of human resources rose to greet me and introduce me to Mr. Big. I extended my hand to Mr. Big and as we shook hands, he stared straight at me without acknowledging my greeting and tersely stated, "Sell me!"

Probe and Prosper!

Was this a request? No way. It was a challenge!

Although I was tempted to *tell* him how productive and profitable I'd make his team, I didn't. I knew that would be a crucial mistake. Instead, I looked directly at him and said, "Do you mind if I ask you a few questions?" He said, "No, fire away!"

I then asked:

- "What do you think about the action plan?"
- "How does it coincide with your objectives?"
- "What would you add to or delete from your learning-system?"
- "What do you want your people to leave with?"
- "How soon do you want your people to benefit from and begin to apply these new skills?"

As he answered these and other questions, I jotted down his responses. The entire meeting lasted about 50 minutes. Of those 50 minutes, I spoke for maybe 10 minutes. The rest of the time, I asked simple, direct questions and just listened to Mr. Big's long and expansive answers.

At the 50th minute, Mr. Big gazed over his glasses and delivered his royal decree, "All right Blackman, I'm confident. I'm convinced. Let's do it!" I thanked him for his time, cooperation and most importantly, *his* valuable input. I didn't talk him into buying, I *listened* him into investing. Despite his challenge to sell him, I didn't. He sold himself!

Werner Heisenberg, a Nobel prize-winning physicist once stated, "Nature does not reveal its secrets, it only responds to our method of questioning." Therefore, let *nature* take its course. Use questions!

Questions reveal needs. Needs lead to solutions. Solutions create business growth. And business growth leads to peak profits! Profits that help you and others attain a more favorable future and improved condition!

47. A Tip from Down Under

Australians have introduced us to Crocodile Dundee, "shrimp on the barbie" and Vegemite sandwiches. However, they're especially proud of their native invention, the boomerang. What happens when you toss a boomerang? That's correct, it comes right back to you. This action also makes the *boomerang* a potent and powerful business strategy.

How would you respond to a customer who asks, "Is that a popular-selling product." If you're like most businesspeople, you'd probably state in a confident and commanding voice, "You bet it's popular, one of our best-selling models!" Their retort, "Oh, that's too bad, I wanted something really special and unique!" You're sunk! And you're unlikely to recover.

However, let's examine this same scenario with the use of the *boomerang*. The customer inquires, "Is that a popular-selling product." The response should be, "Is popularity important to you? Or, are you looking for something unique?" When the customer indicates his or her desire for that "one-of-a-kind" look, you continue to *probe* to uncover what this means, what the customer envisions or wants to accomplish.

The *boomerang* applies to a variety of situations. For example, how would you now respond to a customer who inquires...

Question:

"Does that come in red?"
"Can you deliver it by Monday?"
"When will you finish this project?"
"Is it compatible with our current system?"

Response:

"Would you like it in red?"
"Would you like it by Monday?

"When would you like to finish?"
"Is compatibility important?"

Now I know what you're thinking. This is a drawn-out and repetitive approach. Sure, it requires another question, but it's a question that elicits a response from your *customer's* perspective. There's a big difference between saying, "I can complete it by May!" and your customer stating, "I'd like it all done by May."

Toss It One More Time

I'll never forget one probe session I had with the president of a large and successful insurance agency. During our first meeting he asked, "Jeff, who on my team should attend your series of skill-building programs?" I said, "Well, there are a couple of possibilities. But Milt, if I can ask, who do *you* think should be there and would benefit the most?" He said, "I want the rookies to show up, because they're young, hungry and excited. They're the new blood. The future of our organization! But I also want some of the veterans there too. They're smart, still competitive and they've got great war stories to tell!" I told him that made a lot of sense.

He then asked, "Jeff, what do we highlight first?" I paused, glanced at my notes, in a moment of reflection looked up and then said, "Hmm, Milt, what do *you* think we should highlight first?" He told me, for the next five minutes!

Then he asked, "Jeff, if there's one skill you think is important for my people to master as a result of your results-sessions, what would that be?" I pondered his question and then thoughtfully replied, "Milt, that depends. What would *you* like it to be?" He then made an emphatic statement I'll never forget, he said, "Jeff, I'd consider this program to be an incredible success, if my people could just learn how to answer a question with a question!"

I smiled and said, "Milt, why is that skill so important to you?" And of course, he told me!

I had repeatedly used the boomerang with Milt. But why was he willing to always respond? Very simply, he was logically and emotionally involved with our probe. He knew the motivation for my questions was to help, not to harass. The questions were designed to discover, not to disturb.

However, let me offer one caveat or warning. Don't boomerang everything. For example, if your client happens to innocently ask, "What time is it?"—your response shouldn't be: "What time would you like it to be?"

Probe and Prosper!

48. It Isn't Over 'til It's Over

I often ask clients and seminar participants, "How do you know when you've finished the *probe*?" Their typical responses are: "when you've run out of questions," "when the customer wants to see what you've got," "when you think you know all there is to know" or "when they start asking you questions."

All of these answers are logical, but not necessarily correct. Why? Because it isn't over 'til the customer says it's over! Before I ever begin to *reveal* or show a client how I can help them, I inquire at what I think is the likely end of the *Probe*, with this question: "What else would you like to share with me, before I suggest a results-strategy, possible solutions or an action plan?" If the response is, "You've got it all," then, and only then, do I move on to the next stage, which is the *Reveal*.

In the next four sections, we'll explore four more strategies that'll revolutionize how you ask questions and *probe* in the future.

49. The Fairness Doctrine

Have you ever been in the middle of a *Probe* when you're suddenly confronted by a seemingly insurmountable dilemma, such as the loyalty barrier? You know how that one goes, you're finally in front of prospects we'll call *Mr. and Ms. I'm Not Gonna Budge*. You've made previous contacts with the Budges 17 times by phone and email! And now they've granted you an *audience* for only 15 minutes.

Unfortunately, within the first five minutes, they let you know you're wasting your time, because your number-one competitor,

Hard Sell Enterprises, has been taking care of them for 20 years and they're not about to change now!

At this point, many businesspeople would dejectedly and unhappily pack up and leave. Others would try to convince *Mr. or Ms. I'm Not Gonna Budge* as to why switching to their company, product or service makes more sense. But this strategy is a loser. Why? Because the more you try to convince the Budges to budge, the more they'll defiantly and stubbornly hold their ground.

Prospects don't like to be told how stupid their previous decisions are. The harder you sell, the stronger their resistance will be. So what do you do? Easy! Apply the *fairness doctrine*.

Here's how it works. Ask the Budges a series of very specific questions. For example, "What do you like best about your current supplier?" "How have they helped you?" Or, "What benefits do their products deliver?"

While the Budges enthusiastically tell you all the reasons they're happy, loyal, satisfied and not about to budge, you listen patiently and intently. When they're done, and to acknowledge you've paid close attention, you briefly summarize the key points they just mentioned. For example, you might say, "I can now understand why you've been so happy with Hard Sell Enterprises. The things that are especially important to you are their quality, on-time delivery and follow-up." Your prospects are, of course, nodding their heads in agreement, confident you've been defeated and you'll now bolt for an escape route. Instead, you apply the *fairness doctrine.*

You simply ask the Budges a question that begins with these six words, "Would it be fair to say…"

For example, "Would it be fair to say that even if we could provide you with quality, on-time deliveries and follow-through that was as good or *even better* than Hard Sell Enterprises, you still wouldn't want to discuss any further how we could help you? Would it be fair to say that?"

Now, you wait. And if they say, "Yes, it would be fair to say that!"—you now know they're unwilling to listen, change, alter or budge. To this prospect you say good-bye! Why? Because if your *Probe* reveals there's no need to *reveal*, then there's no need to *reveal*.

What's the real value of the *fairness doctrine,* with its "would it be fair to say" question? It lets your prospect know you're willing to leave. Your time, effort and energy will no longer be devoted (at least for now) to this particular prospect.

However, before you leave, there are still several key things for you to say and ask.

Fairness Doctrine Plus Referral Leverage

Now remember, I'll never share with you any strategy unless I myself do it and have had success with it. Therefore, when I have unfortunately discovered that the *Probe* has revealed there's no need to *reveal*, I'll say something like, "John, it's too bad we won't have the opportunity to work together now, but would it be fair to say, what you're really telling me, isn't 'no,' but instead 'not yet'?" At this point, John usually smiles and says something like, "I'd be more than happy, Jeff, to see you again. Why don't you call me in three months?"

I make a note to follow-up, but then I ask John one more question before I go. I say, "John, just out of curiosity, who else do you know, obviously noncompetitive to you and your company who could benefit from the types of business-growth strategies we offer?" Usually, one of three things happens. First, the prospect may say, "Well, I have no idea." I assure you, responses like this are the exception, not the norm. Second, the prospect may say something like, "Let me think about it. If you call me next week, I'll have a couple of names."

The third response is actually the most common scenario. Immediately, the prospect starts to flip through his or her actual or mental contact list or taps into a database and begins to give me names and numbers. This simple strategy has helped me discover countless new prospects who became clients.

I know what you're thinking, "This makes no sense! It's totally illogical! Why would someone who's not going to use you then go ahead and give you referrals?"

Here's why this strategy works. I don't say, "Could you give me a lead? Would you recommend me in the future? How about passing-out a few of my business cards?" Instead, I ask if the individual knows anyone, obviously noncompetitive, who could benefit from what I do. And here's what I think happens with the referral source's psyche. Most people find it difficult to say "no" or for that matter even "not yet." They feel guilty, as if they've "rejected" you. Therefore, in an attempt to remove the guilt, they'll be helpful and accommodate your request. The simple repositioning of the question often and quickly leads to results.

CASE STUDY

Banc One Generates $230 Million in New Business with *Referrals: Your Road to Results!*™

CHALLENGE:

Banc One Financial Services, (before they became part of Chase), sold mortgages. Lots of 'em. Yet they didn't ask customers or prospects for referrals. They were leaving millions of dollars in lost revenue and profits on-the-table. And also denying potential homeowners the opportunity to live their dream, to "buy a home."

This drove me crazy, since I saw the potential for explosive referral results. So I asked Banc One's President, "How come your folks don't ask for referrals?" He said, "It's not part of our culture."

Since Banc One had me on long-term retainer for several consecutive years, I'd frequently "revisit" this topic with Banc One's President and leaders. However, I was always told, "Jeff, we really value our relationship and work with you, yet you've gotta realize, referrals are not part of our culture!"

NEW RATIONALE:

I knew Banc One had the ability to capture a huge untapped market. Since a referral is a "lead" with virtually no acquisition cost. It's an abundance of opportunity. And all you have to do is ask!

C
A
S
E

S
T
U
D
Y

I also knew when your customers, clients and prospects know you, like you and trust you, they'll willingly refer you to others. For they value what you and your company bring to the table. And since you have a commitment *to service*, it's a *dis-service*, not to see—if you can help one's family, friends, co-workers, peers and business associates.

A study by the Mortgage Bankers Association of America even revealed, "That those searching for mortgages are influenced most by advice from friends and family. More than one-third of buyers said they rely on friends for guidance on where to seek a loan." Referrals help *you*...make *others*...look like heroes.

GAME PLAN AND APPROACH:

C
A
S
E

S
T
U
D
Y

I knew "referrals" were in Banc One's best interest, for the company and each loan officer's future success. So I stayed politely persistent. Early in 1998, I suggested to the senior leadership team of Banc One Financial Services, the development of a referrals program or system. It would strategically teach the bank's sales professionals to ask for referrals and then convert these new leads into booked loans.

The leaders finally agreed, yet wondered, "Jeff, how do you know it'll work?" I simply said, "Its success is up to your people. When they execute, the results will be quick and dramatic."

RESULTS:

In late March, 1998, Banc One and I introduced their *Referrals: Your Road to Results*™ program at three branch-centers. While the initial response was excellent, I knew these positive expectations had to be translated into top and bottom-line results. They were! Within the first two months, referrals generated new booked loan volume of $896,331!

Here's what the bank's sales professionals said about the value of referrals:

> **Loan officer:** "One customer has already given me 11 referrals."
> **Loan officer:** "Referrals help you meet and exceed your company and personal goals. You just have to ask for them."
> **Loan officer:** "I love getting referrals, there's automatic rapport and it lets me know my hard work has paid off."
> **Loan officer:** "Referrals are really hot leads. They're basically free deals that lead to higher volume. It's great!"
> **Loan officer:** "Customers are eager to offer referrals, when they realize you were sincere in your effort to help them."

C
A
S
E

S
T
U
D
Y

Based upon these early successes, the bank's senior leadership team enthusiastically declared, "Jeff, let's roll it out! Now!"

To support the "rollout," we created a series of workshops and customized business-growth reinforcement tools, i.e., workbooks, audios, videos, on-going voice mail reminders, etc.

The bank's loan officers learned how to:

- Ask for referrals.
- Develop a referrals network.
- Positively leverage a prospect they were unable to help.
- Obtain valuable information about a referred lead.
- Contact and communicate with a referred lead…and more.

A NEW $230 MILLION CULTURE CREATED:

Referrals became an integral part of Banc One's daily culture. And volume. To see a "classic cut" excerpt from our "Video Vault" and the *Referrals: Your Road to Results!*™ customized video learning-system I wrote and hosted for Banc One, please head to:

http://www.jeffblackman.com/clients/results-case-studies/

This excerpt tells the story of how I helped Banc One generate $230 million dollars in new business, in 23 months, all from referrals! And the size of a typical referral loan was almost 30 percent greater than a non-referral loan. (Banc One sold this portfolio in March, 2000 to Household International.)

Whether you're selling products or services, if you'd like to learn more about how *you too* can create a referrals culture to drive explosive results, please contact Sheryl Kantor: sheryl@ jeffblackman.com or 847.998.0688. And then get ready to ride, your referral road to results!

C
A
S
E

S
T
U
D
Y

The Fairness Doctrine with Change Potential

Let's see what happens with the *fairness doctrine* when your prospects are now willing to listen or at least consider a potential change. Remember, you ask the question, "Would it be fair to say, even if we could provide you with quality, on-time deliveries and follow-through as good or *even better* than Hard Sell Enterprises, you still wouldn't want to discuss any further, how we could help you? Would it be fair to say that?" But this time they say, "No, it wouldn't be fair to say that! If you could do those things better or faster than Hard Sell, I'd at least be willing to listen!" Perfect! That's the response you've been waiting for. Now you begin to *probe* even deeper to discover what they really want to accomplish, do different or do better.

When you apply the *fairness doctrine*, the results are rapid and remarkable. Your "no-budge" prospects open the door to opportunity. And the potential for that opportunity, for you and them, is achieved through a question, not a statement.

50. The Best Alternative

How would you like to replace the competition that's serving the customers you'd like to be serving? Wouldn't that be nice? However, it's unlikely, because as we've already determined, buyers or decision-makers are often reluctant to change, even if the change helps them attain a more favorable future or improved condition. They have a comfort or security level with the past they probably don't want to disrupt.

My suggestion is never try to *replace* your competitor. Instead, position yourself to become the next best *alternative*. Here's the question you ask: "Mr. and Ms. Budge, I can now understand why you've been so happy with Hard Sell Enterprises and why you wouldn't want to replace them. So I'm wondering: 'How can our company, products and services *complement* what Hard Sell is doing for you?'"

This question is extremely powerful. Here's why. It relieves decision-makers. They now know they don't have to replace their current supplier. Together, you and your decision-makers can now determine how you can best complement, contribute to or be a part of their solution, and not the entire solution.

51. The Blue Suit

A blue suit is considered traditional or conservative attire. And for this *blue suit* strategy to work, *conservative* becomes the operative word.

This approach is disarmingly simple, but incredibly effective. Here's how it works: Whatever your product or service, it's probably designed to maximize gain and/or minimize loss. Gain maximization could be improved self-esteem or enhanced revenues. Loss minimization could be peace of mind or reduced operating expenses. No matter what you're selling, the application of the *blue suit* is essentially the same.

Here's how I apply it in my business. My clients depend upon me to be a business-growth specialist. I help them improve the performance, productivity and profitability of their people and company in a variety of ways—through speaking, training, consulting and business-growth tools.

However, before I can help them grow and prosper from new sales, marketing, customer service or negotiation strategies, I must know what they're losing—or not gaining—because they don't have these business skills. Therefore, here's the question I might ask a potential client:

- "Conservatively, as a result of your team not having the negotiating skills you'd like, how much money are they leaving on the table?"

- "If your people knew how to better prospect and manage their time and territory, conservatively, how many more dollars could they generate?"

- "Because you feel your customer service representatives aren't delivering quality service, what negative impact, conservatively, is this lack of service having on your revenues and bottom-line?"

You might also apply the *blue suit* by asking:

- "Conservatively, how many hours are your people devoting to the following activities and what's the value of their time? Conservatively, then, what's the real cost of having them perform these tasks?"

- "Conservatively, how many opportunities or dollars are being lost, because your machinery is malfunctioning?"

Here's how I once applied the *blue suit* strategy with a potential client: I said, "Thanks for telling me you and your people are not effectively using your referral sources. Now, because of this, conservatively, how much annual revenues are you losing?" The president of the company paused, and then in an exasperated tone mumbled, "Probably a half million dollars a year!" I gasped and said, "A half million dollars a year! Are you serious?" He reluctantly nodded his head. Then his vice president exclaimed, "No way!" The president responded, "What, do you think it's less?" The vice president said, "No, it's higher—closer to a million!" I gasped again, "A million dollars a year! Are you kidding?!" He said, "I wish I was. Let me explain."

He then told me in great detail about all the opportunities they had blown. The power of this question is that if forces the prospects to quantify their pain! They assign a numerical and tangible dollar sign to their suffering.

If We Only Had…

Now, here's one more subtlety to the *blue suit* strategy. Once the dollar figure of anguish is shared and you've expressed your surprise, you can ask this question: "If you had that extra million dollars, what would you do with it?"

Now they begin to plan, dream and visualize for you. They talk about return on investment, expansion, new market penetration, enhanced lifestyle or improved image. They freely express their aches and pains and now want to know you can rid them of their ailment and make them well and better.

By the way, that prospect who felt he was losing a million dollars a year became a client when he said, "We better take a look at the calendar, Jeff, and pick a date for you to start helping our people. That way, we can get those lost dollars flowing toward us instead of away from us."

By using the *blue suit* strategy, how many more people can you help attain a more favorable future or improve their condition? And conservatively, how many more dollars does that mean to you?

52. Budget Builders

At what stage of the *Peak Your Profits* and *Opportunity $elling* *system* do you determine or gain some insight into your decision-maker's budget? Now—in the *Probe* stage. Because not only must your buyers have a need to fill, dream to realize or problem to solve, but they must also have the ability to pay for it! You should never place yourself in a position where you have to guess at somebody's budget or investment potential. *Budget Builders* help you avoid this dilemma.

Budget Builders are questions that remove the guesswork and uncertainty about the budget. However, your decision-maker may be unwilling to share with you a budget, a number or say something like, "I have no idea what this should cost—that's why I called you!" or "Money is no object. If it's worth it, I'll pay for it!" If you get responses like these, you can still determine the budget. Here's one way:

You let your buyers know you want them to make the best possible decision. And that decision will obviously be a reflection of their goals, needs and budget. Therefore, if they have no idea what the investment might be, you can share several ranges. For example, you let them know that happy clients who have had a similar need, problem or goal have made investments within three ranges, let's say:

- Range 1 is $5,000 to $10,000.
- Range 2 is $11,000 to $20,000.
- Range 3 is $ 21,000 or greater.

It's important to stress that you should never put an ending parameter or restriction on your final range.

You now ask them, "Which range would you be most comfortable with—1, 2 or 3?" If they say, "Range 2, $11,000 to $20,000," you say, "Wonderful, would you prefer to stay closer to $11,000 or $20,000?" Their responses help guide you in your creation of the best possible solution.

Is the Budget Really Firm?

How do you handle the decision-maker who gives you a *firm* budget? Let's take a look at an example that'll be easy to relate to. Imagine I'm a real estate agent and you're a motivated buyer. We've already determined you want a four-bedroom, two-and-a-half-bath house in a quiet community, close to schools, shopping and transportation and the lot has to be at least a quarter of an acre. You've told me you're only willing to look at homes listed at $350,000 or less.

Armed with this information, the first house I take you to is listed at $375,000. Not only do you detest the floor plan and neighborhood, but you're also disappointed and disturbed with me, because the house was listed at more than $350,000! You feel I took you here just so I'd make more on my commission! Needless to say, I'm in trouble! You feel I didn't listen and you may begin to question my integrity and real purpose.

However, what if *this* scenario took place? Imagine I said to you, "Now let me make sure I understand what's important to you. You'd like to find a four-bedroom, two-and-a-half-bath house in a quiet community, close to schools, shopping and transportation and the lot has to be at least a quarter of an acre. You have also told me, you're only willing to look at homes listed at $350,000 or less. Correct?" You nod affirmatively.

Now, I ask a question that combines the *budget builder* strategy along with the *fairness doctrine*. And the question is, "Would it be fair to say, if I come across a listing that offers you and your family everything you want—the space, the community, the lot size and then some—but it's listed at more than $350,000— would it be fair to say, you'd prefer I not even show it to you?"

Now how do you think you'd react. It's likely you'll say, "Well, I guess I'd be willing to look at it." I say, "Great! How much in excess of $350,000 are you comfortable with?" You say, "Well, up to $380 is probably okay, maybe even $400, but then it really has to be something special!"

Who just increased the budget—me or you? You did! And it was accomplished, once again, with the use of a *question* or a *probe*.

The following five peak-profit points should help you maximize all your future *probes:*

1. Control through questions that reveal problems, needs and dreams or goals.
2. Keep quiet—stare with your ears, listen with your eyes.
3. Take notes—place value in your prospect's words.
4. Restate your prospect's wants, needs and desires and confirm their importance.
5. Let your prospect know your *probing* is crucial to helping you help him or her.

As a *peak profiteer,* may you continue to *probe* your path to profit!

ANOTHER SPECIAL BONUS

Do you ever fight the price vs. value battle? Do you have prospects or customers who immediately ask, "What's the cost?" Or, declare, "C'mon, you can do better than that!" Yep, thought so. So did my clients. Until I taught them when to ask and how to apply an impactful series of power probes and strategies—specifically created to help you confidently deliver and successfully prove your value. Want to see 'em? For free? Of course you do! So take a quick reading break, and right now, send an email to: sheryl@jeffblackman.com with the subject heading: PYP Value Strategies

---

C A S E S T U D Y

CASE STUDY

Winning Wheels!

CHALLENGE:

How to bring together seven non-competitive, distinct companies and cultures, and their respective teams and create a unified learning-system with a series of regional results-sessions, multiple business-growth tools, plus ongoing coaching and reinforcement. (NABDA, the North American Bus Dealers Alliance included U.S. distributors that provided for schools, healthcare facilities, municipalities, religious organizations, hotels, casinos, etc., every imaginable bus — from school buses to passenger vans to luxury motor coaches.)

RESULTS:

Doug Dunn, a NABDA member, and Chairman and CEO of
Alliance Bus Group, wrote to to his fellow NABDA CEOs:
"By far, the best training experience since I got into this
business. Everyone is learning and using these new skills. All
of Jeff's materials are perfect for what we're doing. It'll pay us
all huge dividends for years to come. We're experiencing increases
by individuals who have never (in all their years in the business)
produced as many sales as in the past few weeks. Unbelievable!
I'm seeing a new level of professionalism and pride."

EVEN MORE RESULTS: THEY DOUBLED THE PRICE!

One of our regional results-sessions took place in Chicago on
October 1st. Two days later, on October 3rd, I received a remarkable email from an ecstatic salesperson, Jay, who worked for one
of the NABDA companies. It was simply titled: *Probing Success.*
The following features verbatim excerpts from Jay's email:

C
A
S
E

S
T
U
D
Y

*Jeff, here's a little story on the success of using power probes.
One of my customers, also my alma mater, is in the process
of purchasing a new bus from us. During our initial meeting with them, we discussed options, seats, blah, blah, blah.*

*Then the conversation started to get interesting...asked a
simple question: "What, in your wildest dreams, would you
want your athletes and coaches to accomplish while riding
on this bus that they cannot accomplish on your current
bus?" After some strange looks and confusion, they were
hooked.*

We were brainstorming together, solving all of their efficiency issues, answering all of their questions, and writing some fabulous specs. By the end of the conversation, they had a bus with wireless Internet, satellite TV, power outlets for notebook computers, airline style tray tables, a separate lounge in the back for the coaches to plan and students to study in privacy, individual seat audio controls, an air conditioning system that would run with the engine off, etc.

They were sold, and they sold themselves. At the end of the conversation, we received one of those rare "buying signals."

The purchasing director told us, "I'll get you the P.O." We were able to skip the Reveal, Translate and Negotiate stages.

To say that "this stuff works" is only putting it mildly.

By the way, through this process, they doubled the price of the bus. Now that's peaking your profits!

C
A
S
E

S
T
U
D
Y

CHAPTER 8

Reveal for Results!

*"The best way to succeed in life, is to
act on the advice we give to others!"*

—Anonymous

53. Ready or Not, Here I Come!

You've probably heard numerous businesspeople enthusiastically boast the following:

- "Let me show you what we've got!"
- "Boy, you're going to love this one!"
- "I can't wait for you to see what just arrived!"

However, these exclamations often occur long before the businessperson ever determines *how* he or she can help you. Unfortunately, all too often, businesspeople assume their customer, client or prospect is just as excited to hear about their product or service as they are to tell their tale!

It's seldom true. Few if any customers actually want to hear your enthusiastic chatter until you've assessed their needs. And assessing needs should always occur before—not after—you *reveal* how you can help them attain a more favorable future and improved condition.

In traditional business development, the *Reveal* stage is when many people begin their "selling." And when they do, it's usually a mistake! Why? Because it's premature. They haven't determined yet the prospect's needs, goals and objectives. They don't know specifically whether the prospect has a need to fill, problem to solve or dream to realize.

As a simple rule, you should never tell, demonstrate or reveal, until you have completed the first two steps in the *Peak Your Profits* and *Opportunity $elling system*—the *Open* and the *Probe*.

You'll Trip If You Skip

What happens if you skip a step in *the system*? Let me answer this question with a story.

As a second-year law student, I began going to law school at night. My days were devoted to selling airtime for a radio-brokerage company. The owner of the company shared with me his "alleged" three-step winning philosophy and strategy for successful business development:

- **Step 1.** Make a telephone call to get the appointment.
- **Step 2.** Write-up a contract that included: the stations, the airtime, the length of the spots and even the budget, before ever meeting the potential client and determining any of their needs, goals or objectives.
- **Step 3.** Show up at the appointment and leave with a signed contract.

Now, as you can obviously tell, there was no priority placed upon the *Open* and *Probe*. I literally walked into a prospect's office with a completed contract. It only required a signature. Their opinion, feelings, attitudes and problems were unimportant. Everything had already been predetermined. By me!

The owner taught me, there was really no need to probe, because the meeting should be focused on my presentation and especially on the close, not on the prospect. He also fancied himself as a great motivational master. His pep talks went something like this:

- "Close early and close often!"
- "You'll never smell the rose, if you can't get the close."
- "The buyer is your enemy!"
- "Get their damn signature, then get the hell out of there."
- "You represent *my* interests, not theirs!"

Did I bring in some contracts? Sure, but not often. At that time, I really didn't understand the psychology or the process involved in business development. Using the owner's quick-hit attack, my successes were rare. And as a result, my attitude, desire and self-esteem suffered.

It was only after leaving that job that I realized the major reason for my poor results was that I spent no time developing rapport, building relationships and discovering needs. I immediately *revealed* that I had no relationship power. Both my "little r" and "BIG R" were nonexistent! Thankfully, I learned this valuable lesson early in my business life. Please, don't make the same mistake I did.

You should always *open* and *probe* before you *reveal*. Never guess or assume you know what your prospect's needs are. Let him or her tell you. And if the *probe* reveals there's no need to *reveal,* then don't *reveal*! In other words, if he or she has no problem to solve, need to fill or dream or goal to realize—there's no need to even waste your time with a *Reveal* stage.

54. A Lesson from Childhood

A key to the *Reveal* stage is maximizing your prospect's involvement with your product or service. Imagine buying a car without test-driving it. Buying a fine leather jacket without trying it on. Investing in new speakers without listening to their clarity, power and fidelity. The point is simple: Customers like to get involved.

An involved customer is more likely to buy or invest. Involvement moves a prospect or client closer to psychological ownership. The more customer senses you activate, the greater the likelihood you get *The Yes*. That's why so many companies invest in working products, samples or vignettes.

For example, when you're a customer, would you rather hear about a hot tub's pulsating action or submerge your hand in the warm water to feel the rapid and invigorating stream? Would you prefer a salesperson eloquently describe a home's incredible view, gives you a virtual reality tour, or you simply gaze for yourself and soak-in the grandeur and scenery?

Do you remember when you were a toddler? Have you recently observed one? Toddlers want to touch, taste, smell, see and hear everything that comes into their world. For children, curiosity is encouraged. This *involvement* is crucial to growth. It promotes learning and understanding.

Child educators are especially aware of the importance of *involvement*. At the Children's Museum of Indianapolis, a "touch me—participatory" environment, the executive director once commented, "The most important thing in the room is the audience, not the object. The object is important only if it can unlock something in the audience." The identical concept is true in your business. Your products, services and ideas are only important if they *unlock* something in your customer!

However, as adults, we are all too often reminded, "Handle at your own risk." "Don't touch!" "You break it—you bought it!" These are classic cases of sensory deprivation. And it's the senses that help sell a product or service.

55. Push, Pull, Play and Profit

I'm convinced *involvement* was a principal reason for the initial success of Sharper Image, the nationwide chain of stores founded by Richard Thalheimer, that offered *adult* electronic toys and gadgets in 187 retail locations in 38 states.

Sharper Image promoted participation. You were encouraged to ride the exer-bike, lay down on the massage table, jump on the pogo-stick or crank up the CD. I know this, because I did all of them at Sharper Image stores across the United States.

Aside from having a great time pushing, pressing and playing, I participated in and witnessed a simple, but most effective business-development technique—*involvement*! (In 2006, Thalheimer was removed as CEO by the Sharper Image board. And as the economy worsened, all retail stores closed in 2008 and the company filed for bankruptcy.) Now, under new leadership and ownership, Sharper Image still sells cool, high-tech, futuristic stuff online and by catalog.)

Remember, an involved customer is more likely to buy or invest. And the more customer senses you can activate, the greater the likelihood you satisfy a need, solve a problem, or help someone realize a dream or goal.

Land Rover took *involvement* to a new level. They transformed the typical car "test ride" into an automotive adventure. The Land Rover Experience began in 1990, as Land Rover erected multimillion-dollar boutiques known as Land Rover Centres.

Salespeople were dressed in khaki safari attire, and they accompanied a prospective owner of a Land Rover Discovery, onto an off-road course built in the dealership's parking lot—that included steep inclines and rocky hills. Customers loved it!

And they still love it today! Where Land Rover offers one hour, two hours, half-day and full day "experience drives" all over the world:

- in California: Challenge yourself to hill climbs, log crossings, side tilts and rock crawls on 180 acres of perfectly rugged landscape.

- in North Carolina: Explore the wooded trails, log piles and lush meadows on the grounds of George Vanderbilt's stunning 250 room chateau.

- in Quebec: In the grounds of Chateau Montebello, one of Canada's most luxurious getaways, navigate woodlands trails and obstacles (and keep an eye out for moose).

And, are you ready for this—customers *pay* for these *experiences!*

Involvement is a simple and savvy sales strategy. Yet it's often ignored. Once, I was in a suburban Baltimore guitar store where each guitar displayed a sign warning, "Please do not handle. If you wish to buy me, call a salesperson." Unfortunately, this owner didn't understand the psyche of his customer—the musician who wants to make music! Oh sure, I know the owner is trying to deter the masses from making musical mayhem, but there were so many other ways the message could have been conveyed.

What if the sign on the guitar said, "Together, we'll make beautiful music—Please call a salesperson so you can start to enjoy me!" Or, "I'll make you a star! Please call a salesperson so I can hear your musical talent!" Or, "My strings are lonely, please call a salesperson and bring me to life!"

Confucius Says...

Confucius must have been a pretty good businessman. He once said, "If you tell me I will forget, If you show me, I will remember, If you involve me, I will understand!" So the next time your customer or prospect wants to touch, see, sniff, taste or hear—let 'em! These statistics reveal the full story and value of involvement.

People remember:

- 20 percent of what they hear.

- 30 percent of what they see.
- 50 percent of what they see and hear.
- 80 percent of what they see, hear and do.

One financial planner I know uses a strategy that makes his presentations or *reveals* memorable and profitable. Why? Because Rick has mastered the art of *involvement*. Rick's clients are wealthy, high net-worth individuals, sophisticated decision-makers.

Yet, Rick is the first to admit his approach isn't sophisticated. If anything, it's simplistic. It's also incredibly effective. Here's what Rick does. He takes out a plush felt bag filled with pennies. He gently hands the bag to his clients and tells them the bag represents their "financial future." He then encourages them to pour the pennies onto the conference table. Somewhat skeptically, they do.

Rick then tells his clients (let's call them Harry and Pam) that each penny represents $10,000 and belongs to them—it's their money. Rick suggests they push, pull and slide the pennies across the table to form different piles. Each pile or category represents the couple's goals. One pile could be a retirement fund. Another could be set aside for their kids' or grandkids' education. While another represents a major purchase down the road or significant contributions to various charities.

Rick says Harry and Pam quickly forget they're playing with pennies. Instead, they strategically plan and calculate their financial future. Obviously, Rick's clients are involved!

56. Presentation Power

I'm always amused by statements like, "Our product sells itself." or "There's no need for us to sell, our work speaks for itself."

Wouldn't that be nice! Unfortunately, it's rarely, if ever, true. I once asked a group of accountants if their work really did speak: "Have you ever seen a financial statement talk?" One accountant exclaimed, "No, but I have seen them cry!"

The point is, your work, product, solution or service doesn't talk or communicate. It's your responsibility to help bring its value to life. And that value is conveyed by *you,* during the *Reveal* stage.

An effective *reveal* has five distinct advantages:

1. It maintains or increases your buyer's level of interest and excitement.
2. It justifies or substantiates the ways in which you can help your decision-maker solve problems, fill needs or realize dreams or goals.
3. It allows your buyer to personally experience the value and benefits of your product or service.
4. It diminishes or eliminates potential objections.
5. It gets you one step closer to *The Yes.*

Whether your *reveal* creates involvement by using charts, graphs, signage, posters, PowerPoint or Keynote slides, product samples, brochures, models, mock-ups, personal tests, laptop demos, holograms, artificial intelligence, augmented or virtual reality, webinars, or some other method, the purpose of any tool, is to help you help somebody—and get results.

And to do that, your *reveal*—with its accompanying support tools—should demonstrate to your prospects or customers the end results, benefits, advantages, outcomes or return on investment of your product or service.

Impactful visuals and involvement tools do more than simply enhance your *Reveal* stage, they also help you stay focused and on track. And they maintain or create momentum in your positive progression toward securing *The Yes*.

A Dynamite Dozen

Here are 12 visual and presentation strategies to think about, as you prepare for your next *reveal:*

1. Organize your information in a logical sequence.

2. Don't reveal a piece of information, a feature or a benefit, until the moment you want your prospect or customer to see it, hear it or experience it.

3. Be prepared to share a startling statistic or a previous success story about your product or service that directly addresses your buyer's previously expressed concerns, objectives or problems.

4. Remember, your visual aids merely complement or support your *reveal* or presentation, they don't replace it.

5. Keep things simple. Some of the most effective visuals have only a few powerful words, symbols or a single, dramatic picture.

6. Think trigger-thoughts or key words and symbols. For example, you might say to a prospect, "We help you maximize your return on investment." However, the letters R.O.I. placed next to an ascending arrow might more effectively communicate and reinforce the same message.

7. Whenever possible, don't present or reveal information in the dark or in a dimly lit room, (even if you're using PowerPoint, Keynote or another presentation format). If you can't see your decision-maker's body language, facial expressions and eye movements, you're at a severe disadvantage.

8. Politely request to control your environment. For example, if the sun is glaring in your eyes, ask if it's okay to change seats or close the blinds. Also, try to remove any barriers that might exist between you and your decision-maker(s).

As you know, many offices have a formalized desk and chair arrangement, but there's often informal seating just a few feet away. I'll actually say something like, "Wouldn't we be more comfortable sitting here…," as I point to the informal setting.

No one has ever said "no." If the informal setting doesn't exist, I'll ask the decision-maker if I can pull my chair around and sit at his or her side, so it's easier for us to work together as we review their *action plan*. Again, no one has ever told me to "stay put!"

9. Use your visual aids to highlight key points, glance at them, but don't talk *to them*. Your words should be directed to your prospect or customer.

10. Don't memorize your *reveal* or presentation word-for-word. If you do, you remove the human element from your demonstration. You'll sound canned, rote or almost robotic or automated. The key is to be convincing, yet conversational.

11. Where appropriate, be creative. Add showmanship. Have a flair for the dramatic. (But always acknowledge and be aware of your decision-maker's investment-style and decision-influencers. (Please see Chapter 10, Focus Sections 72 to 76.)

12. The purpose of any visual aid or involvement tool is *not* to simply entertain or enlighten, but instead to move a decision-maker to action and say *The Yes*.

57. Trial by Jury

During the *Reveal* stage, you should begin asking a series of trial questions. What exactly do I mean by "trial questions"? A trial question elicits an opinion, a feeling, a response, an attitude or a gut reaction to your product or service and its features or benefits. These questions should be simple and open-ended. For example:

- "How do you feel about…"
- "What do you think of…"
- "What's your reaction to…"
- "In which ways will this help you…"

For example, let's say during the *Probe* stage, your customer expresses interest in a product that must be durable, but still has a look that's sleek and contemporary. Now, during the *Reveal* stage, when your customer is experiencing or viewing your product, you might ask, "How do you feel about weight, construction and durability?" The response? "It's great!" You might then say, "What do you like best?" Your client's response: "It feels stable, strong and sturdy." You then might ask, "And what do you think of the design?" Once again, the customer provides an extremely favorable response.

The purpose of trial questions is to make sure you're revealing those features as mentioned in the *Probe* stage that are most important and appealing to your decision-maker. And you now get their "opinion" about these features. Every time your prospect or customer gives a positive response, you're moving closer to *The Yes*.

Take Their Temperature

Trial questions are the equivalent of a thermometer. They help you take your decision-maker's temperature. If your questions elicit enthusiastic answers, you're hitting your buyer's "hot" buttons. The *system* moves forward. However, if your questions get a lukewarm or cool response, your buyer's temperature is obviously dropping and it's time to turn up the heat.

But how do you revive a cooling customer? You take a brief step back—to the *Probe* stage. You ask a series of probing or need-development questions. You must discover what your buyer doesn't like. Or what's causing the concern and reluctance. Once this is accomplished, you can then begin to move through the *Reveal* stage toward the *Translate, Negotiate* and *The Yes* stages.

To help you more effectively *reveal,* here are five profit points:

1. Paraphrase the prospect's expressed wants, problems or goals. For example, prior to revealing your specific solution, you might say something like, "Based upon your expressed goals and objectives about quality, delivery and return on investment, let's look at how our gizmo meets and exceeds your expectations." Or, "Mr. Prospect, you mentioned cost reduction is crucial to your success. Now, let's examine how our gizmo helps you drastically reduce costs, while also increasing efficiency and profitability."

2. Reveal the idea, product or service that solves the problem, meets the need or achieves the goal. Here you provide the idea, strategy, solution, product or service that specifically helps your prospect, customer or client attain a more favorable future, improve their condition and get results. As you reveal or present this solution, remember, an involved customer is more likely to buy or invest. Involvement and activating the senses create psychological ownership. And this "ownership" brings you closer to *The Yes* and the opportunity to *peak your profits*.

3. Downplay premature price questions; determine needs first. Prospects and customers have a natural tendency to want to hurry the process. They may exclaim, "Just tell me how much it's gonna be." "How bad is the damage?!" Or "What's this going to set me back?!"

Don't feel obligated to quickly reveal the price or investment. Let your buyer know you'll be more than happy to share that information, but first you'd like to quickly review his or her needs, goals and objectives, and then reveal or demonstrate how your product or service can help.

By the way, when you do reveal the investment, it should never come as a surprise to your decision-maker. Why? Because together, you already predetermined the budget or budgetary parameters in the *Probe* step. A warning, though: you may get premature price questions during your initial *Probe* stage. There are several ways to respond. For example, you might say, "I'm not sure what your investment will be, that really depends upon what you want to accomplish. Can I ask you a few more questions?" Or "If we're not the right company to help you grow your people and your business, your investment will be nothing. It won't cost you a cent. But first, let's determine what your goals are, and together we'll discover how we can help you."

4. Get prospects' thoughts, feelings and reactions to what you've revealed. Here's where you ask your series of trial questions, to discover their attitudes and opinions about your product, service and company.

5. Never *reveal* until you first *open* and *probe*.

Once you *reveal*, it leads to a road of rapid and remarkable results!

CHAPTER 9

Translate and Triumph!

"You make a living by what you get,
but you make a life by what you give!"

—Anonymous

58. *Is* Versus *Does*

Do you stress your products or service's features or benefits? Hope you said both! Why? Because although the features of your product or service are important, they only become valuable to your prospects or customers when they *do* something for or benefit them.

Unfortunately, most business professionals stop selling after presenting the features of their product or service. But the features are of no value to a buyer unless the client feels these features can somehow help him or her obtain an advantage, an opportunity or a benefit. Your job is to *translate* how you can help the customer attain that better future as he or she maximizes gain and minimizes loss.

When my wife and I were looking for our first home, I was both amazed and bemused by the poor business development skills of many real estate agents. One of their common deficiencies was their inability to convincingly present a home's benefits. The typical agent would enter a home and begin uttering mind-startling revelations like, "Here's the kitchen. This is the living room. That's the dining room. Oh, this must be the guest bathroom!" I wanted to congratulate them on their insights and thank them for the fascinating "guided tour!"

Their crucial error was that they never conveyed *what* these things meant to *us*. These realtors failed to translate. And they had so many opportunities. For example:

- "This spacious kitchen offers you plenty of storage, as well as extra work space."
- "The living and dining rooms provide you with lots of room and an easy traffic flow for when you entertain."
- "The guest bathroom has a modern and contemporary 'look' complementing the theme and mood you're trying to create throughout the house."

Remember, don't focus only on the features of your product or service—or the *is*—but concentrate instead on the benefits, results, advantages or outcomes—the *does*.

59. Speak the Language of Your Customer

A literal definition of *translate* might be, "placing words and ideas into a format or language that's easily understood by another."

If you've ever traveled to a non-English speaking country, you may know the frustration of being unable to communicate. Your frantic hand movements and limited vocabulary didn't seem to work, so you raised your voice. You assumed *louder* would help you be understood. Obviously, this strategy doesn't work either.

When someone doesn't understand you or you don't understand them, the result is stress, anxiety and confusion. These problems could be eliminated with a translation.

For you, your *translation* is the definitive act of "translating" or connecting features and benefits. To maximize your results and peak your profits, this is a connection or *translation* you must make. Please look at the grid on the next page.

Features	Benefits

Now, please jot down as many features as possible about you and your business, products or services. Some features might include:

- The number of years you have been in business.
- The size of your inventory.
- The number of trained professionals at your company.
- Those who are recognized experts with specific knowledge.
- Your location.
- Your guarantee.
- Your product line.

Remember, a feature is simply a fact, a piece of information or raw data about you and your business, products or services. It's what something *is*.

Are you done? Good. Whether your list has three, five or ten features, at this point, they're simply a listing of *is's*. And they may not matter to your customer or prospect. The fact that you've been in business for 25 years may be a "so what?" to your customers if they're not sure how that feature helps them. The fact that you have a large inventory may be a "who cares?". If this inventory feature is important to your customer, then it becomes your responsibility to translate its benefit and emphasize its value.

Now, please jot down in the right-hand margin, the benefit(s), results(s), advantage(s) or outcome(s) of each each feature you previously listed, acknowledging benefits may differ for each customer. Are you finished? Excellent. But I bet you're saying to yourself, "So what? All I have are two lists. What now?" Now, you get to *translate*. And this translation process immediately becomes a powerful and profit-producing strategy for your ongoing success.

60. The Connection

Here comes the real fun part of the *Translate* step. Now, you get to *connect* the features with their benefits, results, advantages and/or outcomes. Please write, on the line above the words "Features" and "Benefits" in the grid on page 220, these six letters: WTMTYI.

These letters stand for: "What This Means To You Is!" This is a powerful phrase and concept you'll use again and again to attain new levels of business-growth. Why? Because it helps you persuade both logically with features and emotionally with benefits. And remember, the features you've already revealed and are now translating, are the same features your prospect or customer identified as being important during the *Probe* and reacted positively to during the *Reveal*.

Now, let's take a look at emotion, logic and the *translation* in action. Saab, the Swedish auto manufacturer, knew the significance of selling both features and benefits—or logic and emotion. At least they did! (In the interest of accuracy, Saab sales did plummet in the 21st century and they eventually went bankrupt in 2011.) However, before their demise, they did something very clever.

Saab ran two full-page ads, side-by-side in business magazines. The headline of the left-hand page read, "21 Logical Reasons to Buy a Saab." This headline was then followed by the 21 logical reasons, such as: four-valve technology, advanced ergonomics or a special steel underpanel. (It's also interesting to point out that this page was printed in black-and-white.)

Now, the headline on the right-hand page had only three simple words: "One Emotional Reason!" Beneath this headline, was a color picture of a Saab Turbo whirring through the countryside.

Talk about an impactful ad! It not only delivered the features logically, but it then *translated* emotionally and in living color— What This Saab driving experience Means To You Is...speed, satisfaction and style.

Clients and seminar participants who have adapted and applied the *What This Means To You Is* strategy, continually tell me about their outstanding successes. And the reason is that this is language that focuses on what's of value and importance to your customer.

Now, because you know about *WTMTYI*, you should never present features as isolated or stand-alone pieces of information. Instead, always present, connect or translate them in conjunction with their respective benefits. And when you do, you'll see increased business, commissions, earnings and profits.

61. No Parrot Problem

Now, you may be thinking, "How many times can I say *What This Means To You Is* without sounding repetitious, ridiculous or like a parrot?!" What you want to convey is the *concept*, not necessarily the exact words. There are an unlimited number of ways you might convey *WTMTYI*. Here are some:

- "With this feature, the benefits to you are…"
- "This will help you with…"
- "The advantages to you include…"
- "This will assist you by…"
- "These will enhance your pleasure by…"
- "You'll appreciate added enjoyment, such as…"
- "This feature does this, so that…"
- "You'll discover…"
- "This will minimize your risk by…"
- "Because of this feature, you'll maximize your gain through…"
- "Others have especially liked…"
- "What's really unique about that is…"
- "One satisfied customer called and said…"
- "A happy client wrote this letter stating…"
- "The best part about this, is that…"
- "The gains you'll realize are…"
- "The bonus for you is…"
- "Your competitive edge is…"
- "The possibilities are…"
- "As a result of this, you'll be able to…"

There are countless other ways to convey value, benefits and advantages to your customers, clients and prospects. Don't get hung up on the words. Instead, focus on the *translation*. Once this is accomplished, then the words or phrases flow easily! They'll become automatic in your business vocabulary.

62. All in Favor, Say *Eye!*

Do your products have tangible features? If they do, when you refer to a smooth surface, a piece of decorative hardware or a distinctive design, where does your eye contact go? It should go directly to the product features you're referring to. When your eye contact is directed toward the product's feature or even a word or picture that describes that feature on a page, your customer's attention is also drawn to that feature.

And when you deliver the *benefits* of that feature, where do you think your eye contact goes? Directly to your customer's *right* eye! That's correct! *Only* the right eye. Why? Because it's impossible to look somebody in both eyes! Try it. You'll end up bleary-eyed, cross-eyed or simply perched on the bridge of his or her nose. Therefore, to communicate the benefits in a persuasive, sincere and profitable manner, deliver them to one eye and to the person who matters most: your prospect!

Remember, you're always doing more than selling a product or service. Ideally, you're also building a relationship. Several years ago, on a flight to Texas, I met a woman from Broken Arrow, Oklahoma. She told me she was a sales trainer for a company specializing in fingernail designs for both men and women. When I asked her, "What's unique about training manicurists?" She responded, "How many professions do you know of, where you literally get the opportunity to stare into your customer's eye and hold your client's hand?"

Whether you label it eye contact, hand-holding, personalized attention, customer focus or goodwill, you should be *translating* not only the features of your product or service, but also your value and ability to serve a client for the long-term.

63. Power Words

Writer Joseph Conrad once said, "If you give me the right word and the correct accent in which to speak it, I can move the world!" The power and impact of the spoken word is enormous. It stirs emotion and creates action. Action that enables you to *translate* effectively and to eventually get *The Yes*.

To help you *translate* and get *The Yes*, I've compiled a list of 189 words and phrases you can use during the *Translate* stage or during any other stage of the *Peak Your Profits* and *Opportunity $elling Business-Growth System*.

The following power words and phrases aren't intended to be all-inclusive. It's likely you're already using other winning words or phrases. If so, please let me know, so I can share it with your fellow pros in the future. You bet you'll receive credit for your idea!

proven	partnership	lightest
new	bargain	compact
research	exclusive	prestige
priceless	free	craftsmanship
trouble free	investment	solid
biggest	quality	contemporary
reliable	first	safety
savings	bandwagon	service
sound	special offer	no extra cost
effortlessly	value	superior
reputation	flexible	natural
responsible	European	big selection
multifaceted	accurate	quick
seamless	can't resist	beautiful

classic	invisible	best
preference	special finish	longevity
richness	modular	peace of mind

ANOTHER BLACKMAN BONUS

Would you like to see the complete list? For FREE?
Of course you would! Simply send an email to:
sheryl@jeffblackman.com with the subject heading:
PYP: Power Words

---

64. Toot Your Horn

Another effective way to translate value to a prospect is through the use of testimonial endorsements. Your clients are probably willing to say lots of nice things about you, your company and your products or services. But perhaps, you haven't asked them.

Many businesspeople have told me they're uncomfortable asking a customer or client for a testimonial endorsement. Their customers are busy. And the last thing they want to do is impose or appear to be self-serving. They're scared such a request could jeopardize the business relationship they've already worked so hard to develop.

Years of experience have shown me that these aren't real concerns. When you're truly willing to serve your customers, then they are more than willing to help *you*. Remember, when value, integrity and non-manipulation are high, resistance is low. My files are filled with hundreds of letters and examples from happy clients. The delight, happiness and gratitude they convey is expressed in terms I'd never begin to duplicate.

Aside from written testimonials, clients have also given video testimonials. However, it's important to stress the only way I can secure such favorable comments is by first doing my job: not to only meet my clients' expectations, but to exceed them.

Whether your clients begin to say incredible things about you in print, on video or even audio, your challenge is in using these words of praise to your advantage. Here's how: You can use this strategy either during the *Reveal, Translate* or *Probe* steps. The next time a prospect asks, "Why should we use you? What makes you so special?" or "What will you do for us that others can't?", here's my suggestion: Don't answer. That's right, don't answer, at least not from *your* perspective.

If *you* begin to tell a prospect what makes you so special, from whose viewpoint are you answering? Yours! And, you're somewhat biased, even if what you're saying is true!

Therefore, shift into what I call the *third-party testimonial* strategy. Say something like:

"That's a very good question and a fair one for you to ask. It's also a tough one for *me* to answer because I guess I'm somewhat biased. Instead, let me share with you what other peers/companies in your industry said about our recent work."

Next, you can show them the letters or emails. Even better, capture your testimonials on audio or video. Then feature them at your website, with proposals or action plans, etc.

Testimonials offer tremendous power and credibility. They're especially valuable if your prospect happens to know the person making the testimonial. I actually had one decision-maker exclaim, "Ernie said *that* about you? He doesn't like anybody. You must really be good!" This fellow quickly went from being a suspect to a prospect to a client!

You can also use to your benefit the "live testimonial." Recently, I had a prospect who was still wavering about his decision to work with me. I said to him, "Bob, I know this is an important decision and I want to make sure you're comfortable with it. Therefore, since I know you and Mark are friendly, please call him. We actually spoke yesterday and he shared with me some great news about his success since we began working together."

Bob called Mark. Mark raved about me and his results. Bob became a client!

The *third-party testimonial* strategy helps you toot your own horn—but with some assistance. While you hold the horn, your testimonial endorsers play the notes.

To help you *translate* more effectively, here are the five *Translate* stage profit points:

1. Explain the feature and emphasize the benefits of those features.
2. Stress how the value of the benefits outweighs the investment in the features.
3. Persuade both logically and emotionally.
4. Request confirmation that these are the benefits your customer has been looking for.

5. Complement your benefit claims with proof, power and testimonial support.

Your ongoing use of testimonials, endorsements, power words and *Translate* strategies will…well, I guess what I'm trying to say is, *what they mean to you is…improved performance, productivity and profitability—in your business and your life!*

CHAPTER 10

Negotiation Know-How!

"To get to the Promised Land, you must negotiate through the wilderness."

—Anonymous

65. I'll Get Back to You

"That's more than I wanted to spend!"
"I'm still not sure the color is right!"
"I'm worried that it won't arrive in time!"
"I'll have to talk it over with my husband!"
"I better just check with my partner!"
"Maybe I should ask my wife."

Have you heard these classic stalls, objections and decision-delayers before? Probably all too often. But why are your prospects hesitating? What's causing their reluctance? Believe it or not, it's unlikely to be the cost, color or delivery time. Most often, it's because as a business professional you were unable to prove the *value* of your product or service and you couldn't help the customers to "positively persuade" themselves. They still don't believe you'll help them attain that more favorable future and improved condition.

Remember, before a customer is a *customer*, he or she is a person! And people don't like to tell other people, "No!" Perhaps they fear confrontation or they don't want to hurt your feelings? Basically, they want to be polite and courteous. Our prospects, like us, often don't reveal the "real reason" for their indecision. Instead, customers create smoke screens or escape tactics that give them a gracious and non-offensive exit.

However, when you have progressed this far with a customer and you're now at the *N* or *Negotiate* step in the *Peak Your Profits* and *Opportunity $elling Business-Growth System*, it's because you have already successfully completed the previous four stages— *Open, Probe, Reveal* and *Translate*.

Don't lose your customer now! How do you hang on so that both of you benefit? It's simple—you *negotiate!* Yet only if necessary.

66. A Lesson from Abraham Lincoln

Abraham Lincoln, the 16th President of the United States, must have been a superb negotiator! Abe once said, *"The best way to destroy an enemy, is to make him your friend!"* If Abe was a *Peak Profiteer*, he might have said, "The best way to make a prospect your customer is to make him your friend!"

When you negotiate with a prospect, it should truly be from a win-win position. If either side feels used or taken advantage of, the potential for a successful long-term relationship is unlikely. A negotiation never means lace-up your boxing gloves and prepare for battle! Instead, it's your opportunity to work out problems, reach an agreement and move forward for the benefit of all.

Unfortunately, many businesspeople don't believe in or apply this basic principle. For some reason, they derive a strange satisfaction from arguing or battling. All too often, when a customer sheepishly claims, "That's really a lot more than I wanted to spend," I've heard these caustic gems as responses:

- "Well you know, quality doesn't come cheap!"
- "You get what you pay for!"
- "The top-of-the-line is never a bargain!"
- "Try to find it for less!"
- "You told me you could afford it!"

Responses like these are argumentative. They're confrontational. They're abrasive. Businesspeople who respond this way are truly trying to "destroy the enemy." And if this goal is achieved, your customer leaves annoyed and frustrated, while you have one less deposit to make to the bank!

Feel Your Way to Success

So how do you overcome the *price problem* and other objections? A powerful and profit-producing technique is the *Feel-Felt-Found Formula*. It's a simple, yet very persuasive, strategy.

Let's consider an actual objection: "The price is too high!" So say your customers, Irv and Sallie. To overcome their concern, you might respond by applying the *Feel-Felt-Found Formula*:

1. **Feel.** "I know how you *feel*, Irv and Sallie. It's not an inexpensive investment. Getting the best value is important to you."
2. **Felt.** "As a matter of fact, your friends Bob and Char, who

suggested I contact you in the first place, *felt* the same way you do at first..."

3. **Found.** "...until they *found* this investment was one of the best they ever made, because it not only enhanced their life-style, it also increased the value of their home."

Potent? You bet! Why does the concept of the *Feel-Felt-Found Formula* work? Let's take a closer look at each step of this value-driven business-growth skill:

1. Feel. With the first word *feel*, customers know you're trying to understand them, to relate to them. You appreciate their concerns and validate their reactions—it's okay for them to feel that way or express that objection.

Many businesspeople are immediately combative when prospects resist making a decision, especially when they express a price objection. Some salespeople will argue and attempt to convince or prove to a customer why they are wrong!

The effectiveness of the first step of the *Feel-Felt-Found Formula* is summed up in one word: *empathy*. By using the word *feel* you're empathetic to your customer's concerns. You're not in *agreement*, for example, that the "price is too high, " but you do acknowledge that "it's not an inexpensive investment" and the customer is entitled to have that opinion.

By the way, is the price really too high? Probably not. Why? Because if you properly conducted the *Probe*, your customer has already shared his or her budget. And now, your suggested investment falls within the parameters your customer—not you—has determined.

2. Felt. Customers also like to know they're not alone. They take comfort in knowing others have had a similar concern. They don't want to be the experimental customer—to go where no customer has gone before! The *felt* step offers reference to *others* who've had similar feelings. In the case of Irv and Sallie, these "others" were friends. There's comfort in numbers or knowing there are others, just like us, who've had a common experience.

3. Found. Once the objection is handled, you must accentuate the positive or the benefits directly associated with the investment. These are the benefits that countless others—or specific "testimonial customers" like Bob and Char—have already appreciated.

Here's an important subtlety of the *Feel-Felt-Found Formula*: You'll notice when you make the transition from "felt to found" the transition word is *until*:

*I know how you **feel**, others have **felt** the same way, **until** they **found**...*

Here's why I think *until* is a much better transition or bridge word to move from *felt* to *found*. If instead of *until*, you use the words "but or however", they're "downer" or "take-away" words. How many times have you been set up by somebody who says, "I'm very pleased with your performance, *however...*" Or "You're doing a great job, *but...*" How do you feel? It's the ecstasy and the agony. A quick high and then you're walloped!

The same happens when using these words in the *Feel-Felt-Found Formula*. Unfortunately, the words *however* and *but* diminish the importance of your customer's feelings or opinions. Don't refute, negate or belittle your customer's reactions. Acknowledge them. Understand them. And then let your decision-maker know how others have benefited from the intelligent decision to invest in your product or service.

If serving others, making more money and peaking your profits are important to you, then review, understand, internalize, apply and make a habit of the *Feel-Felt-Found Formula.*

Oh sure, this may be a brand-new strategy. You may be unfamiliar with it. You might even be skeptical about trying it.

Well that's okay. I'm no different when trying something for the first time, so I sure know how you *feel*...As a matter of fact, others have *felt* the same way when this successful business-growth strategy was initially shared with them...*until* they *found* it's one of the simplest, most non-manipulative and profit-producing approaches they've ever used.

Are They Vended?

Years ago, a client in Minneapolis said to me, "Jeff, we're the market leader. So the only way we can grow is by earning the right to take away or 'steal' business from a competitor or another vendor." He then asked, "So how do we deal with the 'vended customer?'"

Whether you are or aren't the market leader, this objection is a common one. And it's expressed by my client's prospects and your prospects in lots of ways. Like:

- "We don't want to make a change."
- "We already have a long-term relationship with somebody else."
- "It would be a hassle to start with someone new."
- "They're not the best, but at least we know what to expect."
- "I like what you offer, but we're not looking for new suppliers."

So how do most folks reply to these attempts to block and barricade? Typically, they go into "sales overdrive." Immediately doing a data-dump on why they're better. Faster. Smarter. Cheaper. *These* are all losing strategies. Customers don't like to be told they're wrong or that they made a bad decision.

Instead, here's a far simpler and more effective strategy that I teach to my clients. It works quickly and effectively, because it lets a decision-maker answer a simple question: Does it make sense?

All you need to do, is say something like:

While many of our customers have...

realized / discovered / enjoyed...
(use or create the word that works for you)

great / significant...
(use or create the word that works for you)

value / results...
(use or create the word that works for you)

from changing / relying on us...

(use or create the word that works for you)

*what we really need to do—is determine, how it
makes sense for you.*

Then, get to work with your power probes to confirm how it makes sense for them. You can also position the preceding with a question. For example:

*Many of our customers have enjoyed significant value from
relying on us. How does changing, so we can work together,
make sense for you?*

When they answer in a positive way, it gets you closer to *The Yes!* Especially, because they're justifying how it makes sense!

67. Empathy. Understanding. Results!

In Mario Puzo's best-selling book, *The Godfather*, Don Corleone calmly states, "Never get angry. Never make a threat. Reason with people." While you may not agree with "the Don's" *method* of negotiation, it's hard to find fault with his philosophy!

The key to a successful negotiation is a sincere attempt to understand the other person's perspective. You should never lose sight of your negotiating objective or goal, but you must also be aware of your decision-makers' desires, needs and motivators.

As we've just discovered, two of the best ways to be empathetic to your decision-maker is by applying the *Feel-Felt-Found Formula* and the *Does it Make Sense* statement or question.

However, you're probably wondering, "How many times can I repeat the *Feel-Felt-Found Formula* without sounding like a broken record?!" The good news is, as often you'd like! It's not just the words you use, but how you use them, and, more importantly, how you say them.

Thankfully, there are many variations of the *Feel-Felt-Found Formula*. For example, here are three adaptations:

1. "I can appreciate that reaction. You're not the first customer to feel that way. Many of my other happy customers have had the same initial reaction, until they realized that..."
2. "You're right...I, too, would feel the same way. As a matter of fact, some of my other customers were also concerned about that...until they discovered that..."
3. "I can see why you'd think that. I assure you that's an understandable concern. Some of my other happy customers also had a similar sentiment...*until* they appreciated the advantages and enjoyment of..."

If you use the *Feel-Felt-Found Formula* as a means to manipulate, coerce or dominate your customer, then you're *not* a value-driven business professional. You've reduced yourself to a peddler! As a peddler, you're interested only in personal gain. But when your interest is to empathetically and creatively serve others, you have elevated yourself to the status and earning power of a *peak profiteer.*

68. Let's Make a Deal!

"Let's haggle! One hand washes the other!"
"It's time to bargain! Gimme a deal!"

"You've got to do better than that!"
"That's not the best you can do, is it?"

These are typical customer euphemisms for "let's negotiate." Is everything negotiable? Yes! But only if two or more parties are willing to work together. Experience proves that when people want to work things out, the details become unimportant and easy. But when people don't want to work together, the details become the stumbling block or the excuse for "deal destruction."

There's a significant difference between a negotiation and a compromise. *Webster's Dictionary* says *negotiate* means, "to confer or bargain, one with another, in order to reach an agreement or to move through, over or around a difficult place or situation." And *Webster* defines *compromise* as, "a settlement of differences by mutual concessions, the sacrifice or surrender of conflicting claims or principles."

Are there drastic distinctions between these two definitions? Not really. But as you know, it's the subtleties of the business-development and negotiation process that influence your decision-maker and determine your ultimate success.

When dealing with customers or clients, would you prefer to negotiate, confer and bargain—or would you rather compromise, sacrifice and surrender? All too often, when businesspeople compromise, it's almost the equivalent of a sacrifice or waving the white flag. Let's examine a typical compromise:

You say: "And this practical and results-oriented product will only be a $9,000 investment!"
Your customer Teddy says: "But I only wanted to spend

$8,000!"

You say: "Let's compromise and split the difference—how 'bout $8,500?"

Your theory: Something is better than nothing!

However, in actuality both you and Teddy are likely to leave this "compromise" somewhat frustrated. How come? Because you both feel short-changed—you got less than you feel you deserved. And Teddy feels he exceeded his budget.

So how do you solve this apparent dilemma? First, try the strategy of the *Feel-Felt-Found Formula*, emphasizing how the value outweighs the investment. But what if this approach makes little progress? Don't worry, there are still other winning strategies.

For example, you can make what's called a *value concession.* Here's how:

> **You may say:** "How do you feel about this product / service / solution? (The equivalent of a trial question.)
>
> **Your customer Nathan says:** "I love it! It's the best I've ever seen!"
>
> **You may say:** "What do you like best?"
>
> **Nathan says:** "It offers me the convenience, space and beauty I want!"
>
> **You may say:** "Knowing that, how do you feel about a thousand dollars standing in the way of all the pleasure and enjoyment your new product / service / solution will offer to you and your family?"
>
> **Nathan says:** "Well, it's still more than I want to spend."
>
> **You may say:** "What do you suggest we do?"
>
> **Nathan says:** "The most I'll go up is to $8,500, not a penny

241

more!"

You may say: "Hmmm, if I was willing to help you out, would you be willing to help me out?"

Nathan says: "What do you mean?"

You may say: "Well, if we agreed that your investment wouldn't be any more than $8,500, would you be willing to write me a testimonial letter expressing your positive reactions to the job we did for you—and be willing to share with me the names of at least five others (friends, relatives or business associates) who are likely to admire your new product and we might be able to help too?"

Nathan says: "Sure, that seems pretty reasonable."

You may say: "Good. Would it also be possible that instead of an initial investment or deposit of 25 percent, it's 35 percent?"

Nathan says: "Well, okay, but only if you can deliver by the first!"

You say: "Great. On or before the first, it'll be delivered!"

In this example, more was exchanged than just money. There was *not* a simple "split the difference compromise." There was a negotiation that occurred because other things of value became a part of the negotiating process.

Would you be willing to allow for the concession of a $500 reduction in exchange for a glowing testimonial, several "warm-to-hot" leads or a larger initial investment or deposit? Perhaps, as long as what *you* receive is worth at least $500 or more to you.

It's also important to avoid reducing your negotiation to solely a price focus. If this happens, your product or service takes on a commodity perception. As a simple rule, while negotiating, you should never give up something unless you get something in return. And that something isn't always money. Therefore, try to avoid price concessions and be prepared to deal in, and negotiate with, value concessions.

You can even make a value concessions checklist, which might include or be influenced by value items such as:

- Delivery dates.
- Product warranties.
- Transportation charges.
- Volume purchases.
- Service agreements.
- Payment schedules.
- Long-term commitments.
- Quality introductions and referrals.

You can also assign a monetary value to each of the items on your value concessions checklist. This strategy helps you better understand what you're willing to give up or negotiate with, as well as what you want to receive or get in return. While your customer may simply want a discount, you should be seeking an exchange for something of equal or greater value.

While these examples only address negotiations or concessions that relate to the cost, these strategies can be applied to other objections or business barriers. And when they are, you move, once again—one step closer to *peak your profits*.

69. To Get Rich, Use the Twitch!

Let's eavesdrop on a conversation between a customer and a salesperson:

The salesperson says: "And it's only $10,000!"
Charlie says: "I'll give you $6,500."
The salesperson says: "Sold!"

How does Charlie react? Happy? Excited? Impressed with his negotiating savvy? Hardly! Instead, Charlie is probably muttering, "What a dummy! Did I get ripped off? Something must be wrong! I'm buying a lemon! I knew I couldn't trust this place—it must be stolen merchandise! I could have bought the thing for six grand, maybe less."

Charlie feels devastated because his first offer was accepted too willingly. Now, what if Charlie and the salesperson negotiated, made value concessions to one another and the final investment was $8,000? As strange as it seems, Charlie is likely to leave *more* satisfied than if he had spent only the $6,500.

Here's a crucial point: Business development is a reflection of *perceived* value, not actual value. Once again, you should always deliver more in perceived value than you take in actual cash value!

It's Twitch Time

Now, let me share a strategy that has helped clients get rich: the *twitch*. The *twitch* is an exclamation, look of surprise or physical movement that conveys your disbelief with the other person's initial offer, meaning you don't jump at or immediately accept the offer.

Here's an old, yet classic *twitch* example. Years ago, I was strolling the streets at a sidewalk sale, when I discovered audio-tape cassette cabinets for only $18, about half of what I normally paid. (Do you remember cassettes? They preceded CDs, DVDs and online downloads. And followed eight-track or reel-to-reel tapes...and two cans with a string!)

I would have willingly paid $18, because this was a considerable savings, but I knew this was a great opportunity to *twitch*.

I asked the salesperson (even though I saw the sign indicating "Prices as Marked"), "How much are the cabinets?" He said, "$18." I then exclaimed with disbelief in my voice, "$18?!" His response: "Okay, $15!" Now, what did my exclamation mean? Who knows? But he believed it meant I thought $18 was too much, so he lowered the price to make the sale.

Here's a warning, though: Be prepared for the customer who might *twitch* you! Don't give in to your instinct to give in! Recognize the *twitch* and begin questioning the twitcher about his *twitch*. You might say:

- "When you said that, or looked surprised, what were you thinking?"
- "Why do you feel that way?"
- "What's important to you?"
- "In order to get that, what do you want to do without?"
- "That might be possible, what would you be willing to sacrifice?"
- "You've already negotiated an incredible deal on these points, now *this* one's really not that important to you, is it?"

Never lose sight of the fact that, for the *twitch* to be effective, it must not be presented in an obnoxious or condescending way.

Its purpose is to quickly and accurately convey the message to your prospect or customer that his or her suggestion or offer isn't possible, but let's see what other alternatives there might be. Your ultimate goal is agreement, not antagonism!

70. Two Dozen and Two

A negotiation is an evolutionary process. It changes with the introduction of a new objective or an unexpected decision-maker. Therefore, planned spontaneity or preparation combined with flexibility and creativity are crucial to your success. The following strategies maximize your success and results.

1. Negotiate only with those who have authority to make a decision.
2. Attempt to accommodate or satisfy the needs of *all* involved in the negotiation.
3. Anticipate and be prepared to make value concessions, if necessary.
4. Know *your* objectives, limits and expectations, and don't compromise them.
5. Know your customer's goals, objectives and expectations, (as you discovered in the *Probe* stage) and understand them.
6. Identify the strengths of you, your company, your product or service and be ready to communicate them.
7. Look at the big picture, the long-term, not the quick hit.
8. When the judge rules in your favor, get out of the court! Or said another way, when you get a favorable decision or *The Yes*, say thank you and leave!
9. When your customer suggests a perceived win-win alternative and you know it helps him or her, but *really* benefits you, *don't* lick your chops.

10. Respect confidentiality.
11. Always try to finish the negotiation on a "positive."
12. Do your homework, have a plan. It helps you be confident and in control.
13. The more participants or decision-makers you have to deal with, the longer it'll take to hear *The Yes.*
14. The fewer participants or decision-makers, usually the sooner you'll hear *The Yes.*
15. If there's "bad" news, get it out early, don't delay.
16. The best time to *get* something is when you *give* something.
17. Be aware of deadlines (real vs. assumed).
18. Negotiate "fresh." Get a good night's sleep, avoid alcohol beforehand. Terminate a marathon negotiating session by simply setting a time for the next session.
19. Know how to respond to a totally unacceptable offer, either with a question, the *twitch* - physical or auditory disbelief, or silence.
20. Continue to get affirmation or agreement on the issues.
21. Promise a lot and deliver more. Deliver something unexpected, but of value and appreciated. Never promise anything without delivering it.
22. Be organized, and look and stay organized.
23. Whenever possible, negotiate in-person.
24. When more than one decision-maker is present, acknowledge all of them.
25. Be wary of the decision-maker who appears dumb. It could be a ploy.
26. Be willing to walk away from a bad deal.

Remember, a successful win-win negotiation is characterized by positive attitudes, relationships and impressions. Mark McCormack, author of *What They Don't Teach You at Harvard*

Business School and a one-time guest on my radio talk-show, told me, "One of life's big frustrations is that people don't do what you want them to do. But if you can control their impressions of you, you can make them want to do what you want them to do."

To help others do what you want them to do, here are the five profit points for the *Negotiate* stage in the *Peak Your Profits* and *Opportunity $elling Business-Growth System*:

1. Provide solutions, not confrontations.
2. Acknowledge your prospects' or customers' concerns and assure them, you understand the importance of their decision.
3. Isolate the obstacles. Discover exactly what's delaying a customer's decision.
4. Ask your prospects and customers for their opinions, suggestions and ideas, as to the best way to resolve the situation.
5. Let prospects and customers know you want them to make a wise decision they won't regret.

71. We Are Different, One and All

A frustrated client once exclaimed to me, "Jeff, a negotiation would be easy if my customers saw things from my perspective! Negotiations aren't difficult, it's the people negotiating!"

My client's frustration is typical. However, the ability to work with people rather than against them is often the difference between success or failure.

As you've probably discovered, each person is different! There are over 7 billion of us walking, talking and thinking beings roaming the earth. And no two of us are exactly alike. Oh sure, there are the obvious physical distinctions, yet what really influences the business-development or relationship-building process is how you develop rapport with others or adapt your style to a decision-maker's style. People aren't genetically encoded to make decisions the same way.

Decision-makers like to buy from businesspeople who see the world from their perspective. Buyers are usually more comfortable with others who essentially walk, talk, look, move, think and feel like they do.

Clients often say to me, "Look Jeff, I'm not going to be a chameleon and constantly change. I am who I am." I agree. Yet the goal isn't to have you change, but instead to adapt. To be flexible. To better understand others. Because when you've customized and adapted your style to complement your decision-maker's style, he or she is more likely to commit and deliver *The Yes*.

Understanding Others

Since the dawn of time, we've developed labels or categories as part of our ongoing effort to better understand our fellow man. From the ancient Greek philosophers to the modern-day social scientists, we search for new and better ways to understand why others do what they do.

Whether it's as simple and unscientific as drawing behavioral conclusions based upon a person's attire or as sophisticated as connecting electrodes to an individual's skull to assess brain wave patterns, we continue to search for new clues.

As part of my observations and practical business experience, I've developed over the past 36-plus years a methodology to help you better communicate with, sell to, negotiate with and serve, different types of buyers.

You'll recognize and be able to adapt to the *Investment Styles* and *Decision Influencers* of your buyers. You'll learn no one style (either as a buyer or as a successful businessperson) is better or worse than another. Just different. You'll discover what one decision-maker finds appealing and valuable, another could find bothersome and useless.

72. The Four Styles of Decision-Making

Now, please look at the *Investment Styles* and *Decision Influencers* worksheet on the next page. You'll see four different types of decision-making styles: *Charmer, Driver, Pacer* and *Analyzer*. Each style is further divided into 14 decision influencers:

1. Behavior.
2. Surroundings or environment.
3. Business style.
4. Temperament.
5. Attentiveness.
6. Talks about.
7. Approach.
8. Decisions made.
9. Time usage.
10. Body language.
11. Attire.
12. Needs.
13. Monitors progress by.
14. Response to pressure.

OPPORTUNITY $ELLING®
Investment Styles & Decision Influencers

CUSTOMER • CLIENT • PROSPECT _____

☑ Check ONE description in each row that BEST DESCRIBES your customer, client or prospect

Behavior:	☐ Extroverted	☐ Forceful	☐ Relaxed	☐ Direct / To the Point
Surroundings:	☐ Disorganized / Personal Things	☐ Plaques / Signs of Achievement	☐ Cherished Memories or Personal Effects	☐ Organized / Diagrams
Business Style:	☐ Sociable / A People Person	☐ Outcome Driven / Bottom Line	☐ System Orientation	☐ Hard Data / Facts
Temperament:	☐ Amiable	☐ Fidgety	☐ Evenly Paced	☐ Stand-Offish
Attentiveness:	☐ Wandering	☐ Restless	☐ Accepting	☐ Listens Critically
Talks About:	☐ People & Events	☐ Accomplishments	☐ Processes / Systems	☐ The "Company"
Approach:	☐ Empathy / Caring	☐ Takes Charge	☐ Goes Along	☐ Evaluates Others
Decisions Made:	☐ By How They'll Look to Others	☐ Fast / Realistic	☐ Over Time and After Deliberation	☐ Only If All The "Data" Is In
Time Usage:	☐ Often Wasted / Behind Schedule	☐ Always Pressed	☐ RespectsIt / Not Pressed	☐ Uses It Well / Precisely Scheduled
Body Language:	☐ Animated	☐ Restless	☐ Precise / Deliberate	☐ Reserved / Controlled
Attire:	☐ Contemporary	☐ Impeccable / Well Tailored	☐ Conforming	☐ Conservative / Subdued
Needs:	☐ Visibility	☐ Achievement	☐ Others' Approval	☐ To Be Right
Monitors Progress By:	☐ Recognition	☐ Measured Results	☐ How Others Feel About Them	☐ Self-Satisfaction
Response to Pressure:	☐ Battles With Emotion	☐ Battles With Reasons	☐ Complies	☐ Escapes With Logic

(Total No. of Checks): ☐ **CHARMER**   ☐ **DRIVER**   ☐ **PACER**   ☐ **ANALYZER**

Now, please take a few minutes and complete the worksheet for either a current or prospective customer or client. This should be a living, breathing, thinking human being. Somebody you know enough about to develop an accurate analysis. *Please write down that person's name on the line provided on the worksheet and then check off only one characteristic per each horizontal row that best describes that individual.*

Are you done? Good! Count-up the number of checks you have in each column. Then enter that number in the box next to each decision-making style. For example, for *Charmer* you might have eight checks, for *Driver* five, for *Pacer* zero and for *Analyzer* one check. (The total number of checks for all the columns must be 14.)

Now, please circle the decision-making style with the most amount of checks in a particular column. In our example, that would be *Charmer* with eight checks. This indicates that this decision-maker's dominant behavioral or buying style is *Charmer*. Now, we'd underline the secondary buying style, which would be *Driver*, because it has five checks. If you have a tie, that's fine, simply circle or underline both words. It's likely that almost every decision-maker you engage with and "analyze" has a dominant and a secondary style.

To develop better relationships with each of these styles, here's what we'll do in the next few *Focus Sections*. First, we'll explore some of the ways you can identify a decision-maker's style. And then, we'll discuss the do's and don'ts for communicating with and selling to each of the four styles.

73. "Charm" Your Way to the Bank!

Let's have some fun with the *Charmers*. And that's appropriate, because *Charmers* have the tendency to be fun, outgoing and friendly. Their behavior is extroverted. They're sociable. Their body language is animated. They're "people persons."

It's also easy to tell when you're talking to *Charmers*, whether it's in-person or over the phone, because their voices convey enthusiasm and excitement. They're up-beat and amiable. They love to talk, especially about people and events.

Charmers give you an opinion about the weekend ballgame or the movie they saw. They show you pictures from their recent vacation or gladly tell you the latest political joke! Since *Charmers* love to talk, let 'em! Yet, *because* they love to talk, they're often behind schedule and wonder how their days seem to magically disappear.

You'll also know when you're in the presence of a *Charmer*. He or she usually has a strong sense of style. His or her clothes are contemporary with often a dramatic combination of colors.

A *Charmer's* surroundings or office environment are also unmistakable. It's usually disorganized and filled with personal things. One *Charmer* I know has her office filled with miniature toys from fast-food restaurants. Stuffed animals adorn the walls. Banners with humorous sayings hang from her ceiling. Her credenza features an incredible assortment of blinking lights and noise makers! She lets you know from the moment you enter, if you want to do business with her, it better be fun, interesting and entertaining!

Listen with Your Eyes, Stare with Your Ears

When dealing with a *Charmer* (or any decision-making style), you'll begin to discover this individual's dominant and secondary behavioral or buying styles during the *Open* and *Probe* stages. Use your observation and listening skills to learn a lot about your decision-maker. As she responds to your open-ended need-development questions or power probes, she begins to reveal not only how she makes decisions but why she makes them that way.

Potential questions to ask a *Charmer* might be:

- "What do you like best about your job or career?"
- "When you're not working or having fun at the office, what do you do in your spare time?"
- "How did you first get started in this business?"
- "What opportunities in your industry really excite you?"
- "Tell me about that fish on the wall, how long did it take to reel-in that one?"

You might also comment about some interesting item in the *Charmer's* office—an intriguing photo or trophy. The first time I asked the fishing question to one of my clients, she enthusiastically and dramatically told me a five-minute story. Linda loved to fish and hunt! She even had framed in Lucite on her desk, the shell or casing from the bullet she used to bag her first bird on a duck hunt!

Now I'm not much of a fisherman or hunter, but every time I spoke to Linda in-person or on the phone, I always asked her about her most recent or upcoming adventure. As a *Charmer,* she loved the opportunity to tell a story!

Obviously, decision influencers and investment style strategies aren't gender exclusive. They have equal applicability to both men and women. Never assume all men are into sports and power tools and all women are wild about cooking and fashion. They're not!

Assumptions lead to mistakes and lost opportunities.

When you're *revealing* and *translating* to a *Charmer*, whether male or female, be sure to explain to him or her why the decision to use your product or service is one that makes him or her look and feel good. To a *Charmer*, recognition is a strong motivator.

I know one *Charmer* who owns a shiny, bright-red Ferrari. When I asked him what he likes best about it, he said, "When I hop out, I look really cool." He, like many *Charmers* is motivated by recognition, perception, visibility and by how he looks to others.

One of my *Charmer* clients was crazy about ties. Whether they were paisley or print, hand-painted on silk, elegant or inexpensive, designer or whimsical, he was unequivocally nuts about ties. The first few minutes of our conversations were always devoted to his unique neckwear or the latest tie addition to his wardrobe. When I'd spot a distinctive tie in a store window, I'd call him. When an article about ties appeared in a newspaper or a magazine, I'd send him a copy. Now, was all this "tie-time" just ridiculous banter? No, it became an important part of our connection and ongoing relationship. It was just one of the many factors that kept our relationship fresh, fun and strong.

With *Charmers,* Sociability Equals Success.

During your initial contact with *Charmers,* it's okay to engage in "small talk" or friendly conversation. As you move into the *Probe* or discovery stage, your questions should allow them to share their feelings, hopes and aspirations. While in the *Reveal* and *Translate* stages, be sure to stress how your product or service makes them look good. How it enhances their social status or influence. And how it helps them to be positively perceived by others.

While *negotiating* or pursuing *The Yes* with *Charmers,* maintain an optimistic, upbeat and enthusiastic approach. Always let *Charmers* express their feelings or concerns and assure them it's okay to feel the way they do. Remember, when dealing with *Charmers,* make business fun.

To have fun, yet to still succeed and profit, here are 14 more strategies to effectively work with *Charmers*:

1. Stroke their ego in a warm, positive and sincere manner.
2. Talk about *their* interests.
3. Share your knowledge about their achievements and sincerely compliment them.
4. Reinforce or acknowledge their ideas and suggestions.
5. Plan on their tardiness.
6. Plan on the meeting, presentation or sales call to take longer than expected.
7. Entertain them. Breakfast meetings are especially good, because it's easy for you to excuse yourself for a meeting at your office or for your need to move-on to another appointment.

8. Suggest they invite "others" to your meeting, especially if those "others" have the ability to execute, implement or make a decision.
9. Ask them to share their feelings or vision about your product or service.
10. Help them anticipate the success, the notoriety, and the recognition they'll receive as a result of using your product or service.
11. Always suggest a timetable for completion.
12. Stress your commitment to personal service and follow-up.
13. Allow *Charmers* to go off on tangents, but be sure to get them back on track.
14. Go for the "sizzle" not the steak. Promote the emotional benefits rather than the analytical benefits.

Now, here are 7 things *not* to do with *Charmers*:

1. Don't be disturbed when *Charmers* aren't on time.
2. Don't have the expectation this sale will be quick and easy or that *Charmers* will focus only on you and your product or service.
3. Don't diminish their abilities, their role in the company, the size of their office or their surroundings.
4. Don't bog them down with lots of details.
5. Don't stress the legal implications that might arise from using your product or service.
6. Don't stress the terms or the conditions.
7. Don't expect an immediate commitment.

Plus, here are power statements to use with *Charmers*:

- "Next time, let's plan to get together for breakfast and review your ideas."

- "By using this product or service, you'll be even more successful."
- "Others have achieved tremendous recognition when using this product or service, and with *your* confidence, energy and vast network of colleagues and friends, you'll surpass their accomplishments."
- "Your ideas, and the ease with which you communicate them, really impresses me."
- "You're really a lot of fun to work with!"

74. "Drive" or Get Out of the Way!

Drivers are forceful. Direct. Outcome-driven and bottom-line decision-makers. They're fidgety and restless. They have no time to waste on hype or chit-chat. Their focus is on *results.*

It's easy to tell when you're in the presence of a *Driver.* Let's call our typical driver Sue. Sue is the type of person who takes charge and acts in a decisive manner. She has a tendency to be well-dressed. Not contemporary like the *Charmer,* but instead impeccable and well-tailored.

Sue's office environment is also often a testament to her accomplishments. It's filled with plaques, trophies, awards and other signs of her achievement.

One of my clients, David, is a *Driver* off the charts. All 14 of his decision-influencers exhibit *Driver* behavior. When David and I speak on the telephone, our conversations are short, direct and to the point. He acts in a bold and swift manner. He needs answers to his questions now. And stationed immediately outside his office are not one, but two secretaries who help him maximize productivity and results.

To David, being in constant contact with the world and having immediate access to information are essential to his success.

Initially with a *Driver*, i.e., in your *Open*, minimize your socializing. Be straightforward. Let him or her quickly know the purpose for your meeting or call. Your probe questions should focus on the *Driver's* desired results, outcomes and specific objectives.

When *revealing* and *translating* your product or service, appeal directly to the *Driver's* expressed desires of gain-enhancement, loss-reduction or goal-achievement. When *negotiating* or moving toward *The Yes* decision, give him or her specific choices that help meet and exceed their objectives quickly, efficiently and profitably.

Strategies for Results

When dealing with *Drivers*, here are 10 additional strategies to remember and use:

1. Know *Drivers* prefer to meet on their "turf."
2. Your attire should be stylish, but conservative.
3. Be direct, to-the-point, get down to business quickly.
4. Focus on results, the payoff, the bottom line.
5. Be sure to provide options that are precise and clear-cut.
6. Provide specific answers to specific questions.
7. Stress how the benefits save money, increase results, maximize productivity or reduce costs.
8. Discuss timetables, the agenda or an action-plan.

9. Keep *Drivers* apprised of your activities, but be straightforward.
10. Sell the "steak" not the sizzle—the specifics, not the abstract.

And here are 7 things *not* to do with *Drivers*:

1. Don't engage in "small talk" or activities that appear "social," (unless the *Driver* initiates it.)
2. Don't expect to secure *The Yes* based upon your charm, personality or wit.
3. Don't make unexpected changes in your proposal or action-plan.
4. Don't deal in abstract concepts.
5. Don't appear ambiguous, indecisive, wishy-washy or wavering. (A *Driver* perceives these types of behavior as weaknesses.)
6. Don't get bogged down in extensive details, the *Driver* won't be interested. (I'll never forget the *Driver*, a President of a large and successful insurance agency, who two minutes after I began presenting an action-plan, stood and said to his Vice President, "Mike, let's do it! You take care of the details with Jeff, I'm off to another meeting.")
7. Don't provide *Drivers* with extensive explanations about how you helped others, their interest is minimal. *Drivers* are more concerned about how you can help them.

Here are potential power statements to use with *Drivers*:

- "You'll see that the information is organized in an efficient, quick and easy-to-read way."
- "This is breakthrough knowledge. It's immediate and accurate. You're the first person to see this report."

- "This is innovative and unique, which gives you a competitive advantage, starting now."
- "This will produce results faster than anything else available."
- "This will reduce your time commitment, yet increase your gains!"

75. *Pacers:* I'm thinking. I'm thinking!

Pacers must devote time, deliberation and careful thought to a buying decision. If you're a *Driver,* who makes decisions fast and deliberate and you're selling to a *Pacer,* you could experience a high level of frustration. Why? Because the *Pacer* has mastered the line, "I need to think it over." As a *Driver,* you say to yourself, "What's left to think over? How much time does a rational person need to make a decision? A child could have already made this decision!"

It's crucial to never push, prod or pull a *Pacer* into making a decision. If you try to rush them, they rebel by simply once again refusing to decide. Believe me, I've learned this from painful experience.

I'm a *Charmer/Driver,* who is friendly, yet decisive. Therefore, in the past I've been exasperated by *Pacers.* However, over time, I've learned how to work with them, not against them.

To quote the Rolling Stones, "Let time be on your side!"

If a *Pacer* now says to me, "I'd like to think it over." I immediately let him or her know that makes sense. I then say this is an important decision and the last thing I want them to do is to rush into this decision. However, when a *Pacer* tells me, "I still need time to think it over." I then ask him or her this important and unexpected question, "How much time do you need?"

This question surprises a *Pacer*. Nobody ever grants a *Pacer* the privilege of additional deliberation time. And if a *Pacer* says he needs two more days before he can decide, I'll say, "Are you sure two days is enough?" (The benefit of this question is twofold. First, he knows I'm willing to give him more time if it's necessary and second, it also helps him realize he has now given me a time commitment for his decision.)

But what often happens when I give a *Pacer* more time to decide, is he actually begins to divulge what his real concern is, now. And then together, we can solve the problem and handle his reluctance. Not in two days or two weeks, but immediately. Together, we pursue a positive plan to get to *The Yes*.

Reduce the Risk

Pacers must be assured their decision is a good one. They don't want to be on the leading-edge like *Drivers*. Nor are they concerned about status as the *Charmer* is. Instead, they seek the comfort and the assurance there are countless others who are already benefiting from your product or service.

Pacers are wonderful people who are usually relaxed, evenly-paced and somewhat conforming. They're resistant to change. They like a stable environment and value reliability.

Here's excerpted language from an actual letter sent from our Director of Marketing to a decision-maker who's a *Pacer*:

Bill, when Jeff works with you and your people, you can be assured of the following:

First, the peace-of-mind in knowing Jeff's ideas are proven and practical.

Second, you can have a high comfort level, since Jeff has been a very successful presenter at other divisional meetings within your company.

Third, the knowledge that countless others are already benefiting from Jeff's "how-to" tools and strategies.

And fourth, the security of selecting somebody with high credibility. As you know, Jeff is working with other businesses in your industry. He's also a contributing editor to your industry's leading publication, and he has already conducted extensive research within your industry.

The letter worked! Bill finally made *The Yes* decision. The program was an extremely successful keynote for about 1,500 people. Not only was the audience elated and enthused, so was Bill. Immediately following the program, he thanked me profusely and even said, "I always knew I could rely upon you!"

Bill, like many *Pacers* may have "always known," yet his behavioral and decision-making style requires him to ponder and deliberate his 'yes' decision for a long time.

Let's review some of the valuable language from this letter, and see why it got the desired result. The language was carefully selected—just for a *Pacer*. Words and phrases like:

- "You can be assured of…"

- "The peace of mind in knowing…"

- "A high comfort level"

- "A proven presenter"

- "Security"

- "High credibility"

- "Countless others are already benefiting…"

Even when Bill thanked me with, "I always knew I could rely upon you!"—his focus was on reliability.

Strategies for Success

Initially, in your *Open* stage with a *Pacer*, be relaxed, informal and somewhat low-key. Your probe questions should focus on results characterized by reliability or dependability.

When *revealing* or *translating* your product or service, appeal directly to the *Pacer's* need for compliance or stability. And when *negotiating* or moving toward a "yes" decision with a *Pacer*, let him or her know you value their thought process and deliberation. And you'll sincerely work together, so he or she can make the best decision.

Here are 9 more ideas, to help you better serve *Pacers*:

1. Meet at their office, they're comfortable in their environment.
2. Dress conservatively.
3. Acknowledge their involvement or participation in clubs, groups, and associations.
4. Assure *Pacers* they're not the "first on the block" to use your product or service.
5. Stress how numerous others have been happy.
6. Always emphasize consistency and reliability.
7. Focus on how your product or service improves their job performance.
8. Allow them time to make a decision.
9. Be sure you work within the "rules, regulations and policies" of how they traditionally make a decision.

Here are 7 things *not* to do when working with *Pacers*:

1. Don't sell the "sizzle."
2. Don't use highly animated body language or conversation.
3. Don't sound or look "too slick."
4. Don't push *Pacers* for a decision.
5. Don't make them be innovators, guinea pigs or first-time buyers.
6. Don't urge any emphasis on change.
7. Don't present broad descriptions and generalizations.

Potential power statements for *Pacers* include:

- "We'll be sure to keep your performance and productivity levels high."
- "Our product or service allows you to work smarter, as you

concentrate on successfully performing your job or task."

- "In our 38 years in business, others have found us to be reliable and dependable. They say we're 'folks they can count on.'"
- "If you're like other happy customers, you'll especially enjoy the security of knowing what to expect. There will be no surprises."
- "You can have the peace-of-mind in knowing, happy, long-time customers tell us we're their stable, go-to partner."

76. *Analyzers:* Facts Fascinate, Data Delights!

Analyzers are similar to *Drivers.* They too have a tendency to be direct and to-the-point. However, *Analyzers* are especially dependent upon raw data. They get excited by hard facts, diagrams, spreadsheets, grids and numbers. This type of information is essential to support their decisions. They know numbers never lie. Facts tell the story. The truth is in the eighth number after the decimal point!

Analyzers often listen very critically. They're precise with their language. They can be somewhat conservative or even reserved. While the *Charmer* might be friendly and sociable, an *Analyzer* could be perceived as being cool or standoffish.

Analyzers also have a tendency to be highly organized. Everything in their office has a place. I actually knew an *Analyzer* who always had freshly sharpened pencils and blank legal pads on his desk. This let him immediately calculate numbers, assess cost factors and accurately determine rates of return.

He once walked into his office and declared, "I'm missing a

pencil!" Believe it or not, he was! He actually knew precisely how many he had. Where was the pencil? As a practical joke, it was taken by a *Charmer*!

Analyzers demand information that's accurate and logical. I'll never forget an *Analyzer* I once met with, who drew for me a diagram of what he called the "communications network." It was an intricate configuration of lines, arrows and boxes. With great self-satisfaction and precision, he explained why this drawing was crucial to business development and success. I listened intently and took lots of notes.

One week later, when we met again, guess what drawing I had reproduced on the cover of the action-plan I was presenting? Of course, it was *his* diagram of the "communications network." When he saw it he said, "Jeff, since you understand the theory as to how this diagram works, it's logically obvious you're the right person to help us."

Lead with Logic

With *Analyzers*, logic rules. While in the *Open* stage, don't dwell on small talk. Get right down to business. Let *Analyzers* know through your *Probe* questions that you value their opinions, expertise and knowledge.

When *revealing* and *translating* your product or service, appeal directly to their need for data, accuracy, precision, proven success stories and logic. And when *negotiating* or moving toward *The Yes* decision with *Analyzers*, be prepared to offer additional facts and figures. This helps them acknowledge the practicality and reality of making a wise investment decision.

Here are 10 additional strategies, when selling, serving or negotiating with *Analyzers*:

1. Be sure to stress the facts, the details, the raw data and the numbers.
2. Be precise in your language, presentation and action-plan.
3. Avoid typographical errors or poor grammar in any communication.
4. Let *Analyzers* reach their own conclusions about how your product or service solves their problems.
5. Address their desire for logic.
6. Be prepared for criticism or close scrutiny.
7. Establish methods to monitor results and measure performance.
8. Emphasize you and your company's commitment to quality control.
9. Focus on the return on investment or value of your product or service.
10. Accept input from *Analyzers* without being critical.

Here are 7 things *not* to do when dealing with *Analyzers*:

1. Don't engage in intimidating or aggressive behavior.
2. Don't force them into making a decision.
3. Don't attempt to be too sociable.
4. Don't convey broad or abstract concepts.
5. Don't dismiss or gloss over their logical input to your solution.
6. Don't fail to offer well-known and accurate analytical testimonial support.
7. Don't forget to provide previous results or case studies that

are easily documented and substantiated.

Power statements for *Analyzers* include:

- "Please analyze in detail this data and draw your own conclusions."
- "You can assess the accuracy of the numbers to aid your decision."
- "Let's be sure to clarify the impact of this data on your operation."
- "That's a wise decision. It meets your exacting standards."
- "Logically, that's a smart course of action."

Now I'm confident you're a firm believer in, and an ardent supporter of, the *Golden Rule*: "Do unto others as you would like others to do unto you." That's a pretty good philosophy. It serves you well. But is it a good rule to follow in the world of business development? Well, yes and no!

Yes, in the sense that you should always treat your prospects, customers and clients with courtesy, dignity and empathy. However, aside from that, it makes absolutely no sense to treat others the way *you* would like to be treated. How come?

Because as you know, each of us is a unique being, with different desires, needs, goals and objectives. We're not clones. Knowing that, why would *I* possibly want to treat *you* the way *I* like to be treated, unless we *both* are driven and motivated by the same or similar factors?

By effectively, strategically and sincerely adapting your business and behavioral style to better work with and understand the preferences of a *Charmer, Driver, Pacer* or *Analyzer*, you begin to realize new and incredible levels of negotiations and business development success.

- If you're a *Charmer*, this success brings you greater visibility and recognition.

- If you're a *Driver*, your new achievements bring you quick and immediate bottom-line results.

- If you're a *Pacer*, you can be assured you're applying reliable strategies that countless others have also had success with.

- And if you're an *Analyzer*, you'll logically conclude, your adaptation to these 14 specific decision influencers and four types of investment styles yield quantifiable results!

CHAPTER 11

Thumbs Up, Approval: The Yes!

"Every person is the architect of their own fortune."

—Appius Claudius, Roman general, 53 B.C.E.

77. Confess: You Love *The Yes.*

It's the most powerful and sought-after word in business development. Your ability to get prospects, customers and clients to say it has a significant impact upon your future and theirs. Hearing it has numerous benefits. *What it means to you is*—happier customers, improved self-esteem, enhanced confidence and an increased bank account. No matter how it's said: "We've got the green light.", "Let's move forward.", "Make it happen.", "Let's do it." or, as a new client of mine recently exclaimed, "It's a go!"— your objective as a *peak profiteer* and *Opportunity $eller* is to get your decision-makers to say *The Yes!*

In my travels around the world, businesspeople complain to me that "closing" is their greatest downfall. They assure me their inability to "close" is the major contributor to their frustration, anxiety and poor performance. They plead, "Teach us how to close." And I wonder why. Because to me, a "close" makes no sense. "Close" is a word of completion, conclusion or termination. Yet as you well know, once your prospect says *The Yes*, your sale or relationship is just beginning. It's far from "closed." Therefore, I won't teach you how to close. But I'll share with you proven and profit-producing strategies to help you repeatedly secure *The Yes*.

78. Remove the Pressure

Many businesspeople assume *The Yes* is the toughest *Opportunity $elling* stage in the *Peak Your Profits Business-Growth System*. It's not. It's actually the easiest. But only if you've executed the previous five stages correctly.

All too often though, *The Yes* stage is characterized by pressure. But pressure upon whom? Most people say the customer. But it's shared by the customer *and* the salesperson. Why? Well, the customer begins to engage in thoughts like these:

Uh oh! This is where I get taken advantage of. It's time for me to part with my hard-earned cash. Do I really need this? If I save these bucks, then I can get what I really want or need. My parents told me never to trust somebody trying to sell me something. Where's the nearest exit?

And the salesperson's internal mutterings often begin with:

Without this deal, I'll never make quota! There goes that vacation. There has to be a better way to make a living. The boss is gonna say, 'Not again—what's wrong with you?' I knew this customer was indecisive from the start. I can always spot a time waster. Why did I get involved with these people?

However, as a *peak profiteer*, there's no need for "pressure" upon either your prospect or you. Especially when you use the *VINe Principle* (for a quick review, please see Chapter 3, *Focus Section* 13). This means you're always:

1. Value-driven.
2. Integrity-based.
3. Non-manipulative.

Remember, *The Yes* is simply the next step in the natural progression of the business acquisition process. And because it's unlikely that you would have gotten all the way to *The Yes* without the development of some type of a relationship, now is *not* the time to suddenly switch to guerrilla war tactics to secure a positive response.

79. Have a Game Plan

Your objective in *The Yes* is twofold: first, to have your customers say yes, and then to have them acknowledge and appreciate the value of their wise investment decision. It's not the time to beat them into submission! To wear them out! To make them yell "uncle"!

To effectively secure *The Yes*, you should have a game plan. Have you ever seen a professional football player carrying his playbook? (Now, it's on an iPad or a tablet.) Yet it used to be a behemoth book! Football players who tipped the scales well in excess of 300 pounds, needed that much muscle just to carry this "monster" creature that weighed about the same! But the playbook, (in any form) is more than a series of X's and O's. It's actually a strategic plan that sets forth not only a team's specific actions, but also their anticipated responses to the other team's actions.

In essence, it's a lot like the business strategy of getting others to commit to action by saying *The Yes*. Just like a well-trained athlete, you, too, must be disciplined with not only your actions but also be prepared for the actions of others.

However, like the playing field, the business arena also has specific roles. Here are eight guidelines that should be followed to maximize your likelihood of hearing *The Yes*:

1. All decision-makers should be present.
2. Anticipate objections and be prepared with appropriate persuasive and profitable answers.
3. Remember, customers never invest in what something *is*, but instead, they invest in what it will *do* for them.
4. The purpose of *The Yes* stage is to not only put more dollars in your pocket, but to first help somebody else attain a more favorable future and improved condition.
5. Never lose sight of the fact that you're dealing with another human being who makes decisions based on emotional reasons.
6. A "yes" only occurs when you have a decision-maker with a motivated need. Therefore, be sure to focus on *this* particular buyer's motivation(s).
7. Realize "no" often means "not yet."
8. Anticipate a "yes." Positive expectations bring positive results.

As you may recall, during the *Reveal* stage (please see Chapter 8), you began asking a series of *trial questions*. This same crucial strategy should also be used here in *The Yes* stage. Once again, *trial questions* elicit opinions, feelings, responses, attitudes or gut reactions to your product or service and its features and benefits. Trial questions should be simple and open-ended. For example:

- "How do you feel about…"
- "What do you think of…"
- "What's your reaction to…"
- "In which ways will this help you…"

At this point in the business development process, *trial questions* allow your buyers to offer both logical and emotional reasons or explanations as to why they want to own, use, enjoy and benefit from your products or services. Every time decision-makers give you positive responses, that's your signal to move closer to *The Yes* and an eventual sale.

80. He Said What?!

Have you ever seen book titles or magazine and online advertising headlines that scream:

- "1,001 Ways to Close A Sale!"
- "No Means Yes!"
- "Power-Close Your Way to the Bank!"
- "They'll Never Say No Again!"
- "Close the Deal Before They Toss You Out!"

I get a great kick out of such boastful and absurd claims. Because despite their "guarantee" of success, success is actually unlikely. Can you imagine memorizing "1,001 ways to close a sale"? Plus, these contrived closes usually operate from the basic premise of "When your customer says this you respond with Close 52—'the imminent emergency close'! But if your customer says this, you respond with Close 712—'the behind-your-back, slam dunk, in-your-face, puppy dog close'!" It's ridiculous—and unfortunate. Because if these misleading and hard-sell pressure tactics are used, they backfire. Not only is this opportunity lost, but any future business relationship is also jeopardized.

I don't know about you, but I have never had two prospects or clients who carry the same "script." Let alone a "script" that's the same as mine! Plus, if you do try to memorize 1,001 ways to close a sale, there's a real good chance your prospect will deliver Objection 1,002!

I was once given a book boasting on its front cover that it was "the most powerful book ever written on closing." It's also the most manipulative. In a chapter entitled, "The Greatest Closes on Earth," it shares closing strategies with names like "the sharp-angle close," "the three-devil close," "the intimidation close" and "the negative close." Each closing tactic also has an example of its use, preceded by a brief description. Let me share with you, verbatim, four of these descriptions:

1. With this close, the closer throws the customer's objections right back at him and makes him eat his own words.

2. This close actually tells the customer to go to hell when he says he has to think about buying the product.

3. This close is designed to embarrass and shame the customer into buying the product through pressure and emotion.

4. WARNING: When the closer uses this close, he had better be on his toes and far enough away from the customer, so if the customer becomes violent, the closer can take defensive precautions.

The preceding descriptions aren't jokes. They're not fabrications. They're sadly presented as legitimate strategies to get business. If these strategies are used, I think the only thing you're likely to get is total and deserved rejection and humiliation!

Tricky, manipulative or coercive closes serve no purpose for, have no place in and aren't part of the *Opportunity $elling* stages and the *Peak Your Profits Business-Growth System*. Remember, when you properly conduct the first five stages of *Open, Probe, Reveal, Translate* and *Negotiate* and then effectively ask a series of open-ended trial questions, then asking for and receiving *The Yes* is simply the next natural step.

81. Ask and Isolate

Believe it or not, many businesspeople don't ask for the order. In one survey by the Evans organization of 10,000 buyers, it was reported that 96 percent of the buyers surveyed said that the salespersons selling them didn't even ask for the order or seek any type of commitment. Incredible, but true! And in a survey by the Dartnell Corporation, it was revealed that 90 percent of the sales population quits the sales process before the prospect is ready to buy, despite the fact that 80 percent of the sales happen after the fifth contact.

Therefore, positive action that moves you closer to *The Yes* is essential at all times, especially during this final stage. When your prospect, customer or client exhibits enthusiasm or responds favorably to your trial questions, you might say:

- "I share in your excitement, all we need is your okay here."
- "You've made a wise decision, let's take care of the easy paperwork now."
- "Let's schedule your delivery for this week…"
- "With your approval now, you'll start your enjoyment immediately…"

However, even with enthusiasm and excitement, customers can still be very clever about the creative ways in which they delay decisions. They're hesitant about offending us with a defiant "No!", so instead, they say things like:

- "I'd like to think it over!"
- "Boy it sounds interesting!"
- "We'll give it our top consideration!"
- "It looks real promising!"
- "I'll be sure to put in a good word for you!"
- "This looks like a real strong possibility!"
- "It'll require some careful thought!"
- "Everything sure seems to be in order!"
- "You've done a great job presenting this!"
- "We'll get back to you as soon as possible!"
- "I think we might, could, perhaps, maybe be able to do it!"
- "Just as soon as we've made up our minds, you'll be the first to know!"

Do these delaying tactics sound familiar? Thought so. But what do they mean? Who knows? I have no idea! Therefore, you must find out what's causing the hesitation and reluctance.

If you allow your customers to escape without knowing what's causing their indecision, you haven't done *your* job! You must determine the reason or reasons for their unwillingness to give you *The Yes* now.

Dig for Doubt

If customers tell you, "I'd like to think it over," don't argue with them. Instead, acknowledge that you understand their desire to think it over. After all, it *is* an important decision. But then discover *what* they'd really like to think over. You might say: "What specifically would you like to think about?" (And after the answer, add, "In addition to that, is there anything else?")

Once you've isolated the obstacle, you're then in a better position to respond, reassure and get *The Yes*. You should try to never exit without knowing why a customer hasn't yet invested or said *The Yes*. If you do, you're no longer relying upon knowledge, but instead guesswork.

Another successful strategy for responding to "I'd like to think it over," is the following:

> *I understand why you'd like to think it over—it's an important decision. Let's list the point you'd like to consider. Any others?*

The decision delayers can even be written down—by *you*, not your customer. Then you might say:

> *If I could answer or address these points to your total satisfaction, would you be ready to go ahead with your decision?*

279

Or:

> *If I could resolve these issues to your total satisfaction, would you be ready to approve this action plan?*

Or:

> *If you're not comfortable, I'm not comfortable. Therefore, if together we can eliminate your concerns...to your total satisfaction, would you then be willing to give this idea your approval?*

There are two important keys to this very effective strategy. The first is that your customer knows his or her concerns must be answered to "total satisfaction" and second, once these concerns are answered, he or she should then be ready, willing and able to give you *The Yes*. Once again, the concept is more important and valuable than the specific words used. Therefore, aside from saying, "If I can address these points to your total satisfaction..." you might say:

> *If I can address these issues and remove your doubt...*

Or:

> *If we explore the choices, so you're completely comfortable...*

Or:

> *Your unconditional satisfaction is essential. Together, let's see how we can help you achieve that...*

Here's an important subtlety to this strategy. If you've written down your customer's concerns, once each point is properly answered or addressed, cross it off! This shows tangible evidence that, one-by-one, the customer's objections, hesitancies and decision delayers are being eliminated. And with the elimination of each point, you move closer to *The Yes*.

By using such language, your focus isn't on a slick comeback to an objection, but instead on your prospect's real concerns and total satisfaction or complete comfort. And that's where your focus belongs.

The Yes stage isn't time to engage in a tug-of-war or battle-of-wits. If you do, you're likely to defeat yourself. But if your decision-makers perceive they're part of a cooperative, problem-solving, satisfaction-producing scenario, they'll be willing to work *with* you, not *against* you.

82. Silence May Not Be Golden

I've always been fascinated by the advice that goes something like this: "Ask for the order and then shut-up!" Reason: The first person who talks loses! Now, if *you've* heard this alleged wisdom espoused over the years, guess who else has? Of course, your *customer*. So what happens? I've heard stories about businesspeople who sit in silence for five minutes or longer. Both buyers and sellers are operating under the mistaken fear that the first one who talks loses. That's absurd! Do you really think at this point in your relationship, the first person to talk loses if you:

- Have developed a cooperative, collaborative relationship?

- Have progressed positively through the first five stages of the *Peak Your Profits Business-Growth System*?

- Have effectively determined problems to solve, needs to fill or goals to realize in the *Open* and *Probe*?

- Have involved your decision-makers and they responded favorably to your *trial questions* during the *Reveal*?

- Have repeatedly stressed the benefits and what your product or service means to them in the *Translate*?

- Have isolated and removed concerns to their *total satisfaction* in the *Negotiation* and *The Yes*?

- Have conveyed throughout the entire process that you'll deliver high perceived value and help them attain a more favorable future and improved condition, and now, as part of that natural and positive progression, you seek their commitment?

Of course not! However, just in case your decision-maker hits the mute button and goes silent, here's a very simple but effective strategy. Look at your buyer, and then with almost a chuckle in your voice, say something like, "You know, this reminds me of something my wise uncle once said, and that is, silence means consent!" Your decision-maker is likely to smile or laugh as well. Now, you can address his or her concern, if there really is one, and together move toward *The Yes*.

83. A Fearsome Foursome

A key to securing *The Yes*, especially when your decision-maker is still reluctant to commit, is to build value—quickly and dramatically. You must also show a willingness to be a creative and flexible problem-solver. Therefore, here are three more strategies to build value—the *Mouse Method*, the *Reduction Rule* and *Value Focus*. Plus, an additional strategy on cooperative problem-solving—the *Trial Balloon*.

The Mouse Method

The *Mouse Method* is based on a strategy I heard articulated by Michael Eisner, the onetime leader of the Walt Disney Company. One afternoon while driving my car, I was listening to a business-radio station, where Eisner was being interviewed. The reporter, in a rather defiant tone, asked, "Mr. Eisner, recently you have increased admission to the Magic Kingdom by $4 per person. Isn't it becoming rather pricey for a typical family of four to see the Mouse? How do you justify that?"

Was Eisner challenged or intimidated by this question? No. Instead, he responded, "You're right, admission has gone up by $4 per person, and I can see why you may think it's an inappropriate increase." (It's interesting to note, Eisner didn't refute the reporter's claim or express disturbance. Instead, he simply agreed. That in itself is a powerful persuasion strategy.) You, too, can overcome an objection or a potential problem through initial agreement.

Now before I tell you what else Eisner said, let me tell you what he *didn't* say:

- "We *have* to hike-up the price! Do you have any idea what it costs to run that place?"

- "Hey, even a Mouse has to make money!"

- "I've got to protect myself! Do you know what my liability exposure is if somebody gets hurt on a ride?"

- "Look, you can't begin to grasp the size of my payroll and daily overhead!"

Instead, here's what Eisner said: "You're right, admission has gone up by $4 per person, and I can see why you may think it's an inappropriate increase. It has gone up, though, for a good reason. Over the past few years, we have significantly increased the entertainment value of a visit to the Magic Kingdom and to our other attractions. So the real question a mom and dad need to ask themselves is this: Do they want $16 to stand in the way of what's likely to be their greatest family vacation experience ever?"

Wow! What an answer. Eisner didn't focus on the cost of admission, but instead on the return on that investment. Remember, when value is high, integrity is high, non-manipulation is high, and yes, sometimes even when price is high, what's low? That's right—resistance. So, learn from our friend Mickey. When your customer is in doubt, use the *Mouse Method* to build value.

The Reduction Rule

Here's how the *Reduction Rule* works. Let's say your product sells for $365 and it's a consumable product to be used once a day.

On an annual basis, the investment is $365. But by using the *Reduction Rule*, the investment is only $1 a day. And $1 a day sounds very affordable, especially if it's providing your customers with enhanced value, increased gain or reduced loss.

The *Reduction Rule* is used on a regular basis for a variety of products and services. For example, newspapers, magazines, newsletters, online subscriptions and information services continually ask if you can afford to be uninformed and out-of-touch, by *not* subscribing to their publications or services. What they're really asking you is, "What's the cost of ignorance?" Therefore, for only 8¢ a day, you can have the world at your fingertips! The *Reduction Rule* is also used to sell, for example, a $1,000 product or service in four easy payments of only $250.

One of the key advantages of the *Reduction Rule* is that the reduced or diminished dollar reference makes it easier for the buyer to justify value in his or her mind. The decision-maker is able to better rationalize his or her decision. Let me give you an example. On January 26, 1986, I watched my beloved Chicago Bears beat the New England Patriots 46 to 10 at Super Bowl XX in New Orleans. How much did I pay for my ticket? $150. (I know, a bargain today!) But at the time, here's how I rationalized what I thought may have been an irrational, impulsive and spendthrift decision.

I said to myself, "This is a lot of money to spend to simply attend a football game. However, it's an extremely reasonable investment for an experience of a lifetime. And if I live for at least another 50 years following this game, that's only $3 a year! Actually, that's less than a penny a day for a cherished memory. There's nothing left to think about. It's my civic duty to watch the Bears in the

Super Bowl!" As you can tell, my decision had nothing to do with football, but instead history! I used the *Reduction Rule* on myself and it worked!

Value Focus

Value Focus is especially useful when your product or service increases gain or reduces loss in some quantifiable or measurable way. Here's an example of how I use *Value Focus* with my clients. Let's say a client, Gary, shares with me during the *Probe* that he's willing to budget and commit $50,000 over the next six months to a business-growth learning-system for his team. Whether Gary's budget allows for $50,000 or only $5,000, his investment is unimportant, unless I deliver value that returns to him and his company dollars greater than the investment.

So how can I build value and show the potential for results? It's easy with the *Value Focus*. For example, I might say:

"Gary, let's take a look at the real value or bottom-line results you'll enjoy because of this investment. First, you said over the next six months, we'll enhance the confidence and skill-level of at least 100 salespeople. The typical sale is $10,000, and your gross margin is 25 percent."

"Therefore, your typical sale is worth $2,500 to your company. And you mentioned to me earlier, if these news skills, strategies, attitudes and behaviors help your salespeople make just one more sale a month, the impact would be profound. Let's do the math together and see just how profound the results could be."

"If each salesperson made just one more sale a month, that's 12 more sales a year. And with 100 salespeople, that's 1,200 more sales per year. Plus, with an average gross profit value of $2,500 per sale, that translates into $3 million a year!"

"Now, even if your system was only 50 percent effective, that's still a return of $1.5 million! What would those kind of results mean to your top line, bottom line and future success? By your own projection, you could have a total return on your investment within less than one month. How do you feel about that?"

As you can tell, once again, my primary focus is on helping Gary acknowledge, anticipate and envision his results. Not in some abstract way, but in a quantifiable and measurable way, with numbers, projections and his future—created by *him*, not me.

The Trial Balloon

If your decision-maker is still hesitating, you might consider slightly altering your offer, deal, transaction or agreement to secure *The Yes*. The *Trial Balloon* strategy lets you present possibilities, but without your commitment. You don't make a definitive declaration as to what your changes might be, but pose your possibilities in the form of suggestions or questions. The three key words to launch your *Trial Balloons* are "*What if we...*" The reason this language is so valuable is that the "we" shows your sense of cooperation, collaboration and willingness to work on a solution together with your decision-maker. Examples of *Trial Balloons* might be:

- **What if** we kept the delivery date the same, but extended the maintenance agreement?
- **What if** we did _____ and you did _____?

- **What if** we keep your investment the same, but change your initial investment to _____?
- **What if** we changed your investment payment schedule from ___ months to ___ months?

Like a trial question, a *Trial Balloon* also seeks an opinion, feeling or reaction from your decision-maker. And a positive response from your decision-maker to your *Trial Balloon* creates a dialogue that helps you get *The Yes.*

To help you achieve ongoing business growth and peak profits, be sure to apply the five profit points of *The Yes* stage:

1. Expect a positive response.
2. Once again, emphasize the results, benefits, advantages and outcomes, rather than the investment in your product or service.
3. Ask several open-ended trial questions to get your prospect's opinions, feelings, reactions and attitudes.
4. Ask for a "yes" decision. If there's hesitation, find out why, resolve it and then ask again for a "yes."
5. Congratulate your customers or clients on their wise investment decisions.

The real fascination of business development is its ability to communicate, persuade and move others to action, and *that* is an art! As you perfect your "art," you'll hear numerous prospects, customers and clients give you *The Yes!*

CHAPTER 12

Customer Commitment

"Service is the difference between a
good company and a great company."

—*Anonymous*

84. Who Pays Your Salary?

Why is it we sometimes ignore those who pay our salary? How come we often neglect the lifeblood of our business? Why is it we forget about the people who help us buy our home, car, clothes and raise our family? Are we selfish? Rude? Arrogant? Uncaring? No!

Maybe, it's just that we often get too excited about the "chase," the opportunity to clinch the new deal, reel in the big one or land that tough-to-get prospect! We forget about the significance of *the customer*!

Webster's says a customer is, "one who trades *regularly* at a particular business, a patron, a buyer." The key word is "regularly." Regularly implies a sense of trust in, confidence toward or knowledge about one's products or services. There's a level of expectation. And it's met over and over.

To better understand customer satisfaction, happiness and loyalty, throughout this chapter we take a closer look at successful companies that benefit and profit from their commitment to customer service. And we even explore one industry giant hit—and hit hard—when it stopped listening to its customers.

Whether our example is about a well-recognized Fortune 500 company or a closely-held family business you may have never heard of before, you'll soon see why the service principles, philosophies and strategies that elevated these companies to phenomenal levels of success will also work for your company.

A *Time* magazine cover story once carried this headline: "The Hapless American Consumer: Why is Service So Bad?" Could it be, at one time, uncaring businesspeople elevated greed to a new and lofty level? Was *I* and *me* more important than *you*? It seems some businesses could flourish in spite of themselves and how they treated their customers. The marketplace acknowledged it might take months or even years to find a customer and only seconds to lose one, but it didn't matter. Why? Because money would be made on the next customer.

But then folks like you and me (customers) got smart, fed-up and vocal! We started talking. The Technical Assistance Research Programs Institute, discovered 91 percent of unhappy customers never buy again from an "offending" company. But they continue to voice their displeasure and frustration to nine other people! That's right, nine other people will quickly learn about the service violator. And each one of them could tell nine more people! As you can see, this mathematical progression quickly causes severe damage to a business.

Customers have become more sophisticated and more demanding. They have higher expectations. And they can afford to be that way. Because they know if you're not willing to serve them, your competitors are.

If the business deity was once greed, now and throughout the 21st century, it's service! *Business Week* magazine declared the 1990s "The Decade of the Customer." One cover story stated in large, solid-black, capital letters, "KING CUSTOMER" followed by this sage reminder, "Forget market share. Stop worrying about your competitors. The companies that are succeeding now put their customers first." (That simple message is still true today, three decades later!)

Whether your company is young and growing, established and secure, large or small, your commitment to service is crucial. Why? Because with it, you boost retention and profitability. Without it, you jeopardize your future. Probably even your existence!

Big Blue's Big Boo-Boo

Here's an example of the cold, hard truth. It requires we briefly take a peek at the past. In the winter of 1993, I spoke at a conference for 200 sales and sales management professionals. These folks worked for a division of a company you're very familiar with. They make computers. Big ones. And lots of 'em. The company has been dubbed by the media as "Big Blue." Many of us know it as IBM.

Now, this particular division of IBM had done especially well. However, on the morning I spoke, these IBM professionals knew they worked for an organization that in the past year had lost the most money, (at that time), in U.S. domestic corporate history—$5.5 billion! And *The Wall Street Journal* revealed that morning that over the next year, IBM would cut their staff by some 35,000 to 50,000 people.

What happened to IBM in the early 1990s? Or Sears? Or GM? Did these icons of industry simply become fallen dinosaurs? While their decline was evident, it was unlikely their extinction was imminent. (As of this writing, Sears recently identified 100 unprofitable stores, and announced they'll begin "closing sales" at 72 of these stores "in the near future.") However, a key contributor to IBM's woes then may have been the simple fact that they didn't listen to their customers.

In May 1993, IBM had a three-day customer conference in Chantilly, Virginia. The conference title offers tremendous insight into IBM's admission of anguish and aspiration for future success. It was called, "The New IBM—A Dialogue for Partnership." Did that imply the "old" IBM didn't dialogue, didn't partner or didn't listen?

During that meeting, IBM met with more than 100 of their biggest North American customers. Apparently, for years many IBM customers complained IBM ignored their product and service needs. They hoped the "new" IBM would be more responsive, more focused on customer concerns and satisfaction.

Why did IBM hold this meeting? Because they knew these customers represented a collective annual purchasing power of almost $30 billion.

Since 1993, IBM has obviously rebounded. They continue to manufacture and market computer hardware, middleware and software throughout the world. With operations in over 170 countries. However, even though IBM's revenue now tops $80 billion, at times in recent years their revenue has declined. This is due to fierce competition in their traditional businesses, as well as new businesses like cloud computing, analytics, mobility and security.

However, IBM obviously escaped from an earlier hole they should never have dug in the first place. Had they maintained a customer focus, they might have avoided drowning in that $5.5 billion worth of red ink.

Remember, when it comes to customers, a successful business always requires three basic business tenets:

1. Acquisition.
2. Satisfaction.
3. Retention.

Even the "mighty" can't ignore these.

85. Valuable Lessons

According to the International Customer Service Association:

> *Corporate America recognizes that it costs nearly five times as much to get new customers as it does to keep existing ones. Thus, more resources are being committed to all aspects of customer service; salaries, training, human resources and equipment. Senior management is finding*

service more integral to their competitive advantage and to their bottom-line profits.

This constant commitment to service has nothing to do with phony smiles, clever phrases and hanging banners with slogans. It means the ability to compete and to compete profitably, now and throughout the 21st century. It requires a passion. A missionary zeal. A relentless pursuit to satisfy your customers.

Few companies possess this collective commitment. However, one company that has made customer service its fierce battle cry is a client of mine, Federal Express.

FedEx is still a young company. On April 17, 1973, its first night of operation, FedEx shipped only eight packages. Seven were trial runs. In 1983, it was the first corporation in U.S. corporate history to hit the $1 billion mark in annual revenues within its first decade of operation. Today, FedEx has more than 425,000 worldwide employees and contractors in 220 countries and territories, who make sure when "the most important package is yours" and "it absolutely, positively has to get there"…it does! And they do it, over 14 million times a day.

When Federal Express won the Malcolm Baldrige National Quality Award, Chairman and CEO Fred Smith didn't say the Baldrige was testament to his company's expertise, an apt award for years of dedication or even a prize well-deserved. Instead, he said, "I just hope we don't take this damn thing too seriously!"

What a great quote! In essence, what Smith said is, "Okay, the status is nice, but it sure doesn't matter to our customers that we won some award if their packages arrive late or on the wrong day!" Smith knows he and FedEx can't allow the past to block their vision and customer commitment for the future.

Although FedEx now has a network of companies with annual revenues in excess of $60.3 billion, its quest for service excellence hasn't peaked. It has just begun. I know firsthand.

As part of my preparation and research for programs I conducted with FedEx senior managers, I observed, read about and heard about this service passion. These folks eat, live and breathe service. Believe me, it ain't hype. They mean it! The American Management Associations' Management Briefing, "Blueprints for Service Quality, The FedEx Approach" states:

"There are no 'secrets' at Federal Express. The company's impressive growth and its distinguished service quality achievements have little to do with 'magic' formulas. Their foundation lies in sound managerial theories and practices, the staples of management literature and of the wisdom espoused by quality 'gurus' for years, even decades."

What sets Federal Express apart is this:

1. "A constant, clearly stated service quality goal—100 percent customer satisfaction, enunciated frequently and pursued doggedly in innumerable ways, large and small.

2. A mathematical measure of absolute service failures as a catalyst to promote continuous quality improvement.

3. Employees who feel empowered through open communication, training opportunities, quality improvement tools, and

excellent leadership. They thus gain the freedom to take risks and innovate in the pursuit of quality and service for both internal and external customers.

4. Finally, and most fundamental, FedEx has a people-first environment that acknowledges employee satisfaction as the primary corporate objective, and nurtures a culture from which customer satisfaction and profits spring."

Regarding this last point, Fred Smith explains the FedEx corporate philosophy this way, "When people are placed first, they will provide the highest possible service, and profits will follow." Smith summarizes this philosophy in his theory of *PSP* or *People-Service-Profit*. If you take care of your people and serve your customer, then you'll profit. Federal Express has always had this unwavering commitment to service, whether it was that first night when they shipped eight packages or yesterday when delivering over 14 million.

When I asked FedEx employees what *service* means to them, here are some of the responses I received:

*   *100 percent customer satisfaction. Period.*

*   *Providing timely and accurate responses or solutions that properly meet the customers' needs, and doing so with a friendly and positive attitude.*

*   *Keeping promises.*

*   *Prompt, educated and friendly service.*

- *Being readily available and efficiently prepared to handle problems, questions or suggestions. To maintain a relationship in a proactive way.*

- *Helping our customers attain their goals.*

- *Doing whatever it takes to give customers the perception that they are receiving more value than the investment they are placing in the partnership.*

- *Customer service means being an equal partner with our customers, making their problems our own.*

- *A willingness to go the extra mile...on your own!*

And as a client said to me, "Remember, in the extra mile, there's no traffic jam!"

Enterprise Ahead of the Traffic

Another client that's also way ahead of the traffic is Enterprise Rent-A-Car. Former senior vice president Wayne Kaufmann once told me, "Our business is simple. You just have to do everything right all the time." Apparently, Enterprise is doing lots of things right!

Kaufmann joined Enterprise in 1963, six years after the company was founded by Jack Taylor. In 1963, Enterprise's fleet size was 27 cars. From those humble beginnings, they've emerged as the industry leader.

As part of my initial work with Enterprise and their leadership team, I learned Enterprise:

- Had surpassed Hertz as the largest car rental company in North America, based upon fleet size and number of rental locations. (Today, Enterprise Holdings is the world's largest transportation solutions provider.)

- Had in excess of 2,500 branches. (Now, more than 9,900 fully-staffed neighborhood and airport locations in over 90 countries.)

- Had a fleet of more than 260,000 cars. (Now, more than 1.9 million vehicles worldwide.)

- Had over 20,000 employees. (Now, 100,000.)

- Had annual revenues over $2.5 billion. (As of fiscal year end in July, 2017, Enterprise Holdings had revenues of $22.3 billion. Enterprise Holdings operates the Enterprise Rent-A-Car, National Car Rental, and Alamo Rent A Car brands through its network of independent regional subsidiaries and franchises.)

- Had an unwavering commitment to customer service.

Enterprise even created the Enterprise Service Quality index or ESQi. It's a measurement tool that reflects their employees' service behavior, as judged and rated by Enterprise customers. And ESQi is just as important as other statistical information for utilization rates, transaction times or new accounts.

Andy Taylor, when he was Enterprise's Chairman and CEO, told me, "ESQi is only one element of our success, but it's an essential one. I refuse to give my competition my service advantage." He went on to share this philosophy: "Our business really isn't about cars, it's about giving our customers' freedom, flexibility and independence." (Today, Andy is Executive Chairman of Enterprise Holdings.) Yet he has always known, loyalty is a key profit and growth driver.

Taylor told me his philosophy would help Enterprise reach or exceed its goal—doubling annual revenues. According to Taylor, the key to this goal's realization was staying on track. He said, "Jeff, if you get off track, you'll be buried. To stay on track, keep your customers happy, keep your people happy and then you'll make money!" Enterprise is happily making money...and on track!

Long ago, they surpassed Andy Taylor's $5 billion goal. For once again, for Enterprise Holding's fiscal year ending July 31, 2017, revenues were $22.3 billion. They also owned 38 percent of the United States airport business, and globally, conducted 70 million customer transactions.

Plus, in the fall of 2017, the Enterprise, National and Alamo brands landed the top three spots in the J.D. Power North American Rental Car Satisfaction Study for the fifth year in a row. And Enterprise, National and Alamo were the only brands to finish above the industry average.

Pam Nicholson, President and CEO at Enterprise Holdings said, "These kinds of milestones are achieved only one way in an industry as competitive as ours. They are a direct result of our employees' incredible work ethic and their all-in focus on customer service excellence and efficient operations." She added, "Our total revenues not only continued to increase significantly during FY2017, but they actually more than doubled during the last decade along with our fleet size. In addition, since 2007, we have grown our share of the U.S. airport business 10 percentage points."

In the next section, you too will learn specific service strategies to grow, to achieve new milestones and to stay on track.

86. Stay on Track!

To help you stay on track, here's my first suggestion: Ask yourself and those you work with what "customer service" means. Discuss it. Define it. Then determine if you and others within your organization are indeed satisfying and making that definition come true.

Then, devise and execute a customer service action plan. After all, it's important to know where you are, if you want to get to where you want to go! You can develop your customer service action plan by answering these nine questions:

1. If you asked your customers to list your company's strengths, what would they include?
2. Of all the strengths listed, which three would your customers list as the strongest?
3. What are your organization's weaknesses in the minds of the customers you serve?
4. Of your weaknesses, which three are most frequently mentioned by your customers?
5. What strengths do you have that those you serve don't know about?
6. What strengths do you have that your competition doesn't?

7. What assets do you have that prospects, customers and clients want?
8. What assets do you have that prospects, customers and clients need?
9. What's your mission?

Put Your Mission Into Motion

You should consider developing both corporate and personal mission statements. For example, here's the corporate mission statement for Blackman & Associates:

> *Blackman & Associates is devoted to providing you with value-driven learning-systems, services, growth-tools and training. All designed to help you attain a more favorable future and improve your condition. In fulfilling this mission, we help you maximize your performance, productivity, profitability and results.*
>
> *Our dedication to this mission is best demonstrated by our personal attention and commitment to quality service. The depth of that service is best expressed by those many clients and people we serve.*

And here's my personal mission statement:

> *The purpose of my being a business-growth specialist is to help my clients attain a more favorable future, improve their condition, maximize results and drive growth.*

Now, to help you develop your mission statements, please fill in the blanks to the following statements:

Corporate Mission Statement:

The purpose of our company being a _____
is to help our customers or clients _____

_____

_____

Personal Mission Statement:

The purpose of my being a _____
is to help our customers or clients _____

_____

_____

Years ago, I had the pleasure of visiting with Greg Lewis who, in 1985, founded Motivation Excellence, an incentive marketing company in Schaumburg, Illinois. From its inception, Greg had a simple goal: providing exceptional incentive travel experiences with "gold star" service. This service passion struck me when Greg and I met, as I saw the following mission statement greet me as I entered the lobby. It stated:

We, as a team, are committed to exceeding our clients' expectations by developing programs to provide solutions for their needs.

We, as a team, will accomplish this by providing unparalleled client service while building client relationships into long-lasting partnerships.

We, as a team, will develop and nurture a fun, challenging, fulfilling, and rewarding environment of mutual respect,

trust, pride and growth...a creative environment produces
a creative product.

We, as a team, will prosper through recognition as the best
incentive marketing team in our industry when measured
by ourselves, our suppliers, our industry and our clients.

Greg recently retired. As of January 22, 2018 Motivation
Excellence is now under the leadership of new owner and CEO,
David Jobes. He's a 26-year company veteran, and was previously President. Yet it's evident that this "gold star" service
commitment which Greg started, David will continue. For the
Motivation Excellence website proudly and confidently declares:
"We anticipate that this change will only bring positive outcomes
for everyone moving forward. Our dedication has always been
to both our clients and employees alike, and that is what we will
continue to focus on in the years to come – providing exceptional service with incredible results."

It's obvious that delivering exceptional or "gold star" service
and building quality relationships were, and still are, drivers for success at Motivation Excellence. The same is true for
Enterprise.

When I began working with the folks at Enterprise Rent-A-Car, I
discovered that building relationships with internal and external
customers is also an integral part of their mission. If you hop
online, you'll quickly see that the Enterprise mission is:

To be the best transportation service provider in the world,
to exceed our customers' expectations for service, quality
and value, to provide our employees with a great place to

work and to serve our communities as a committed corporate citizen.

That's good stuff. Yet here's an earlier, expanded version of *The Enterprise Mission* that's even better stuff:

Our mission is to fulfill the automobile rental, leasing, car sale and related needs of our customers, and, in doing so, exceed their expectations for service, quality and value.

We will strive to earn our customers' long-term loyalty by working to deliver more than promised, being honest and fair, and 'going the extra mile' to provide exceptional personalized service that creates a pleasing business experience.

We must motivate our employees to provide exceptional service to our customers by supporting their development, providing opportunities for personal growth, and amply compensating them for their successes and achievements. We believe it is critical to our success to promote managers from within who will serve as examples of success for others to follow.

Although our goal is to be the best and not necessarily the biggest or the most profitable, our success at satisfying customers and motivating employees will bring growth and long-term profitability.

Once you've assessed your strengths, weaknesses, marketable assets and mission, you should then determine the specific goals that are appropriate for you, your team and your organization. Whatever your goals may be, they should acknowledge that your aim is to make it a joy for prospects, customers and clients to do business with you.

When decision-makers think about your company, they really don't think about your company's headquarters or bricks and mortar locations or online presence. Instead, they think about the relationships they have with *you* and the *others* at your company who serve them.

87. The Top 10

Whatever products or services you market and sell, or industry you compete in, there are still certain commonalities or "business-growth and service truths" crucial to your ongoing success. Leonard Berry and his colleagues at Texas A&M University researched and identified 10 dimensions of "service quality." They are:

1. Reliability.
2. Responsiveness.
3. Competence.
4. Accessibility.
5. Courtesy.
6. Communication.
7. Credibility.
8. Security.
9. Understanding.
10. Tangibles.

Let's explore each:

1. Reliability. This is your ability to provide consistent, reliable service. You get it done right the first time. And you always honor your promises to your customers.

2. Responsiveness. This means you provide service in a timely fashion. And "timely" is defined by your customers. It could be seconds or weeks. To be responsive, it's essential you understand your customers' needs, goals or problems. Then once you do, you must be appropriately responsive.

3. Competence. Here, you have the knowledge and skill-level to perform the service. And a surefire way to deliver it, on-time and as expected. Competence is characterized by sound judgment and intelligent decisions. Customers like to do business with smart businesspeople who act like winners.

4. Accessibility. How accessible or approachable are you and your people? Are you easy to reach? Or are your customers always stuck in a relentless game of phone and email tag? Are customers continually being transferred from one person to another? Do they have to search your store or office to find you or anyone else to help them?

Customers are typically reasonable, patient people. Yet extended waiting or delays on a regular basis often causes them to search for another individual or company who promptly and efficiently solves their problems.

5. Courtesy. Courtesy is an essential business basic, but all too often, it's forgotten. Courtesy is characterized by common sense. It means you're polite, considerate and understanding of your customers and your fellow employees, who are your internal customers.

Courtesy includes respect for property, not just your customers', but yours. Meaning you treat your products, merchandise, samples, display areas and support materials as prized possessions. Why? Because if your customers sense you don't care about *your* things, they begin to wonder how you'll treat them and their things.

6. Communication. Here, you keep customers informed in a language they understand. Listen to your customers. Educate them. Never forget, information is only of value to your customers if they know about it and understand it. (A computer salesperson recently suggested I invest in "5K Retina display with 5120-by-2880 resolution, 8-Core, 3.2 GHz Intel Xeon W, Turbo Boost, 19MB cache, 3584 stream processors, 9 teraflops single precision, 32GB of 2666MHz DDR4 ECC memory that's configurable to 4TB SSD.") I'm not sure, but I think the preceding means, this computer system is really fast and way cool!

7. Credibility. With credibility, your word is your bond. Customers know you're trustworthy and believable. If you say it, it's gospel. If you do it, it's done right! Remember, it takes years to develop your reputation, yet only seconds to lose it. To achieve your desired results and goals, first, help your customers achieve theirs.

8. Security. Here, you and your people (along with your products or services) provide customers with a comfort zone or peace of mind. With you, they're assured of performance and results. You, your talent and expertise remove the risk, concern and doubt that may accompany their decisions. Remember, your customers are always looking for ways to maximize gain and minimize or eliminate loss.

The movie *The Lion King* gives us the phrase: "Hakuna Matata." It means "no worries, it's a problem-free philosophy." Somehow, you must continually convey to your customers and prospects, that with you and your company, they'll receive "Hakuna Matata."

9. Understanding. You must make a sincere effort to understand your customers' needs, goals and objectives. Learn their specific requirements. Provide individualized or customized attention. And always recognize and acknowledge by name your regular, loyal and repeat customers.

10. Tangibles. Here, you concentrate on the image being conveyed by your company, products, services, physical facilities, promotional materials, website, and especially you and your people. Like it or not, this stuff matters.

One of my clients, Raj, is an extremely successful banker. While in graduate school, Raj helped defray expenses by delivering pizzas. However, he wasn't your typical pizza delivery man.

Raj knew, at an early age, the importance of tangibles and image. Raj requested and received from his employer extra shirts and hats with the company's logo. His strategy was simple: He knew if he looked sharp and presentable, people would likely be more willing to invite him into their home, instead of making him stand outside on the stoop in the cold or rain.

And he also knew he'd likely receive larger tips and repeat sales. Raj was right on both accounts. He even had business cards printed. And guess what happened? Customers would order pizzas and request only Raj deliver them!

It may not be fair, but like it or not, you're always being judged by your prospects and customers. Be sure their judgments are in your favor.

Are these ten dimensions of service easy to find in any company? How about your company? In other business professionals? How about you? Do you successfully deliver all ten dimensions? If not, which ones do you deliver? How often? Are you missing any? Are you weak in any of them? Where will you improve?

Now I'll admit, these 10 dimensions may be tough to find. And especially tough to execute. However, when you focus on fine-tuning or upgrading your skill levels in each of these areas, the positive and profit-producing possibilities and results are profound.

To be competitive, you can't rest upon your laurels or previous accomplishments. Acceptance, comfort and complacency breed mediocrity. Today, demanding consumers expect quality, value and service. And with each purchase or decision, they vote...with their money. It's your job to make sure they don't switch their votes.

88. Service Lives!

As I travel across the globe, helping companies grow their people and business, I spend lots of time in hotel rooms. And excitement is no longer generated by free Wi-Fi, a vast movie selection, oatmeal soap bars or fuzzy shoe shine mitts! However, good or especially great service stirs my juices!

Years ago, I stayed at the Hyatt Regency in Indianapolis. It was clean, comfortable, spacious and uneventful. Until I called the bell stand. At 9:45 a.m., John cheerfully greeted me. He assured me within five minutes he'd be at my room with a cart to escort me and my learning materials to a meeting room. Four minutes later he arrived.

John acknowledged me with a warm and friendly smile. He also inquired about my visit. He then asked, "Notice anything special about the 17th floor?" I said, "No. Why?"

He then proudly told me, "Mr. Blackman, you slept on the Sports Floor!" Surprised, I replied, "I did?!" John said, "You see this bed, was it roomy? Comfortable? It should be. How 'bout your shower head? See how high that is? Like your bed, it's designed for a seven-footer!"

Enthusiastically, John exclaimed, "Mr. Blackman, Indianapolis is the home of the NBA Pacers and the NFL Colts. And to better serve their opponents, our guests, we invested millions of dollars and redesigned 34 rooms on this floor to make road-life easier for these gifted athletes!"

Wow! Talk about a service commitment. John then told me the Hyatt had taken lots of new NBA and NFL business away from competitors who weren't as customer-focused. Plus, he added, "The Hyatt is where the media and fans now hang and spend big bucks."

Good News Travels Fast

One week later, just prior to the start of the NCAA Basketball

Tournament and March Madness, I was preparing for a program in a hotel room at Purdue University in West Lafayette, Indiana, not far from Indianapolis. As I watched the Indianapolis news, the sportscaster reported from the floor of the Hoosier Dome, the site of key tournament games.

However, he didn't wax rhapsodic about state basketball legend, Coach Bobby Knight or projected tourney favorites. Instead, he reported on where the teams would be staying—the renovated Hyatt with their extra-long beds and extra-high shower heads.

Talk about perceived value. Invaluable publicity. And a tremendous testament to customer focus and service. You see, when you discover an individual or a company that not only meets expectations, but exceeds them, you want to tell the world! (While a Hyatt Regency Indianapolis manager recently told me that the Sports Floor no longer exists, it still doesn't diminish Hyatt's commitment to, and execution for, a market segment with unique customer needs.)

89. The Race is Never Over

When Xerox won the Malcolm Baldrige National Quality Award, their victory didn't come easy. They underwent a grueling scrutiny, including some 400 hours of analyses and on-site inspections by Baldrige examiners. Throughout this process, Xerox discovered five basic principles about its quest for quality and customer satisfaction:

1. You have to look at your company through the eyes of your customers—even if it hurts. You have to let them define quality for you.

2. You need commitment from the top down, from the CEO to the mailroom.

3. You have to establish benchmarks that really stretch you. Set difficult, but attainable goals. Then meet them.

4. Get suppliers involved. When Xerox began their Leadership Through Quality process, 92 percent of parts received from suppliers were defect-free, a fair standard for their industry. Ten years later, they had attained 99.7 percent defect-free parts.

5. Xerox is committed to sustaining quality. Above all, they've learned: in the race for quality, there's no finish line! Since the quality, sales and service race is never over, it's essential to "win" every transaction, encounter or opportunity with a customer. A "win" can be a sale, a solved problem, a positive impression or simply a willingness to listen.

These "times of truth" are chances to create customers for life! Therefore, be sure to eliminate the following "losing language" from your service, sales or business vocabulary. In responding to prospects, customers or clients, never say:

- "Sir, you don't understand…"
- "Ma'am, I'm really busy, you'll just have to wait…"
- "Sir, as I told you before…"
- "Look lady, I don't have to listen to this…"
- "You can't be serious…"
- "We can't do that, and we won't do that because…"
- "Can I be honest, candid, frank with you? (Does this imply you were previously dishonest, not candid or not frank?)
- "No problem!" (When it's really a big problem!)
- "Trust me!"
- "You don't need anything today, do you?"

- "I just happened to be passing by..."
- "I'll get back to you."
- "We're out of stock."
- "It's on order."
- "Our policy states..."
- "It's not my problem..."
- "No way. Impossible. Never. Forget it."
- "I'm going on break. Someone else will have to help you."
- "You shouldn't..."
- "You are acting like a..."
- "You'll have to..."
- "You should have told me that..."

The preceding language conveys arrogance, impatience and indifference, which could all lead to insolvency! Instead, use winning words and phrases like:

- "How can I help you?"
- "Of course we can do that..."
- "That's easy!"
- "Let's devote the time together to find out exactly what you need..."
- "I apologize for the delay, I really appreciate your patience."
- "Do you mind if I put you on hold? Thanks for waiting."
- "Hmm, I don't know the answer to that question, but I'll be sure to find out and call you no later than four o'clock today..."
- "It's my pleasure..."
- "Glad you're here. How can I help?"
- "I know exactly how to solve that problem!'
- "We had another customer with that same challenge. Here's what we did..."

- "There are several alternatives. Here's what I suggest..."
- "Our in-house expert recommends..."
- "You'll be really happy when you..."

Not only are the words you choose and use important, but so is the inflection, or tone, in your voice. Always try to convey warmth and interest. Subtleties really matter. Empathy and sincerity are valued by your customers. Remember, it takes months, even years, to find, sell and serve a customer, but only seconds to lose one!

90. This Isn't Chicken Feed!

Some businesspeople forget the customer or client is your reason for being in business. I assure you, this principle was never forgotten at Quill.

Quill became North America's leading business-to-business, direct marketers of office supplies, business furniture and technology products. It was located in Lincolnshire, Illinois (a northern suburb of Chicago), and it achieved tremendous growth and success since their start in 1956.

Quill's founder and president, Jack Miller, began the business with a phone in his father's chicken store and a $2,000 loan from his father-in-law. By 1998, this privately held company had annual sales in excess of $630 million. (In May of 1998, Quill was sold to Staples for $685 million!)

I've had the pleasure of knowing Jack Miller since the winter of 1987. And over the years, I've also had the opportunity to chat with him numerous times; at his office, at his home, or during an interview for my radio talk-show. Jack has been recognized as one of the "movers and shakers" or "who's who" in Chicago business. With me, he's always low-key, humble and interested in how my family and business are doing. Yet, also, always focused on how to best serve his customers.

Jack and his brothers Harvey and Arnold identified commitment to customers as one of the keys to Quill's incredible track record. At Quill, customer service wasn't rhetoric, it was reality! Jack's office was a testament to this basic business tenet and to his success. But perhaps what fascinated me most about his office, was that he was surrounded by "ideas!" On countless engraved wooden plaques were sayings, quotes and slogans focusing on excellence, selling, commitment and service. One of them declared, "We're happy, but not satisfied!"

Jack and his brothers turned these slogans into measurable action. They were always looking for ways to better serve their 700,000+ customers. For example, Quill, long before others were doing it, set up customers with an electronic ordering system accessible through compatible personal computers and equipped with special software that Quill supplied. The system enabled customers to not only benefit from computerized ordering, but to also review their past purchases as well as share business ideas with Quill and their fellow customers.

Quill also made a commitment to significantly enhance or speed-up their delivery system. Virtually every stock order received by 6 p.m., was shipped that same day. And it arrived the next day. An incredible commitment, when you realize, at the time, Quill handled over 12,000 orders each day. This commitment to speed and convenience was also practiced when an order was placed. Quill answered over 93 percent of all incoming calls on the first ring.

The Bill of Rights

Quill's dedication to the customer was especially evident when walking through the halls of their corporate headquarters. Throughout its corridors were large framed posters that boldly proclaimed, *The Quill Customers' Bill of Rights*. It was first published in 1970 when Quill had 32 employees. It was restated, approved and reprinted on April 1, 1987, when Quill had grown to more than 850 employees. And in the 1990s, Quill grew to more than 1,300 employees. It's still incredibly powerful, what we can learn and apply today about service, from a document created 50 years ago by a small company. Here is...

The Quill Customers' Bill of Rights

The undersigned officers and the more than 850 employees of Quill Corporation express a desire to clearly state the principles and ideals which guide all of us at Quill in our relationship with our customers.

We feel this unusual step is necessary at this time because we find ourselves when we are customers, both as individuals and as a company, frequently dissatisfied with the way we are treated. Disinterest, discourteousness, bad service, late deliveries and just plain bad manners are too common.

We can't tell others how to run their businesses (except by not buying from them). But we can and will run Quill as we feel a business should be run. Therefore, the following is a list of what we consider are the inalienable rights of our customers. We expect to be held to account whenever we

316

deny any of these rights to any customer.

1. *As a customer you are entitled to be treated like a real, individual, feeling, human being, with friendliness, honesty and respect.*
2. *As a customer, you are entitled to full value for your money. When you buy a product you should feel assured that it was a good buy and that the product is exactly as it was represented to be.*
3. *As a customer, you are entitled to a complete guarantee of satisfaction. This is especially true when you buy the product sight unseen through the mail or over the phone.*
4. *As a customer, you are entitled to fast delivery. Unless otherwise indicated, the product should be shipped within 8 to 32 hours. In the event of a delay, you are entitled to immediate notification, along with an honest estimate of expected shipping date.*
5. *As a customer, you are entitled to speedy, courteous, knowledgeable answers on inquiries. You are entitled to all the help we can give in finding exactly the product or information needed.*
6. *As a customer, you are entitled to the privilege of being an individual and of dealing with individuals. If there is a question on your account, you are entitled to talk with or correspond with another individual so the question can be resolved immediately on the most mutually satisfactory basis possible.*
7. *As a customer, you are entitled to be treated exactly as we want to be treated when we are someone else's customer.*

How will you create the equivalent of a *Bill of Rights* for your company and customers?

91. I'm Here to S.E.R.V.™

"You're nuts. No way!"

"I'm livid!"

"Let me talk to the boss. I'm really mad!"

"I can't believe this. Who's in charge?"

"This must be resolved. Now! Or I'm taking other action!"

Despite your best efforts to always deliver quality and profitable customer service, you may still encounter the tough, demanding or complaining customer. Yet your greatest marketing and sales opportunities may begin with the preceding, or similar, caustic questions or confrontational exclamations. Plus, there's no need to surrender, especially when you know how to S.E.R.V.™ your customers.

Most customers and decision-makers are honest, reasonable people. If there's a problem, they seek fair and fast solutions. Thankfully, we don't have to encounter or battle often the feared *customer from hell!* Although, they do exist.

A painting contractor once told me an amazing story. He said he just completed painting the interior of a customer's palatial home. The home was gorgeous and so was his work. Or so he thought.

While he admired his skill and artistry, his customer, who we'll affectionately call, Mrs. Pita, (pain in the _ _ _) declared, "While it may look perfect, it must first pass, *my nylon test!*" Somewhat confused, he said, "Excuse me, what's your nylon test?"

She then removed from her pants pocket a wadded-up pair of nylons or pantyhose. She rolled them into a ball and said, "I'll run the nylons over the baseboards, walls, crown molding and ceiling. If there's a snag, you'll fix it!" Though shocked by her unrealistic expectation, he politely listened. The few bumps or snags she found, he quickly remedied. He told me, "Jeff, the faster I finished, the sooner I could flee!" So how do you handle the occasional or potential tough or nasty customer?

Here's how, with the four-step S.E.R.V.™ problem-solving formula.

The steps are:

1. **S**   Specify.
2. **E**   Evaluate.
3. **R**   Remedy.
4. **V**   Verify.

Each step also has three specific action strategies for resolving problems:

1. Specify. *Specify* the difficulty, dilemma or problem to be solved. Specification lets you solve your customer's problem, whether it's real or simply perceived. Effective *specification* requires you to:

a. Know the facts.
b. Listen without bias.
c. Re-affirm, or repeat, the facts to your customer to demonstrate you truly listened.

2. Evaluate. In this stage you find out:

    a. Who goofed or made the mistake?
    b. What did or didn't happen?
    c. What should have happened that didn't?

The goal here isn't to assign blame, but instead to empower or authorize someone within your company (*you* or somebody else) to take positive action on behalf of your customer.

3. Remedy. To *remedy* the problem, you should do three things:

    a. First, ask your customer what he or she wants, or what he or she suggests to solve the problem.
    b. Offer your suggestions.
    c. Work together with your customer to reach agreement.

4. Verify. Here, you *verify*:

    a. The course of action to be taken.
    b. That your customer is satisfied or happy with that action.
    c. That you value your customer and their business.

The S.E.R.V. formula is another effective tool to enhance your relationship with a customer. It works at both the "little r" and "BIG R" levels. However, will the S.E.R.V. formula always work? Nope. But it's not for lack of trying.

Unfortunately, no matter what you do or say, there are always those select few customers who are the chronic complainers. The relentless whiners. They can never be satisfied. Their goal is to inflict pain and suffering. They like to add fuel to the fire. They're charter members of *Club Unhappy* and hope to recruit you too.

However, they're the minority. And remember, nobody ever won an argument with a customer!

Five Action Steps:

1. Have you and your team learn and apply the S.E.R.V.™ formula.
2. Write down potential or common complaints.
3. Practice the four S.E.R.V. steps with these complaints. Role play. Rehearse. Get comfortable. Get conversational.
4. Be in control. Never be intimidated.
5. Remember, your business is all about customer acquisition, satisfaction and retention. You got 'em. Now, keep 'em!

92. Remember the Alamo!

As you can probably tell, I'm passionate about service. My clients expect a lot, and they get it. They deserve a lot, and we deliver it. Thankfully, they tell me, that we provide quality service. Their expectations aren't only met, they're exceeded. While my standards are high for service delivery, they're also high when *I'm* a customer.

I'm really a pretty easy guy to please. However, if I feel I've been wronged, I take swift, aggressive action. It's never threatening or abusive. It's always polite and factual. The following pages feature an excerpt from a letter I wrote in 1990 to Chuck Platt, president of Alamo Rent A Car. Its contents are likely to both amuse and shock you. (And this was obviously long before Alamo became part of Enterprise Holdings.)

Date: November 20, 1990

To: Chuck Platt, President, Alamo Rent A Car

From: Jeff Blackman, a frustrated/disappointed Alamo Customer

Re: Alamo Rent A Car Maui, Jane S. and Mark H. *(Names have been changed)*

Dear Chuck,

The Aloha spirit is not alive and well at Alamo…at least on Maui.

On November 14th, my wife, four-month old daughter and I had just completed two wonderful weeks devoted to business and pleasure in the islands.

While staying on the "big island" of Hawaii from November 4th to 9th, we also used Alamo Rent A Car. There, your customer service agents are attentive, courteous and helpful. They were extremely accommodating. Unfortunately, the same accolades cannot be expressed about the level of service (or lack thereof) on Maui.

After dropping my daughter and wife off at the Kahului Airport, I then returned the car (at approximately 6:45 p.m.) to your facility. After handing the "check-in service ticket" to customer service agent Jane S., I thought I'd quickly be on my way. I was mistaken!

Jane claimed I owed $11.46 more. I said, "For what?!" She told me that because the car was returned one hour late, an additional amount was now owed. I immediately told her that no late fee was ever discussed.

Chuck, of course I understand why you have a late fee, and yes I do think it's "good business"—BUT only if a customer is told of its existence and exactly what their potential liability/responsibility might be. I never was!

While renting the car, customer service agent Francis P. (who was very helpful) stated that the car was "due back on November 14th" and that I was paid in full "unless the gas tank wasn't returned full." No specific due-back time on the 14th or any late return penalty was ever referred to.

When I expressed my dismay, Jane tersely stated, "It's in your contract!" To which I disbelievingly queried, "Are you familiar with an adhesion contract?" She responded facetiously, "I don't know legal jargon. I'm not a lawyer!"

I said, "I do, I am a lawyer!"

She told me to "contact corporate." After several frustrating minutes with Jane, it was obvious, she wasn't the right person to solve this problem. A solution hopefully would have been offered by on-duty supervisor Mark H. It wasn't!

Chuck, while your promotional posters exclaim the benefits of the Buick as being excitement, romance and adventure, if similar posters were used to describe Mark's attitude toward serving the customer, they might proclaim disinterest, insincerity and confrontational!

When I explained the situation to Mark, instead of acknowledging my frustration or understanding the problem, he actually said, "Can I talk now?" Mark then repeatedly stated, "That's in your contract." He gleefully indicated that everything that was circled (by Francis) and initialed (by me): the decline of the collision damage waiver options, the VISA card payment and the optional refueling charges, I was responsible for. I agreed.

But when I asked him why there was no request for me to initial the "return date-time-Alamo office" box, Mark suddenly fell silent. Chuck, at one point after referring to the language on your contract, Mark actually said to me, "You do know how to read...don't you?!"

When it became apparent that neither Mark nor Jane were "empowered" with the ability to solve a problem or at least offer other alternatives, I requested the president's name and address.

Chuck, the best thing about this experience, is that it has given me one more story to share with all my audiences worldwide! Though trained as an attorney, my living is made as a broadcaster and professional speaker.

And ironically, the four speaking engagements that I just conducted on Maui and Oahu all dealt with the importance of service. Service that's essential to a company's long-term success and profitable performance.

Unfortunately Chuck, none of the strategies for effectively handling a service problem were employed by Jane or Mark. And they had so many opportunities. For example:

Mr. Blackman, we're sorry this happened. What do you suggest we do?

Mr. Blackman, let me make sure I understand why you're disturbed, so that together we can properly solve this for you.

Mr. Blackman, we apologize for any inconvenience. Unfortunately we're required to charge you this additional amount now, but what can we do to help you possibly recoup this money or to express your complaint to "corporate."

Mr. Blackman, because you were a loyal customer on two islands for two weeks, why don't we just forget about such a minimal amount. Thanks for your business. Have a nice trip home!

As I made it clear to Mark and Jane, and I'll express to you, I'm not interested in the $11.46! Considering my "time is money investment"—just writing this letter isn't a financially sound decision! But it was written because as you and I both know, the commitment to service starts at the top! A wise person once said, "The goal of customer service is to make people want to do business with you." This customer currently has no intention to do business with Alamo again in the future.

Perhaps that's a decision that you can change!

Creatively yours,

Jeff Blackman

P.S. By the way, Chuck, out of fairness, I informed Jane and Mark that a copy of the letter sent to you would also be sent to them. Jane nodded, but Mark said, "Don't bother, it doesn't matter, I won't read it, don't waste your time." He later facetiously exclaimed, "Have a nice flight!"

JB/srk

It's obvious from this experience that facts can be more frightening than fiction! Now I know what you're wondering, "What happened?"

Within two weeks of sending this letter, I received calls and letters of apology from several members of Alamo's executive management team. They assured me service is a priority and that Jane and Mark are exceptions to the typical Alamo employee. They also informed me that Jane had been reassigned and that Mark had been fired. And as a gesture of goodwill, they gave me a free weekend car rental.

Because of $11.46, poor communications and bad attitudes, two employees sacrificed for Alamo a potential revenue stream for a lifetime. However, out of fairness, there was one especially positive outcome from this Alamo debacle. Alamo sent me the equivalent of its "commandments" or "bill of rights" for customer service. While it's evident these beliefs weren't embraced by Jane or Mark, hopefully they were by other employees and they should be of value to you.

An Alamo Best Friend Always…

Has an enthusiastic smile.
Treats others with respect and courtesy.
Uses proper language.
Acts professionally.
Helps others.
Is properly dressed and well-groomed.
Deals with others with honesty.
Eats, drinks, smokes or chews gum in the break areas only.
Uses a person's name.
Is dedicated to excellence.
Says thank you.
Makes other people feel important.

Are You Always A Best Friend?

---

93. Horror at Herman's!

Herman's World of Sporting Goods capitalized on the health and recreation boom in the United States in the late 1980s and early 1990s. At one time, it had 270 stores. Unfortunately, this vast success was short-lived. In May 1993, it closed almost 150 stores west of Philadelphia in going-out-of-business sales. It then filed for bankruptcy in 1994. And liquidated its assets in 1996.

Perhaps the company's "attitude" toward its customers during its "final sales" gives some insight into its downfall. So help me, cross my heart, I'm not kidding, believe it or not, I actually saw the following signs in a Herman's store in Highland Park, Illinois.

I didn't realize it was such a difficult task to put batting gloves in their correct packages. If you can't do this, don't even look at the gloves. And, don't be so rude to leave them on the floor.

Absolutely no returns, refunds or exchanges. Once it leaves the store, you own it. No matter what. We've said it several times, we'll say it again. No returns!

Make sure you have the right size, we're tired of saying no refunds. If you're not serious about keeping your purchase, we don't need your business.

Kinda easy to figure out why they went out of business!

94. A Little Bit Extra

With increasing domestic and global competition, companies and businesspeople that make a commitment to their customers are more likely to survive and thrive. As a successful business pro, you should never stop focusing on expense reduction, market penetration, product improvements, cash flow and increasing earnings.

Yet, you must realize that perhaps the greatest contributor to your profitable growth and your bottom line is customer or client satisfaction. Customers may not demand perfection, but they do demand satisfaction.

Always treat customers how *they* like to be treated. Jack Wilson, my video publisher, would often say, "CS equals CS. Common sense equals customer service." And common sense tells you selling, marketing or negotiating without serving is a dangerous game to play. Because the penalties are severe. And the penalties aren't measured in yardage, points or minutes. The penalties are measured in dollars. Especially dollars being lost.

Companies and employees with a poor commitment to service are not only losing customers, but, unwittingly, they're preparing to lose their businesses. For without a profitable customer, you won't have a profitable business. Customer service must become an immediate priority for you and everyone in your organization. And the time for that prioritization is now.

Consider this study by *U.S. News & World Report* that shows how and why companies lose customers. Customer are lost because:

- 1 percent die.
- 3 percent move away.
- 5 percent form other friendships or business relationships.
- 9 percent switch for competitive reasons.
- 14 percent are lost because of product dissatisfaction.
- 68 percent quit doing business with a company because they

perceive an attitude of indifference toward them by some employee.

That's right, 68 percent of your customers could potentially stop doing business with you, not because your product is inferior or your location is inconvenient, but, instead, because you or your people, simply look, sound and act like you just don't care. It's shocking, but absolutely true.

A customer makes one buying decision at a time, but this "decision" is made repeatedly, for months, years or even decades. Unfortunately, a lost customer rarely returns.

A Business Is Lonely Without Customers

While walking through a store, I overheard a conversation between two customer service representatives. One said to the other, "This would be a great job, if it weren't for all these customers." The problem with his statement is twofold: First, he truly didn't understand what his role is: to serve his customers. And second, and perhaps the greatest violation, is that his management or leaders don't communicate to him and his fellow employees the significance and value of their customers.

In your competitive marketplace, the companies with great customer service prosper. They survive and thrive. To be one of these companies, service must be an essential part of your culture. Outstanding and profitable service does more than simply enhance your image, it improves your top and bottom lines.

A workshop participant once said to me, "You can get your prospect's attention with price, but you can only earn their loyalty through care and service."

Management guru Peter Drucker declared more than 40 years ago, "The only valid definition of business purpose is to create a satisfied customer." Drucker's axiom is timeless. It should be observed, internalized and mastered. Then, it will pave the way to your more favorable and profitable future.

So how can you and your people continually deliver great service? It won't be accomplished with the creation of a customer service desk, a new department or a customer appreciation day. Customer service isn't about a desk, a department or a day. It's a philosophy. An attitude. And it must inhabit your culture and your people as it runs throughout your entire organization.

You should always help customers promptly and enthusiastically. You should always be sincere, attentive and caring. Because with this kind of attitude and philosophy to service, you create an abundance of customers for a lifetime of success. And that success allows you to *peak your profits.*

CASE STUDY

Exceeded Expectations! A Home Run!

CHALLENGE:

How to bring together and unite a group of hard-charging leaders, salespeople and technicians, with strong technical expertise—and help them reinforce and execute a company initiative focused on delivering incredible "gold star" service.

GAME PLAN AND TEAMWORK:

I had the pleasure and privilege to work with a Denver-based client in the mountains of Colorado. We were at the Peaceful Valley Lodge and Resort in Lyons at an elevation of 5,400 feet. Such a "lofty" location was the perfect setting. Because my client, Linx, is ascending. Fast!

They've been named to *Inc.* magazine's INC. 5000 list of America's fastest-growing companies in 2008, 2010, 2011, 2012, 2014, and 2015.

Linx is a "system integrator" for network cabling, audio visual and security systems. Yet what they really do, plain and simple, is make sure your stuff works!

So when you move to a home or office, renovate a current one or erect a new building, school, hotel or hospital, they assure your phones, computers, televisions, conference rooms and security are up and running. Immediately! The first time!

C
A
S
E

S
T
U
D
Y

While some of the United States' most recognizable and respected companies rely upon "Team Linx" for their talent, expertise and technical know-how, what they especially value is the execution of the *Linx Gold Star Service* commitment.

And that commitment starts at the top with Linx's president and co-owner, Erik Isernhagen, and his dedicated leadership team. Erik and his team are smart. Hardworking. Fun. And focused.

With them, their project managers, project foremen and support teams, they all know that little things matter. For example, for my two-hour trek from Denver to Lyons, my travel mate was Erik. (Yep, the president picked me up at the airport.)

C
A
S
E

S
T
U
D
Y

For the room set-up, the afternoon/night before our results-session, we had a talented crew re-arranging tables and chairs; Erik, Jay, Ivan, Tom, Dale and Damon. (That's right, the executive leadership team was the "official" set-up team!)

GOLD STAR SERVICE:

To give depth, meaning and significance to their service commitment, Linx has created eight points of what they enthusiastically and passionately call: *Linx Gold Star Service.*

Whether you sell a product or a service, are a manufacturer or a retailer, an established, veteran corporate player or a young, hungry entrepreneur, these eight points should have immediate applicability or adaptability for you and your business.

Linx Gold Star Service requires:

1. INTEGRITY
- Be the client's advocate.
- Do what you say you are going to do...follow through.
- No shortcuts to quality...do it right the first time.

2. LISTENING
- Take the time to listen to what our client wants.
- Be the expert at discovering our client's hidden needs.
- Active listening...restate what the client asked for to ensure you got it right.

3. EXPERTISE
- Professionally trained staff.
- Explain technology in laymens' terms.
- Set realistic expectations that are jointly shared.
- Understand client needs and tailor solutions that meet the client's definition of value.

4. COURTESY
- When on the jobsite, act like a guest.
- Be polite and respectful.
- Leave the site clean at the end of every day.

5. ATTITUDE
- Be likeable.
- Hustle with a "Can-do" attitude.
- Enjoy what you are doing.

CASE STUDY

6. COMMUNICATION

- Provide clear, consistent, meaningful and prompt communication.
- Identify how the client wants to receive their information. (Content, Frequency, Format)
- Express our desire to serve...Give our clients the comfort of understanding we won't stop working until they're happy.

7. PROFESSIONALISM

- Be prepared, considerate and on-time for appointments.
- Maintain a clean and professional appearance.
- Strive for perfection, deliver excellence.

8. OWNERSHIP

- If a client expresses a need to you, or around you, you own it.
- Our client hired us to do a job...deliver it regardless of challenges.
- Partner with our customer to get the job done...we're on the same team.

*****

May the preceding help you too...to reach for the stars!

RESULTS:

Following our work together, Linx president and co-owner, Erik Isernhagen wrote:

"Jeff, tremendous. Exceeded expectations. A home run! I can

334

see why you've never lost your 'money back guarantee' bet! Your content was great and your delivery was exceptional. I very much appreciate that you worked with me ahead of time to ensure relevance to our company's focus. Our key people, (typically skeptics), haven't stopped referencing you. By the way, I was reading the comments back to you, trust you saw how many made mention of the impression you left. These guys aren't all that touchy-feely or expressive, so those comments are meaningful!"

Jeff, comments include:

Jeff was outstanding. His ability to get us all involved was superb. This meeting demonstrates our commitment to exceeding customers' expectations.

Valuable and rewarding. Jeff was truly eye-opening.

Jeff, thanks for your insight/direction. We were very fortunate to have you out here!

I've learned things that will help me personally and professionally. Jeff was awesome!

C
A
S
E

S
T
U
D
Y

CHAPTER 13

A Profit Potpourri

"The secret is to know something that nobody else knows."
—Aristotle Onassis

95. According to Our Records

If there's anything I've discovered, it's that a successful business requires lots of little things be done right. It's often the nuances or the subtleties that mark the difference between disaster and triumph. This section is devoted to those "little things." It's a profit potpourri of ideas that allows you to distinguish yourself from your competition. It's also chock-full of simple, yet very effective strategies to help you better run and manage your business. And that helps you maximize your results and *peak your profits.*

As you know, it's tough to stay in business if you don't get paid or are paid late. Delayed payments are a killer to cash flow. It's especially frustrating when you have to chase money. Thankfully, bad debts have never been a major problem at Blackman & Associates. However, on occasion, we, too, have to politely and persistently pursue dollars due.

There's no magic to getting money, but the following steps have proved successful for us:

1. If payment isn't received within one week of the due date, a copy of the bill is emailed to a client. (Along with a "read receipt.")
2. If ten days later, payment still hasn't been received, another copy of the bill is emailed. Written on the invoice, as well as in the email, is: "This must have been accidentally over-looked. Thanks for having your folks in accounting take care of it today." (Once again, the email includes a "read receipt.")
3. If seven days later, payment still hasn't been received, a friendly phone call is made to the "accidental debtor" or the person responsible for accounts payable. Our request is direct, yet friendly. It goes something like this:

"Hi, could sure use your help. We're sure it was an oversight, but would you believe…we still haven't received payment for invoice #, in the amount of _____?! How would you like to take care of that payment today: By check? Wire transfer or ACH? Credit card? What's easiest for you? Thanks. Appreciate it."

Typically, people are extremely apologetic and some say they're even embarrassed. Payment is usually received immediately.

4. If seven days later payment has still not been received, a letter like the upcoming one, is emailed. (With a "read receipt.")
5. If payment still hasn't been received by the specified date, then the matter is turned over to my attorney for collection. This is a last resort, but an effective one. (And I can't remem-ber, the last time this was necessary.) It's amazing how a polite correspondence from "Legal Louie" quickly motivates action and payment.

And what if payment still doesn't arrive? Then, it's decision-time.

- You can sue. Or turn it over to a collection agency. (These remedies will be influenced by the amount you're owed, "hassle" factor and expense.)

- You can forget about it. (This, too, will be influenced by the amount you're owed, but it's often the right decision to "move-on," even though this is a frustrating decision.)

Date:
To: Client's name
Company:
From: Sheryl Kantor
Blackman & Associates, LLC

Re: Your past due account. Final Appeal.

A "final appeal" for collection should be brief, friendly and successful. This letter is brief.

It's also friendly. We wish to keep your goodwill.

Despite repeated requests (by email and phone), your payment still hasn't been received. (Please see the attached invoice from "date" in the amount of $_____.)

We want to protect your credit rating. Unless payment is received on or before (always give a specific date), you'll require us to turn your account over for collection.

Please send your payment today. Thank you.

Sheryl Kantor
Blackman & Associates, LLC

- You can watch old gangster movies to get ideas on "persuasion." (Often very entertaining, but not very realistic.)

- You can call a debtor and offer at a future date to be a pallbearer at their funeral. After all, you have carried the individual for so long, now you can finally finish the job! (Just kidding about this strategy, but it sure is appealing!)

As a client of mine once said, "Until you get paid, your quality product or service is merely a gift!"

96. What's Your P/E Ratio?

Do you own stock? If so, your objective is usually pretty simple. Buy low and sell high! You desire positive results and a return on your investment.

Your decision to buy shares in a company could have even been influenced by the company's P/E or price/earnings ratio. Just like a stock can increase in value, you too can increase in value. Therefore, it's important that you also focus on *your* P/E ratio.

The P is your:

- Performance.
- Productivity.
- Pride.
- Persistence.
- Passion

The E is your:

- Energy.
- Excitement.
- Enthusiasm.
- Effectiveness.
- Execution.

A publicly-traded company produces an annual report that always features an opening statement, "To our shareholders." Your "shareholders" are your prospects, customers, clients, leaders, teammates, partners, community, industry and stakeholders.

Your opening statement, "To our customers," might go something like this:

> *By nearly all measures, I've attained the qualities of a stellar performer—market leadership, superior customer satisfaction, a solid clientele, plus loyal and profitable relationships. I'm now leveraging those strengths to realize my remaining goal: sustained and enviable growth, service and results.*

On a daily basis, use your skills, attitude and behavior to drive your choices and do whatever it takes to enhance your P/E ratio and increase the "value" you bring to your company, customers and marketplace.

After all, just like a stock, you too are, or can become, a "blue chipper." Which means you're reliable and of the highest quality!

97. A-to-Z, Be the Best You Can Be!

One of the great joys of being in my business, is that I get to do research everywhere—while visiting at a client's office, traveling on the road, surfing the Internet or even simply reading the Sunday newspaper.

And I once discovered a gem in Abigail Van Buren's column *Dear Abby* in the *Chicago Tribune*. It was called, *To Achieve Your Dreams, Remember Your ABCs* by Wanda Hope Carter. It features an A-to-Z listing of simple thoughts to pursue your dreams.

And it inspired me to create a new A-to-Z listing of motivational messages—to help you achieve happiness, success and results in your business and life. Here's my:

A-to-Z, Be the Best You Can Be!

Attitude and action drive your results.
Belief and behavior are a powerful combination.
Confidence helps pave your path to prosperity.
Defeat is part of life. Learn from it.
Enthusiasm creates opportunity and results.
Focus on your goals and priorities. Avoid distractions.
Go for it!
Hope may not be a strategy, but it's sure a meaningful motivator.
"I did!" is far better than, "I'll try."
Jump at the opportunity to help, to volunteer, to say, "I can do that!"
Knowledge creates growth. But remember, it isn't what you know, it's what you do with what you know.

Love and laugh. Often!

Money matters. It gives you choice, freedom and flexibility.

Navigate life's journey, through the successes and the setbacks. It'll make you stronger.

Opportunity is always knocking. Be ready to answer.

Persistence and positivity are often the difference between winning and losing.

Quick isn't always the best solution. Patience pays.

Respect others. Be kind, courteous and gracious.

Success and happiness are yours to pursue and achieve. Make it happen!

Truth is your friend. It doesn't require a good memory.

Unique is who you are. Embrace it. Share it!

Value your self-worth. If you don't, nobody else will.

Words matter. They can help or hurt. Choose wisely.

Xamine where you're at. Where you'd like to be. And how you want to get there.

You make a difference. Expect great things in your future.

Z isn't the end. It's a fresh start. Be the best you can be, living A-to-Z!

Here's one more A-to-Z strategy. Organize from A to Z (in an accordion file or even better, scanned into your computer) "items of interest" to your prospects, customers and clients. My A-to-Z files (hardcopy and digital) are filled with newspaper and magazine articles, print advertisements, catalog pages, brochures, annual reports, promotional literature, links, videos, music or cartoons that may be of some, great or even no interest to me, but are of significant value to my clients—current and prospective.

I've gathered information on:

Advertising	Cruises	Hot Dogs
Architecture	Dining	Led Zeppelin
Autumn	Diversity	Phone Gadgets
Baseball	Dry Cleaners	Pizza
Bed & Breakfast Inns	Exotic Getaways	Recipes
Birds	Financial Planning	Spring Training
Branson, Missouri	Golf/Tennis Schools	Thanksgiving Tips
Coffee	Great Resorts	Wine
Credit Reports	Hospitality	Yiddish

While the preceding topics may seem like potential categories for a game of *Jeopardy*, what they really represent is a valuable collection of "little r" stuff that's of value to clients, prospects and friends.

I once had a client who told me he was planning a long weekend with his wife and he wanted to stay at a bed and breakfast in southern Wisconsin, but he had been too busy to search the Internet.

I assured him I could help. I simply went to the "W" section of my A-to-Z file and grabbed the *Wisconsin Bed & Breakfast Inns Directory*. Within minutes, I sent him several possibilities. He was, of course, appreciative, but he was astounded I had finger-tip-access to this information.

You generate great relationship-building and business-development power when you send a prospect or a client information that's of interest to him or her with a simple note or email like, "Thought you'd find this interesting." "Knew you'd enjoy this!" "Saw this, and thought of you!" "You're gonna dig this!" By the way, even if you send others information that's a few years old, if they've never seen it before, it's brand-new knowledge.

98. Your Action Plan

The "action plan" on this page helps you with current and prospective clients—to plan, prepare and profit.

Client's name: _____

Step:	*Approach / Strategy:*
Preparation:	With this client's decision-influencers and behavioral tendencies, I must be sure *to do* and *not do* the following:
Open:	What type and how much interaction should I initiate with this client?
Probe:	What type of questions do I ask to uncover needs, problems and goals, as well as find their motivators or "hot buttons"?
Reveal:	As I reveal how our products, services or solutions can help this client, I'll focus on:
Translate:	This client would be most influenced by the following types of benefit statements:
Negotiate:	I should anticipate these concerns, objections, fears and hesitancies, but I'll reduce them by:
The Yes:	What approach works best to commit this decision-maker to action?
After The Yes:	Knowing this client's style, his or her service expectations are likely to be:
	Requiring me to respond with:

---

99. Psyche-Kick Phenomena!

It's a word that frightens professional athletes. Its mere utterance causes tailspins. If mired in one, results turn to rubble. Opportunity turns to despair. It's the feared, detestable and horrible "slump"!

Like the cleanup hitter who can't buy a homer, or the quarterback who can't complete a pass, a business pro wonders how long he or she has to wait before hearing another "yes."

Often, a slump isn't the result of physical activity, but, instead, mental activity. Of course, a successful business professional must continue to effectively sell, market, negotiate and serve, but often these activities are influenced by the mental mindset or attitude you bring to these business skills.

When Todd Sauerbrun joined the Chicago Bears football team, he was a highly regarded punter. In the National Football League draft, Sauerbrun was selected high for a kicker in the second round and the 56th overall. While punting in college at West Virginia, he broke several NCAA (National Collegiate Athletic Association) records. With his proven history of success, Sauerbrun was expected to be a valuable addition to the Bears. However, to Bears' fans and coaches, Sauerbrun's rookie season was a huge disappointment.

For many outstanding athletes, there's a transition time when they make the jump from college-ball to the pros. However, football critics and analysts claim the same transition time isn't necessary for a punter. After all, he's kicking the same size ball, on the same size field and often in better conditions. So if the physical nature of Sauerbrun's job and body hadn't changed, what had?

His mind! After the first five games of the season when Sauerbrun's punting was abysmal, he said, "I'm very confused right now, but overcoming it. I've got to stop thinking of the bad things and be positive or not think at all. It's been tough."

According to Robert Schleser, director of the Institute for Sport and Performance Psychology at the Illinois Institute of Technology, "Sauerbrun needed to develop confidence based on successes. Competition anxiety is a function of failure." This assessment is interesting and on-target. During a broadcast interview, I heard Sauerbrun tell a reporter, "Just before I kicked the ball in college, I'd think about which record I was going to break. But here in the pros, I tell myself, just don't make a mistake!"

Maury Buford, a former Bears punter said, "The physical part of kicking doesn't change (from college to the pros). A lot of kids can punt the ball a long way. It's the mental aspect they can't handle."

Gary "Coach" Zauner is a former successful college kicker, who has served as a kicking specialist for high school, college and several NFL teams. He warns you can't train every kicker the same way, but he does "work with them on positive mental images and mental toughness."

Zauner also agrees with other coaches that one of the real keys in a successful kicker is that he simply believes in himself. That's a very valuable message, whether you're a kicker or a businessperson. (Note: Despite Sauerbrun's horrific pro start, he became a believer. And a Pro Bowl punter. Sauerbrun was in the NFL for 12 seasons—with the Chicago Bears, Kansas City Chiefs, Carolina Panthers and Denver Broncos.)

100. Fly the Friendly Skies!

My preferred airline carrier is United. As a million-plus-miler, I've logged lots of time in their friendly skies. Most flights are uneventful. This one was unforgettable.

About 10 minutes before landing in Phoenix, I noticed the flight attendant passing out small cards to certain passengers. My curiosity turned to disbelief and then admiration when she handed me *my* card. I was now the proud owner of the business card of Gary L. Prosser, Captain of this United flight. However, the message on the back of Captain Prosser's card is what made this experience so memorable and meaningful.

It said:

Mr. Jeffery Blackman – in 4C

We are <u>truly</u> delighted you are flying with us. We acknowledge the great many miles you have flown through the friendly skies and we <u>very</u> much appreciate your business. <u>Thank</u> you!

Gary Prosser and Crew

Are you "truly delighted" your customers or clients are investing in your products and services? Have you "acknowledged" the great many dollars they've invested in you and your company?

Do you "very much" appreciate their business"?

Have you told them "thank you"?

CASE STUDY

A Memorable Maverick!

Since this chapter is focused on little things with a BIG impact, I thought this "case study" qualified! It's not about an experience with a client. Instead...

Daily, I'm never quite sure where I'll discover that valuable nugget or significant keeper. That's why I always keep my eyes and ears open for "moments of significance" that I can then share with readers and clients.

Here's an example:

I was in Dallas conducting results-sessions for some of the top financial advisors in the world. The night before I spoke, I attended a reception and dinner, where the featured guest speaker was Dallas Mavericks owner, Mark Cuban.

As you probably know, Cuban is a self-made billionaire. Before he bought the Mavericks in 2000 and became an NBA (National Basketball Association) team owner, he made a boatload of money by founding two companies, Micro Solutions and broadcast.com, which he sold to Yahoo.

Now I've seen Cuban interviewed lots. He's a frequent guest on sports broadcasts and has been featured/profiled in numerous newscasts. Plus, he's a celebrity investor on ABC's hit TV-show, *Shark Tank*.

As one of my radio producers used to say, Cuban "gives good air!" Meaning, he fills the airwaves with entertaining anecdotes, quotes and opinions.

Cuban's detractors would say he's brash, arrogant and cocky. Well, okay, he may be all of those things, yet after hearing him speak (really answer questions for seventy-five minutes) and chatting with him briefly, I also found Cuban to be extremely likable.

C
A
S
E

S
T
U
D
Y

Dressed in blue jeans and a baggy white shirt, Cuban sat comfortably in a director's chair on a stage, answering questions and sharing stories about his humble beginnings, work ethic, customer commitment, charitable donations, player negotiations and new business ventures.

He was direct. Smart. Funny. Honest. Entertaining. And memorable. Being memorable is something Cuban especially values. Here's why.

When he was asked, "What's your goal for your team/franchise?" he replied with what I'll label as an unrehearsed burst of brilliance:

"My business really isn't about basketball or, for that matter, winning games. My purpose is to create memories so fans will forever remember their experience at a Mavs game. The next day, I want their throats to still be raw from screaming. Their hands still red from clapping. And their feet still sore from stomping."

That's brilliant!

Cuban is singularly focused on the outcomes, results, benefits, advantages, value and memories his "product" produces.

Of course, he knows the importance of winning, yet it must be in a unique and memorable environment. One that's unforgettable. One that generates positive word-of-mouth. One that helps sell over 17,000 seats per game. Cuban knows memories drive revenue. To best create those indelible mind impressions, Cuban is an active participant. He can be seen cheering his players and screaming at refs from the sidelines. Or cueing the audio engineer at a Mavs game to pump up the volume. He knows music that's loud, thumping and stirring revs-up the crowd.

Cuban is also easily accessible. Daily, he answers hundreds of emails from fans. He knows this type of "personal relationship" with customers also creates the right memories.

What memories are you creating for your customers or clients?

CASE STUDY

CHAPTER 14

Your Journey

"It is something to be able to paint a particular picture, or to carve a statue, and so to make a few objects beautiful; but it is far more glorious to carve and paint the very atmosphere and medium through which we look. To affect the quality of the day—that is the highest of arts."

—Henry David Thoreau

101. A Lesson From A 6-Year-Old

To gaze into the future often requires a brief peek into the past. And I see before me a little boy. A little boy who at the age of 6 stands in his first-grade classroom. He's asked by his teacher, Miss Northrup, to pronounce two words: listen and rabbit. The little boy confidently and proudly exclaims, "Wis-sin and wabbit!"

And ev-wee-buddy waffs. So he repeats the words again, this time even louder. Once more he bellows, "Wis-sin and wabbit!" And this time, ev-wee-buddy waffs even woud-uhr and wong-uhr.

He goes home, ti-uhd, de-pwessed, and fwus-twated. And says to his peh-ents, "My teach-uh, Miss Nawth-wup is cwazy. She cwaims I need speech co-wection wessins. She's wong. And I'm going to pwoov it!"

So that little boys begins to work very hard, every day, to correctly pronounce his Rs and Ls. Until one day, after three years of speech correction lessons, he's able to enunciate, articulate and communicate. And I assure you, I know that little guy, really, really well.

Eventually, he grows up to become an attorney, a Hall of Fame Speaker, a bestselling author, a TV and radio broadcaster and... the author of a book called *Peak Yaw Pwofits!*

Yep, I'm that little boy. At the age of 6, (unbeknown to me at the time), my life and career choice were being shaped and influenced. I've often wondered what my life would be like if I had properly pronounced "listen and rabbit." (Maybe I would have played shortstop, batted third and led the Chicago Cubs to a World Series Championship, long before 2016. Okay, maybe not!)

The reason I share this story, is because it's about a journey. A journey of results. Confucius said, "Every great journey begins with a single step." This journey for *Peak Your Profits* first began in August of 1994, when I said to my wife Sheryl, "I'm going to write another book." She responded the way she always does, "Great! I know it'll be a winner!" There was no agent. No publisher. No title. No first word. However, I was committed to the journey, the process, the result.

And now, some 377 pages later, with this newly revised and upgraded 5th edition, we're sharing this journey together. It's a journey that is and always will be tremendously self-fulfilling for me. And I hope it's a journey that is and will be just as incredibly rewarding for you. With the thousands of revisions, upgrades, edits and new content, this latest edition of *Peak Your Profits* that you hold in your hands, is truly a better and more powerful book. (Thanks again to my publisher, Melissa Wilson and my editor, Jon Malysiak, for their keen insights and wise guidance. With your candor and counsel, you challenged me. Together, we always found a way to make "it" better. Plus, laugh!)

To borrow from Henry David Thoreau, it may be something to paint a picture or to carve a statue, or even to write a book. But it's far more glorious to affect the quality of one's life. I wrote this book so your life and the lives of those you serve would be positively enhanced. In these pages are the strategies to help you and others attain a more favorable future and improve your and their condition.

I'm confident you have the skills, enthusiasm and desire to make your dreams and others' dreams come true. That requires discipline and commitment, but it's worth the effort. It's worth the time. It's worth the energy. It's worth investing in *you* and *your* journey.

By the way, our relationship doesn't end here. I'm always available to help you reach your next level of success. If you'd like to explore in greater depth how I can help you, your company or any group or association you're involved with grow and prosper, please let me know. If you call me, I'll call you. If you write me, I'll write you. If you email me, I'll email you. These are promises! Our relationship has really just begun.

May your journey be filled with health, happiness and prosperity, as you continue to *peak your profits!*

About the Author

HELPING OTHERS WIN BIG! Those who want to win BIG in today's competitive marketplace call Jeff Blackman. He's a speaker, author, success coach, broadcast personality and lawyer. He heads Blackman & Associates—a results-producing business-growth firm in the Chicagoland area.

Jeff's clients call him, a "business-growth specialist." His customized *Referrals: Your Road to Results* learning-system helped one financial services client generate $230 million directly from referrals, in only 23 months!

DELIVERS RESULTS! Since 1985, Jeff has shared his positive and profit-producing messages with numerous Fortune 500 companies, closely-held businesses, entrepreneurial driven organizations and association audiences throughout the world.

Whether Jeff works with you once, or once-a-month in an on-going learning-system, he helps you outdistance your competition and reach new levels of unprecedented success. His high-energy and high-content messages have immediate take-home value.

HALL-OF-FAMER, AWARD WINNER & HONORS. On August 4th, 2008, in New York City, Jeff was inducted into the National Speakers Association's *Speaker Hall of Fame.* He was awarded the *CPAE: Council of Peers Award for Excellence* designation. To date, only 242 professional or celebrity speakers have been selected and honored worldwide, including; Ronald Reagan, Colin Powell, Zig Ziglar, and Norman Vincent Peale.

Jeff is also one of approximately twelve percent of professional speakers to receive the CSP or *Certified Speaking Professional* designation from NSA. And in June, 2008, Vistage, the world's leading CEO organization, named Jeff *Fast Track Speaker of the Year,* based upon the quality and impact of his content and delivery. Jeff also graduated with honors from both the University of Illinois and the Illinois Institute of Technology Chicago Kent College of Law.

BESTSELLING AUTHOR. Jeff's bestselling books include: *Opportunity $elling®, RESULT$, Carpe A.M. • Carpe P.M. – Seize Your Destiny™, Peak Your Profits*—which was also published in Malaysia and Singapore, and selected by Fast Track as one of "the best business books on tape" and, *Stop Whining! Start Selling!,* which achieved "Bestseller" status at Amazon within one month of its release.

As an audio-author, Jeff's results-strategies were featured on Nightingale-Conant's *Sound Selling.* POPP Publishing released/distributes Jeff's audio business-growth system: *Opportunity $elling® - Six Profit-Producing Steps to Multiply Your Earnings* and the *RESULT$* CD.

Jeff has also written and hosts two video learning-systems published by JWA Video; *Profitable Customer Service* and *How to Set and Really Achieve Your Goals.*

BROADCASTER. As a radio and TV talk-show host, some of Jeff's guests have been: Oprah Winfrey, Jerry Seinfeld, Albert Brooks, Penn Jillette, Ted Koppel, astronaut Jim Lovell and Olympic gold medalist Bruce Jenner.

HAPPY HUSBAND. DEVOTED FATHER. NUTTY FAN. Jeff is a happy husband, devoted father, veteran softball player, avid biker, and a loyal or nutty Chicago Cubs fan! He and his family are also crazy Chicago Blackhawks, Bears and Bulls fans. (They also love the Cubs, yet over the years, have spent lots of time consoling Jeff!)

On Sunday nights, the Blackmans can often be spotted together at a local hip, happenin' or dive restaurant…eating, talking and laughing!

Blackman & Associates, LLC
2130 Warwick Lane • Glenview, IL 60026
Phone: 847.998.0688 • Fax: 847.998.0675
jeff@jeffblackman.com • www.jeffblackman.com

Visit Jeff's website and subscribe to his FREE e-letter, *The Results Report*. Plus connect with Jeff on LinkedIn and Facebook and follow him on Twitter: @BlackmanResults

Keynotes, Coaching, Workshops & Learning-Systems by Jeff Blackman

DRIVE GROWTH AND RESULTS. Jeff:

- Ignites and inspires you to attain new levels of success.

- Helps you outdistance your competition.

- Enhances your performance, productivity and profitability.

- Accelerates your growth.

- Dramatically increases your results.

Unique, creative, honest, hard-hitting and humorous, Jeff's customized high-content, results-oriented and profit-producing messages in sales, marketing, negotiations, customer service, leadership and change have immediate application.

If you hire speakers or influence the selection of speakers at your company or professional association, please contact Jeff to learn more about how he can help you, your team or members *peak your profits.*

What do clients value most about Jeff? His:

- Energy and quick connection with an audience.

- Quality content and real-world solutions.

- Warm, friendly and impactful style.

- Commitment to customization and exhaustive research.

- Focus on quantifiable, measurable results and outcomes.

- Powerful, profit-producing messages.

- Sense of humor and spontaneity.

- Positive, fun and meaningful audience interaction.

- Dedication to long-term success with ongoing reinforcement.

Plus, he's fun and easy to work with!

To maximize your results, please contact:

Sheryl Kantor • Director of Marketing
Blackman & Associates, LLC
sheryl@jeffblackman.com • 847.998.0688
www.jeffblackman.com

Stop Whining! Start Selling!
(Book)

100 Profit Points
827 Growth Strategies
And 1 Giant Winner: YOU!

Stop Whining! Start Selling! became an Amazon bestseller within one month of its release. Jeff delivers the kinds of revenue growth strategies that turn you or your company into a profit powerhouse—fast!

These principles have been tested before tough and cynical audiences—Jeff's clients. And, they've learned how to stop whining, start selling, and keep winning! They're generating consistent, profitable, and explosive results. Now, so can you.

Jeff shows you how to whip your competition, create loyal and devoted customers, shorten your sales cycle and sell value to maximize profits.

You'll learn strategies like:
- 179 potential power probes.
- 13 proven principles to overcome objections.
- 35 insights on dealing with top decision-makers.
- 22 proven methods for asking for and getting referrals.
- 21 strategies for turning time into money.
- Plus, additional strategies on prospecting, creativity, goal achievement, time or self-management and more.

Stop Whining! Start Selling! is available at your local bookstore or your favorite online provider.

Please visit jeffblackman.com/growthtools for more information and more tools—in written, audio and video formats.

And please be sure to sign-up for Jeff's free e-zine, *The Results Report*. You never know what timely topics Jeff will write, rant or rave about.

Each issue is packed with powerful, conversational, information-loaded, real-world stuff—to help you generate immediate results. Plus, it's fun to read! To subscribe and join Jeff's virtual family, simply go to jeffblackman.com.

Opportunity $elling® / Six Profit-Producing Steps to Multiply Your Earnings
(Audio Learning-System)

Jeff delivers more than 5 hours of profit-producing ideas from his proven business-growth system, including:

- The system's 30 profit points.
- 8 core profit-principles to compete and win.
- 16 strategies to improve your listening skills.
- 12 questions to ask yourself about relationship building.
- 15 tips and techniques on questioning and probing.
- 12 presentation strategies and 8 guidelines to assure the sale.
- 11 profit phrases to translate features into benefits.
- 5 strategies to create your differential competitive advantage.
- Why ethical practices are crucial for increased earnings.
- 25-plus negotiation strategies.
- The 10 dimensions of service.
- More than 50 suggestions about adapting to a buyer's decision-making style and more.

This audio business-growth system is literally filled with hundreds of proven and profit-producing strategies. Plus, you also receive:

- A *Mental Motivator* pocket-card that outlines all six steps of the system, along with the 30 profit points.
- An *Opportunity* sales chart.
- Investment style worksheets.
- 150 profit-words and power-phrases.
- A special bonus: a free copy of Jeff's sales quotation book.

Please visit jeffblackman.com/growthtools—for more information and to order. Plus, discover more business-growth tools—in written, audio and video formats.

And please be sure to sign-up for Jeff's free e-zine, *The Results Report*. You never know what timely topics Jeff will write, rant or rave about.

Each issue is packed with powerful, conversational, information-loaded, real-world stuff—to help you generate immediate results. Plus, it's fun to read! To subscribe and join Jeff's virtual family, simply go to jeffblackman.com.

RESULT$
Proven Sales Strategies for Changing Times
(Book or Book & Audio CD)

RESULT$ is the shot-in-the-arm to guide you to spectacular success. No scholarly-type rhetoric. No long-winded theories. Just fast-paced, street-smart, straight to the point, ethical actions and "proven sales strategies for changing times."

Fill your mind and bank account with lots of good stuff, as you:

- Reach for the moon.
- Maximize relationship power.
- Say goodbye to gab.
- Vote for value.
- Breed hope and happiness with hustle.
- Turn fear into fortune. And more...

Get ready to be a sales superstar, as you produce RESULTS!

Carpe A.M. • Carpe P.M. /
Seize Your Destiny
(Book)

This results-oriented and inspirational powerhouse helps you shape and create your life, exactly the way you want it. Focus your power—with impactful strategies, stories, quotes and questions. Turn knowledge into action. Generate results. For *you*, are a dynamic source of success!

- Both books, *Carpe A.M. • Carpe P.M.* and *RESULT$* deliver short, meaningful and memorable messages. They're the perfect "gift" for you, a teammate, a friend, a family member or even a client, customer or prospect.

To read excerpts from these books or to order, please visit jeffblackman.com/growthtools

And please be sure to sign-up for Jeff's free e-zine, *The Results Report*. You never know what timely topics Jeff will write, rant or rave about.

Each issue is packed with powerful, conversational, information-loaded, real-world stuff—to help you generate immediate results. Plus, it's fun to read! To subscribe and join Jeff's virtual family, simply go to jeffblackman.com.

Opportunity $elling® / Six Profit-Producing Steps to Multiply Your Earnings
(Sales Quotation Book)

A strategic and philosophical blockbuster! Salespeople declare it's "their constant companion, as an on-the-road refresher and mental-motivator." It ignites you, whether you're beginning your sales career, on your way up, or already on top and want to stay there!

To read excerpts from *Opportunity $elling* or to order, please visit jeffblackman.com/growthtools

And please be sure to sign-up for Jeff's free e-zine, *The Results Report*. You never know what timely topics Jeff will write, rant or rave about.

Each issue is packed with powerful, conversational, information-loaded, real-world stuff—to help you generate immediate results. Plus, it's fun to read! To subscribe and join Jeff's virtual family, simply go to jeffblackman.com.

What Do YOU Think? Your Opinion Matters!

To you, my valued reader…

You did it! You finished! Congrats. Am proud of you. Way to go!

Hope you had as much fun reading *Peak Your Profits* as I had writing it. May it always be a source of inspiration and results, for years to come!

Our relationship should also continue to grow. Meaning, if I can help you in any way, please gimme a buzz at 847.998.0688 or shoot me an email at jeff@jeffblackman.com. Whether it's about an opportunity or a challenge, I'm here for *you*.

Also, since your opinion really matters, I could sure use your help. It would mean a lot to me, if you took just a few minutes and wrote a quick review of *Peak Your Profits* on Amazon. What did you dig? How did it help you? What results are you already achieving?

Your honest input will help others also attain new levels of success. Thanks a bunch. Really appreciate it.

May you continue to rock your future and peak your profits!

Jeff

Index

Imagine...

Your goals have now
been achieved
or exceeded.

How do you feel?

Seize the OPRTNTY!

As you...
Peak Your Profits!